Caste as a Form of Social Inequality

CASTE AS A FORM OF SOCIAL INEQUALITY

Mukesh K. Singh

CENTRUM PRESS
NEW DELHI-110002 (INDIA)

CENTRUM PRESS
H.O.: 4360/4, Ansari Road, Daryaganj,
New Delhi-110002 (India)
Tel: 23278000, 23261597, 23255577, 23286875
B.O.: No. 1015, Ist Main Road, BSK IIIrd Stage,
IIIrd Phase, IIIrd Block, Bengaluru-560085 (INDIA)
Tel: 080-41723429
Email: centrumpress@gmail.com
Visit us at: www.centrumpress.com

Caste as a Form of Social Inequality

First Edition, 2011

ISBN 978-93-81293-63-8

PRINTED IN INDIA

Printed at Tarun Offset, Delhi

Contents

Preface

The work provides a critique of the current theories of caste system which locate its essence in endogamy and argues that the present morphology of caste is the result of the changes the institution has undergone over centuries of its existence, but its origins are embedded in the ecology of the Vedic cattle-keepers.

Although many other nations are characterized by social inequality, perhaps nowhere else in the world has inequality been so elaborately constructed as in the Indian institution of caste. Caste has long existed in India, but in the modern period it has been severely criticized by both Indian and foreign observers. Although some educated Indians tell non-Indians that caste has been abolished or that "no one pays attention to caste anymore," such statements do not reflect reality. Caste has undergone significant change since independence, but it still involves hundreds of millions of people. In its preamble, India's constitution forbids negative public discrimination on the basis of caste. However, caste ranking and caste-based interaction have occurred for centuries and will continue to do so well into the foreseeable future, more in the countryside than in urban settings and more in the realms of kinship and marriage than in less personal interactions.

The first three castes had social and economical rights which the Sudra and the untouchables did not have. The first three castes are also seen as 'twice born'. The intention in these two births is to the natural birth and to the ceremonial entrance to the society at a much later age. Each Varna and also the untouchables are divided into many communities. These communities are called Jat or Jati. For example the Brahmans have Jats called Gaur, Kokanastha, Sarasvat, Iyer and others. The outcasts have Jats like Mahar, Dhed, Mala, Madiga and others. The Sudra is the largest Varna and it has the largest number of communities. Each Jat is limited to professions worthy of their Varna. Each Jat is limited to the Varna diet. Each Jat members are allowed to marry only with their Jat members. People are born into their Jat and it cannot be changed. This is the how the caste system is supposed to be in its religious form. But in reality it is much more complicated and different from its religious form.

In modern times, as in the past, it is virtually impossible for an individual to raise his own status by falsely claiming to be a member of a higher-ranked caste. Such a ruse might work for a time in a place where the person is unknown, but no one would dine with or intermarry with such a person or his offspring until the claim was validated through kinship networks. Rising on the ritual hierarchy can only be achieved by a caste as a group, over a long period of time, principally by adopting behaviour patterns of higher-ranked groups.

The book provides well-written and well-researched information on caste as a form of Social Inequality is a treatise on the subject. It provides enough insight into and proper information on related subjects also. The book narrates new perspectives on caste system which would enliven and create an interest in historians, sociologists, anthropologists, students, researchers and layman alike.

—Editor

1

Genesis of Caste System in India

CASTE

The Indian caste system is unique among systems of social stratification. This is not to say either that it is wholly incomparable with other types of stratification, or that no elements of caste are to be found elsewhere. In the first place, caste possesses the common characteristic of being evidently connected with economic differentiation. This is apparent whether we consider the effective caste groups (*jatis*) or the four traditional *varnas* of Brahmins, Kshatriyas Vaisyas and Sudras. The *varnas,* as Senart observed in a classical study, originally resembled feudal estatesin certain respects. They were like estates both in the character, and to a great extent, in the hierarchical ordering of the groups (priests, warriors and nobles, traders, serfs), and also in the fact that they were not totally closed groups; individuals could move from one *varna* to another and intermarriage was possible.

The *jatis,* which developed later and which continued to grow in number through the extending division of labour, the incorporation of tribes, and to a lesser extent, the operation of factors such as religious innovation, are the basic units of the traditional caste system. In modern India there are some 2,500 *jatis* in each major region. The *jati* is the endogamous group, and the principal way of life and maintaining it by the exercise of customary and, in earlier times, juridical sanctions. The economic significance of the *jatis* is plain; they are for the most part occupational groups and in the traditional village economy the caste system largely provides the machinery for the exchange of goods and services. On the other hand, elements of caste can be observed in other societies where more or less strict segregation of particular groups occurs; for instance, segregation of those engaged in 'unclean' occupations, or of those belonging to a particular ethnic group. But such individual features do not constitute a caste system. The only cases in which a caste system has been established outside Hindu India are those of non-Hindu groups in India (e.g. Muslims) or of Hindu settlement outside India, notably in Ceylon.

The sociological problem of caste is, therefore, to account for the existence and persistence of this unique type of social stratification. An explanation may be sought in two ways, either in terms of historical events or in terms of some factor or factors which are present in Indian society and not elsewhere. Any historical explanation is bound to be speculative in the present state of knowledge, and its value would consist chiefly in its incitement to fresh historical research. One of the most plausible accounts so far offered seems to be that given by J.H. Hutton, who suggests that the original Aryan invaders of India, with their distinct ranks, introduced the principle of social stratification into a society already divided into exclusive tribal groups by taboos connected with food, and that they took over and consolidated these taboos as a means of maintaining social distance between themselves and the subject population. In this manner the principle of stratified exclusive groups was reinforced, and provided with a powerful sanction in the shape of a religious and magical doctrine of pollution through food, and later, pollution through contact.

The second way of explaining caste, in terms of some other, specific feature of Indian society, involves a brief consideration of the relationship between *jati* and *varna*. Modern students of caste have emphasized the role of the magical and religious ideas of the *varna* system, as expounded in the ancient religious literature. M.N. Srinivas observes that the notions of *karma,* which 'teaches a Hindu that he is born in a particular sub-caste because he deserved to be born there', and *dharma,* the code of duties (or rules of the caste), 'have contributed very greatly to the strengthening of the idea of hierarchy which is inherent in the caste system'. The concept of pollution, he says, is 'fundamental to the caste system' and every type of caste relation is governed by it.' K.M. Panikkar, however, has argued from the distinction between *jati* and *varna* that the caste system has no basis in Hindu religion, and is rather the product of Hindu traditional law and of the weakness of the central political authority during much of India's history But although this draws attention to other factors which may be important in sustaining caste, it is in the main a plea for a re-interpretation of Hinduism. In fact, the castes and sub-castes are directly related to the *varna* system which, as Srinivas notes, provides an All-India frame of reference into which the myriad sub-castes of any region can be fitted, and at the same time embodies a generally accepted scale of values of and prestige. The distinction which Panikkar makes between the influence of religion and that of law is hardly tenable, for Hindu traditional law is dominated by religious ideas. The notions of *karma, dharma,* and pollution have figured prominently in both religious and legal thought, and together they constitute a doctrine which is undoubtedly one of the principal sustaining forces of the caste system.

We may conclude, the, that an explanation of the caste system would involve reference to some general theory of social stratification, to the specific features of the Hindu religion, and possibly to other factors such as the fragmentation of Indian society and the maintenance of a traditional economy. Such an explanation might be tested, albeit with difficulty, by studies of the effects upon the caste system of the far-reaching economic and political changes in recent times. In fact, studies in this field have hardly begun. The empirical studies of the past decade or so have mainly contributed a more precise knowledge of the traditional caste system. Almost all of them have been carried out in rural areas, where the impact of economic and political changes is weakest; even so, a number of studies reveal significant changes. Wealth and education have become accessible to members of lower as well as higher castes—although not perhaps on equal terms, S.C. Dube has shown how this affects a village community; wealth, education, or personal qualities may bring an individual prestige and power despite membership of a low caste. But the changes have been brought about by external forces, and they do not yet seriously challenge the old order. Dube notes that '... the grip of the traditional system is still firm, and people from lower castes or others with humble origins must behave with considerable tact and discretion if they seek to enhance their influence and importance in the community'. Similarly, F.G. Bailey, in a study of a village in Orissa, shows how the 'extending frontiers' of the economy and the polity bring about changes. With the development of trade, and of a money economy, land ceases to be the main source of wealth; the lower castes enrich themselves through trade and then use their wealth to buy land and so acquire prestige and power. The extension of government and administration also changes the balance of power; the lower castes in the village are no longer defenceless, for they can appeal, outside the village, to public officials and administrative bodies. But Bailey also concludes that caste in the village remains powerful, for it is still effective in hampering social mobility and in its ritual aspect it maintains the traditional hierarchy.

We should expect changes in caste to be greater in urban areas than in the villages, for economic change is greater there, the anonymity of town life facilitates social mobility, and the intellectual life of the town is more favourable to change. As yet, however, the paucity of studies of caste in an urban and industrial setting makes it impossible to determine how far new activities, associations and ideas—trade union, professional or political organizations and ideologies—have weakened the allegiance to caste.

Some information about the prevalence of caste sentiment is provided by K.M. Kapadia in a study of graduate teachers in Bombay State. He shows that while a high proportion of teachers express themselves in favour of intercaste marriages, even for their own children, there are in fact many agencies tending to maintain caste sentiment and caste endogamy. Thus caste foundations and charities are common, and many castes publish journals and organize social functions. One-third of the teachers subscribe to their caste journal and would like to participate in caste social activities. Kapadia concludes that 42 percent of the group display fairly display fairly intense caste feeling.

The lack of urban studies accounts in part for the uncertainties and disagreements about whether caste is being strengthened or weakened in Indian society as a whole. Many sociologists have observed that caste associations have developed rapidly, especially in the towns. M.N. Srinvias writes : 'There is a good case for arguing that caste-consciousness and organization have increased in modern India. Witness for instance the proliferation of caste banks, hostels, co-operative societies, charities, marriage halls, conferences and journals in Indian towns'. The influence of caste in politics is disputed, and it certainly varies from one region to another; there is no doubt that castes play an important part as electoral organizations and as vote collecting agencies, but empirical studies show that local castes are frequently divided on political issues, and that many other considerations influence political allegiance. In the sphere of education and opportunities for occupational mobility it is clear that caste retains its importance; higher education is still mainly open to the higher castes.

On the other side, there are general arguments about the effects of legislation, political democracy, and industrialization, all of which are held to be inimical to caste. Overt caste discrimination has certainly diminished, and the position of untouchables has improved, but it is doubtful whether the factors mentioned have weakened caste consciousness and allegiance. It may be claimed that they have not yet had time to do so; and industrialization, in particular, is not yet far enough advanced to have a decisive influence. But the effects of industrialization cannot be predicted with certainty, and compassions with the Western countries may be misleading. In the European countries which became industrialized during the nineteenth-century, the new industrial workers were not involved in any such close traditional bonds as those of caste and joint family, and they were not hampered in this respect in the formation of economic and political associations of a modern type. Moreover, neither workers nor industrialists were influenced by a traditional other-worldly religion. The actual connections between industrialization and changes in caste (and joint family) have therefore to be studied directly in India, and this calls for a new kind of research, which would be focused upon urban areas rather than villages, and upon the crucial occupational groups of a modern industrial society rather than the traditional caste occupations. M.N. Srinivas, in the survey mentioned earlier, specifies a number of topics which need to be investigated; the interrelation between caste and class, the relation of caste, class and rural-urban residence to utilization of educational facilities, the role of caste and class in bureaucracy, the part played by caste in trade unions and in political life at different levels, urbanization of selected castes in different parts of the country, the relation between caste and economic development, dominant castes in different parts of the country, hyperg-amous castes, and the role of purity-pollution ideas in the caste systems of North and South India. It is only necessary to add that the religious ideas which support caste deserve to be systematically studies.

We have seen that the strength of caste, and the tendencies to change, have been variously estimated, while the evidence is neither abundant nor clear. But whatever may be said about the strength of castes themselves, and of the individual's attachment to his own caste, it may be claimed that the traditional *caste system* has been profoundly altered. In that system each individual caste had its ascribed place and co-operated with other castes in a traditional economy and in ritual. No doubt, there was always some competition between castes and there were changes of position in the hierarchy of prestige; but there was no generalized competition. It is quite otherwise with the modern caste associations, which exist in order to compete for wealth, educational opportunities, and social prestige in a much more open society. These associations are, in fact, interest groups of a modern type; in Tonnies' sense, they are 'associations', while the traditional caste groups were 'communities'. It is easy to understand that they should have grown up on the basis of traditional castes, but equally that they contradict the caste system and may well give rise to, or be absorbed into, the secular groups of a modern society—trade unions, professional associations and social classes.

Origin of Varnas

The origin of caste system is in the *Varnashrama Dharma,* the division of society into four *Varnas* (four castes) viz., *Brahmin, Kshatriya, Vaishya,* and *Shudra*. It was believed and preached that for the prosperity of the world the creator created the four *Varnas*. The creator created these *Varnas* from different parts of his body i.e., the *Brahmin* was born from his mouth; the *Kshatriya* from his arms; the *Vaishya* from his thighs and the *Shudra* from his feet. He created *Brahmins* with *Gayatri* (metre); the *Kshatriyas* with Trishtubb; the *Vaishyas* with *Jagati* and the *Shudras* without any metre. The first three Varnas are twice born (*Dwija*), the first birth being from the mother and the second from the investiture with the sacred girdle. In the second birth *Savitri* is the mother and the teacher is the father because he gives instruction in the Vedas. Therefore, the first three *Varnas* are born twice while the *Shudra* is born only once. Among the *Brahmin,* the *Kshatriya,* the *Vaishya* and the *Shudra Varnas*, each preceding *Varna* (Caste) is superior by birth to the one following. It is popularly held that in the beginning there were only three *Varnas* and the fourth *Varna* of the Shudra is an outcome of the fight between *Brahmins* and *Kshatriyas* for the supremacy in the *Varna* (Caste) hierarchy.

Status of the Shudra

Many restrictions were imposed on the *Shudras* of which a few could be mentioned in brief. The *Shudra* was prohibited from milking a cow whose milk was to be used for *Agnihotra,* from witnessing performance of sacrifice, from taking *Soma* drink, from initiation (*Upanayana* or the wearing of the sacred thread), from studying the Vedas, and from kindling the sacred fire (right of sacrifice). If a *Vaishya* or *Shudra* comes as a guest to *Brahmin's* house he should be served food along with the servants. If a *Shudra* comes as a guest to a *Brahmins* house, he shall be given work, for his hospitality he is punished (100 *pannas*), because the *Shudra* is not worthy of respect on the ground of his age or wealth or knowledge, howsoever considerable these may be. He cannot be anything else but a servant. Even if one is young, if one is learned in the Vedas, he is elder to a *Brahmin*. The *Shudras* were not only prohibited from learning the Vedas, the Vedas could not even be recited before the *Shudras* by law. The recitation of the Vedas was interrupted merely by a look at the *Shudras* women.

The food touched by the first three *Varnas* is impure but not unfit for eating, while if it is touched by the impure *Shudra* it should not be eaten. If a *Brahmin* dines with a *Shudra* at a *Sharadha* a ceremony (ceremony of worshipping dead ancestors) all merits of the dinner will be destroyed. If a *Brahmin* dies of food given by a *Shudra* he is reborn as a village pig or in a *Shudra* family. After the food if he indulges in sexual intercourse with a *Shudra* women and a child is born, it becomes a *Shudra* and shall not ascend to the heaven. Neither the *Shudras* are carried by the twice born nor the twice born are carried by the *Shudras*. A *Brahmin* may not dwell in the kingdom of a *Shudra* or invader or low born men. Such was the discrimination among the *Varnas*. Most of the rules were to the advantage of the higher *Varnas*. The higher was the position of a *Varna* in the social hierarchy, the more was the advantage to that *Varna* from these rules. It is, therefore needless to say that in this scheme of things, the *Shudra* had few privileges because of his lowest position in the *Varna* system.

Discriminative Justice

Law is an instrument made and used by the powerful class to keep the subordinate classes in subjugation resulting in the perpetuation of poverty. According to Plato, law is a convention devised for regulating conduct, therefore, it is an arbitrary power the obeying of which depends on one's capacity to flout it. Even the judiciary was discriminative. For similar offences punishment prescribed was rigorous for the lower *Varnas* in general and the *Shudras* in particular. But for the same offences the *Brahmins* were subjected to very light punishment. One comes across innumerable discriminative laws against the interests of the *Shudras*.

Duties of Shudras

Discrimination by the judiciary against *Shudras*, an idea of the iron hand with which the *Shudras* were ruled. Even the duties of the *Varnas* and their status in the caste hierarchy had one to one correspondence. As a result the *Shudras* were given menial work which in turn placed them in the lowest position in ritual purity. Some of the duties which were assigned to the *Varnas* are given below. It was believed that for the sake of preserving all creations, the most glorious being ordained separate durities for those who spring from the creator's mouth, arm, thigh and feet. For the *Brahmins* he ordered teaching, study sacrifices (as priest) for others and also giving and receiving gifts. Defence of the people, giving alms, sacrifice, study and absence of attachment to objects of senses were ordained for the *Kshatriya.* Tending of cattle, giving (alms), sacrifice, study, trade and agriculture were ordained for *Vaishya.* Serving the upper castes without grudging was the duty of the *Shudra.*

A *Brahmin* may take the belongings of the *Shudra* with perfect peace of mind as nothing belongs to the *Shudra* but to his master. The mere sight of possession of wealth by the *Shudra* injures a *Brahmin.* A *Shudra* giving judicial decision would sink the kingdom into misfortune. The region chiefly inhibited by the *Shudras* is bound to be oppressed by famine and disease. Even if freed by his master, the *Shudra,* whether bought or not by the *Brahmin,* may be compelled to practise servitude as he was created merely to serve the *Brahmin.* Only two classes of *Shudras* were exempt from taxes: (1) Those *Shudras* who used to like washing the feet of the Brahmins and (2) those who were deaf and dumb or were suffering from diseases. In such a case the relaxation was to last till the infirmities continued.

To serve the upper three caste was ordained for the *Shudra.* The higher the caste he served the greater would be the merit. If the *Shudra* pursues his duties without complaining against the system, then he gains in this as also the other world. His mild speech, submissiveness to the Brahmins give him a higher birth. He may serve the *Kshatriya* for subsistence, the *Vaishya* for support of life and the *Brahmin* for the heaven. However, food which was left over, old clothes, blighted part of grains and very old furniture could be given to the *Shudras.*

Shudras were Kings

Originally the *Shudras* were kings and belonged to the ruling class. They were made slaves. The *Kayasthas* of Bengal, the *Lingayats* of Karnataka, the Marathas excluding the 5 and 96 families of Maharashtra, king Shivaji, the Vaidyas of Bengal, who were all converts to Hinduism, Madura Ramayana Chavadi, thousands of Yadavas residing chiefly in Madura and adjoining villages, even Gupte, *Ahirs,* the *Goper* of Bengal, *Chettis* the

Jats, the *Khatiks* of the Punjab, *Jats* Goldsmiths known as *Panchamas* or *Vishya* Brahmin of Marwar and so many other castes were once regarded as *Shudras*. However, they are not treated as untouchables now.

Untouchability in Ancient India

Shudras were divided into *'bhojyanna'* (food prepared by whom is not partaken by *Brahmin*) and *'abbojyana'* (food prepared by whom is not partaken by *Brahmins*). The first includes owned slaves. Historically untouchables were *abbojyanna* and therefore, were not *Dasas* or slaves or domestic servants in ancient times. *Shudras* known as *Chandalas, Vishadas, Vartyas* or untouchables are out of the *Varna* system. They lived outside the localities. For example *Madiga*, an untouchable caste in Karnataka State, *Mang* and *Mahar* castes in Maharashtra, *Adi Dravidas* in Tamilnadu, *Chomars* in North India and *Domes* in Bengal live on the outskirts of the villages. These castes are also known as *'Avarnas'* meaning thereby that they do not belong to the *'Varnas'*. There was no fifth *Varna* in the earlier Smritis but untouchables were referred to as *Panchamas*. *Panchamas* were also regarded as 'Hinas' of four types: (1) *Hina Janmana* (born against rule of marriage), (2) *Vratyas* (failure of *Dwija* in *performing Upanayman*' at proper time), (3) *Mlechas* living in *Mlecha* land (4) *Kshatriyas* who stopped performance of sacred ceremonies. The *Hinas* did not accept the authority of the Vedas, the system of the twice born and the caste system laid down by the *Brahmins*. The Jains and the Buddhists did not accept the Vedas, the *Varnashram* system of twice born.

Dasos or *Dasyus* were non-Aryans and did not belong to the *Varnas*. Hence they were treated as *Avarnas*. They were opposed to *Varna* system and did not follow Brahminic ceremonies. They were conquered and gradually made slaves. They had to suffer a lot. The very name *Shudra* is derived from *shue* (sorrow) and *Dru* (overcome) which means that one who has overcome sorrow. *Dasyus* or *Dasas* are the same as *Nagas*. *Dasa* is a Sanskritised form of the Indo-Iranian word *'Dahaka'* who was the king of *Nagas*. Indra consigned the base *Dasa Varna* to the cave and undertook task of subjugation and destruction of *Dasas*. He made *Dasyus Hinas* and gradually transformed them into *Shudras. Dasyus Hinas* are synonymous and in some places they are described as *Asuras.* It seems several wars were fought between Aryas or Aryans and *Dasas.* During these wars the Aryas prayed to Indra for subduing the *Dasas* in favour of Aryas.

Mlechas

Buddhists are regarded as *Mlechas.* They resided beyond three Aryan countries i.e., *Brahmanarto, Brahmarshi* land next to Brahmavarta central land. They spoke a barbarian language which was different from the Aryan and opposed the *Varna* system and the *Ashram* system and did not believe in the Vedas. They were branded as impure and referred to as foreigners. Those *Mlechas* who accepted the caste system became Hindus. They resided beyond the Vindhya mountain ranges (beyond Aryan culture) in Andhra, Anga, Vanga and Kalinga. Countries like Arattak, Karaskara, Pundra, Sauvira and Pranuna were also known as *Mlecha* countries. After they were conquered, they were given position similar to that of the *Chandlas* in *Aryavarta.* Greeks and Romans were treated as *Mlechas* and were reduced to slavery by Kautilya. This was natural as John Locks states that the conqueror uses one of the following four methods to rule the conquered people:

1. he continues to rule them according to their own laws and assumes himself only the exercise of the political and civil government; or
2. gives them a new government; or
3. destroys and disperses their society; or
4. in fire, exterminates the people.

The *Kushans* were foreigners or *Mlechas* whose kingdom extended upto the Bay of Bengal. They accepted Buddhism. King Julyaina destroyed many Sarglasrons (Buddhist monasteries) and killed *Bhikus* (Buddhist priests) in 2 B.C. *Mlhlrokulc,* a worshipper of Shiva, slaughtered countless Buddhists. Sashanka, king of Bengal, in the middle of 7 A.D. endeavoured many times to uproot the Bodhi tree (Buddhism). In Kashmir, Kshemagupta and Shri Harasha dealt ruthlessly with the Buddhists. At the instance of Kumaril Bhatt the Buddhists were driven out of Kerala. King Sudhanvan issued an injunction that from the Bridge of Ram in Sri Lanka to the

Himalayas, one who does not slay a Buddhist, both old and young, shall be slain. Thus, many Buddhist countries were destroyed because of their not believing in the Vedas and the *Varna* system. After their conquest they were made slaves and were not given the position of even *Shudras* but *Chandalas*—the untouchables.

Therefore, they were kept outside the *Varna* system whereas the Jains who not only accepted the *Varna* system but also the superiority of Brahmins and Brahmins were made the priests of Jaina temples. They had no alternative but to surrender to Brahminism. As a reward the Jains were not regarded as *Mlechas* or *Panchamas*. This was a theological distinction and not a racial one.

The Aryas even surrendered *Mlechhas* for food. The Brahmins were the enemies of Buddhism as they imposed untouchability on broken men when they refused to leave Buddhism. The defeated tribes became broken wanderers to settle themselves along with the settled tribes. They accepted to stay outside the village settlements. Untouchability was born out of the struggle for supremacy between Buddhism and Brahminism which has contributed a great deal to the moulding of the history of India. The *Panchamas* were defeated Buddhist who were made untouchables without any rights whatsoever, under the law of Brahmin countries.

Marriage and Caste Multiplication

Legally, the Shudra could marry only a *Shudra* woman, *Vaishya* could marry a *Shudra* and or a *Vaishya* woman, Kshatriya could marry a *Shudra*, a *Vaishya* and a *Kshatriya* woman, while a Brahmin woman could be a wife of only a Brahmin. Twice born marrying a casteless (*Hinayatt*) woman would descend to the rank of *Shudra*. A child born to a Brahmin by a *Shudra* woman was deprived of Brahminhood. Then both *Anuloma* (higher caste male and lower caste female) and *Pratiloma* (lower caste male and higher caste female) marriages were prohibited. *Dasi* (slave) also included a Shudra woman kept as concubine.

Shudra did not have the right of property. The *Dwijas* took advantage of it and reduced the *Shudra* woman's position to that of a *Dasi* or concubine. The powerful *Shudra* married a

Brahmin woman. In order to prevent such marriages, *Pratloma* marriage was prohibited and persons concerned were regarded as *Chandalas.* Their status was degraded i.e., after the touch of a *Chandala*, one should plunge into water, after talk with a *Chandala,* one should converse with a Brahmin and after seeking a *Chandala*, one should look at either the sun or the moon or the stars for purification.

The offsprings of *Anuloma* marriage were given intermediate caste above the mother's caste and below the father's caste. This law multiplied caste. Some examples can be cited as under :

1. Brahmin man + Vaishya women= *Ambustha*
2. Brahmin man + Shudra woman = *Nishad*
3. Kshatriya man + Shudra woman = *Urga*
4. Kshatriya man + Brahmin woman = *Suta*
5. Vaishya man + Kshatriya woman = *Magadha*
6. Vaishya man + Brahmin woman = *Vaideha*
7. Shudra man + Vaishya woman = *Ayogara*
8. Shudra man + Kshatriya woman = *Kahattar*
9. Shudra man + Brahmin woman = *Chandala*
10. Brahmin man + Ugra woman = *Awrita*
11. Brahmin man + Ambastha woman = *Abhira*
12. Brahmin man + Ayogava = *Shigyana*
13. Nishada man + Shudra woman = *Pukkasa*
14. Shudra man + Nishada woman = *Kukkutta*
15. Kshattar man + Ugra woman = *Sapaka*
16. Vaidehaka man + Ambastha woman = *Vena*

Thus, the entire social system was governed by the Brahminical law which was regressive in its character and was used as an instrument by socially privileged *Dwijas* who were also economically and politically powerful to keep the *Shudras* and the *Avarnas* in subjection and perpetual poverty. An arrangement was made so that the subjected class could never rise even in future by way of depriving them of any chance of economic power. This has continued even today. As a result the *Avarnas/Panchamas* or scheduled castes are deprived of the economic power or property.

HISTORY OF THE INDIAN CASTE SYSTEM

The history of the Indian caste system dates back to the Vedic period.

Origin

The origin of the caste system as it is today is still obscure. A 2001 genetic study, led by Michael Bamshad of University of Utah, found that the genetic affinity of Indians making their way to Europeans is proportionate to caste rank, the upper castes being most similar to Europeans, whereas lower castes are more like Asians. The researchers believe that the Indo-European speakers entered India from the Northwest, admixing with or displacing the proto-Dravidian speakers. Subsequently they may have established a caste system and placed themselves primarily in higher castes.

The study concludes that the Indian castes "are most likely to be of proto-Asian origin with West Eurasian admixture resulting in rank-related and sex-specific differences in the genetic affinities of castes to Asians and Europeans.". Because the Indian samples for this study were taken from a single geographical area, it remains to be investigated whether its findings can be safely generalized. However the findings of this study is considered controversial since the study was limited to one state, Andhra Pradesh, in India during the regime of a Chief Minister who was reprimanded several times by the Indian courts for Anti-Hindu activities. At the end of this article, the acknowledgments state that it incorporates contributions from an anonymous reviewer and because of its financial support, it has to be classified as an *advertisement. The publication costs of this article were defrayed in part by payment of page charges. This article must therefore be hereby marked "advertisement" in accordance with 18 USC section 1734 solely to indicate this fact.* The findings of this article is also in contradiction to later Human Genetic studies conducted with larger samples.

An earlier 1995 study by Joanna L. Mountain et al. of Stanford University had concluded that there was "no clear separation into three genetically distinct groups along caste lines", although "an inferred tree revealed some clustering according to caste affiliation". A 2002-03 study by T. Kivisild et al. concluded that the "Indian tribal and caste populations derive largely from the same genetic heritage of Pleistocene southern and western Asians and have received limited gene flow from external regions since the Holocene." A 2006 genetic study by the National Institute of Biologicals in India, testing a sample of men from 32 tribal and 45 caste groups, concluded that the Indians have acquired very few genes from Indo-European speakers.

According to a 2006 study by Ismail Thanseem et al. of Centre for Cellular and Molecular Biology (India) "the vast majority (>98%) of the Indian maternal gene pool, consisting of Indo-European and Dravidian speakers, is genetically more or less uniform", while the invasions after the late Pleistocene settlement might have been mostly male-mediated. The study concluded that the "lower caste groups might have originated with the hierarchical divisions that arose within the tribal groups with the spread of Neolithic agriculturalists, much earlier than the arrival of Aryan speakers", and "the Indo-Europeans established themselves as upper castes among this already developed caste-like class structure within the tribes."

The study indicated that the Indian caste system may have its roots much before the arrival of the Indo-Aryan immigrants; a rudimentary version of the caste system may have emerged with the shift towards cultivation and settlements, and the divisions may have become more well-defined and intensified with the arrival of Indo-Aryans.

More recent studies have also debunked the British claims that so-called "Aryans" and "Dravidians" have a "racial divide". A study conducted by the Centre for Cellular and Molecular Biology in 2009 (in collaboration with Harvard Medical School, Harvard School of Public Health and the Broad Institute of Harvard and MIT) analyzed half a million genetic markers across the genomes of 132 individuals from 25 ethnic groups from 13 states in India across multiple caste groups. The study establishes, based on the impossibility of identifying any genetic indicators across caste lines, that castes in South Asia grew out of traditional tribal organizations during the formation of Indian society, and was not the product of any mythical "Aryan Invasion" and "subjugation" of Dravidian people.

Hindu Scriptures

Although the Hindu scriptures contain some passages that can be interpreted to sanction the caste system, they also contain indications that the caste system is not an essential part of the Hindu religion, and both sides in the debate are able to find sections in scriptures that support their views. The most ancient scriptures—the *Shruti* texts, or Vedas, place very little importance on the caste system, mentioning caste only rarely and in a cursory manner. A hymn from the Rig Veda seems to indicate that one's caste is not necessarily determined by that of one's family:

Rig Veda 9.112.3 —*I am a bard, my father is a physician, my mother's job is to grind the corn.*

In the Vedic period, there also seems to no discrimination against the Shudras (which later became an ensemble of the so-called low-castes) on the issue of hearing the sacred words of the Vedas and fully participating in all religious rights, something which became totally banned in the later times. Later scriptures such as *Bhagavad Gita* and *Manusmriti* state that the four varnas are created by God. However, at the same time, the Gita says that one's varna is to be understood from one's personal qualities and one's *karma* (work), not one's birth. Some scholars believe that, in its initial period, the caste system was flexible and it was merit and job based. One could migrate from one caste to other caste by changing one's profession. This view is supported by records of sages who became Brahmins. For example, the sage Vishwamitra belonged to a Kshatriya caste, and only later became recognized as a great Brahmin sage, indicating that his caste was not determined by birth. Similarly, Valmiki, once a low-caste robber, became a great sage. Veda Vyasa, another sage, was the son of a fisherwoman. Vasishtha was a shudra and he became sage later.

Manusmriti, dated between 200 B.C.E. and 100 A.D., contains some laws that codified the caste system. Varna is mentioned as caste equivalent in Manusmriti. Manusmriti and some other shastras mention four varnas: The Brahmins (teachers, scholars and priests), the Kshatriyas (kings and warriors), the Vaishyas (traders, landowners and some artisan groups), and Shudras (agriculturists, service providers, and some artisan groups). Another group of untouchables excluded from the main society was called Parjanya or Antyaja. A varna can be viewed as a group of castes or a social division that consists of various sub-castes called *jatis*.

Passages in Manusmriti and other scriptures suggest that the Indian caste system was originally non-hereditary:

Manu Smriti X:65 — *As the son of Shudra can attain the rank of a Brahman, the son of Brahman can attain rank of a Shudra. Even so with him who is born of a Vaishya or a Kshatriya*

The various smritis, like the Yagnavalkya smriti and the Manusmriti strongly disapprove of marrying outside one's caste. The smritis also argue that new, despicable castes are formed out of such cases. According to these smritis, the chamars were born out of the union of a vaideha and a nishada, the chandals were born out of the sexual relations between a Brahmin and a Shudra.

Emergence of Rigid Caste Structures

Megasthenes, the Greek ambassador to Chandragupta Maurya's court in India classified people of India into seven classes: philosophers, peasants, herdsmen, craftsmen and traders, soldiers, government officials and councillors. In its later stages, the caste system is said to have become rigid, and caste began to be inherited rather than acquired by merit. In the past, members of different castes would not partake in various activities, such as dining and religious gatherings, together. In addition, the performance of religious rites and rituals were restricted to Brahmins, who were the designated priesthood. The "Pandaram" priests are an example of an order of Dravidian tamil priests, based in Nepal and South India. The Pandaram maintain the same tradition as the Brahmin priests, including the use of the Sanskrit language (traditionally reserved for the Brahmins) for the rituals. While they are not generally as well trained as the Brahmin priests, they are highly respected within their community and are addressed with reverence.

According to the Manusmriti, every caste belongs to one of the four varnas (Brahmin, Kshtriya, Vaishya, and Shudra).

However, there have been many disputes about the varna of many castes, such as castes being considered Kshatriya by some scholars, while described as Shudra by others. While texts such as the Manusmriti attempted to rationalize ambiguous castes by placing them in varna-sankaras (i.e. mixed varna), the fact remains that Indian society was, and is, composed of numerous geographically diversified but endogamous groups. With many occupational groups practicing endogamy within a particular region, as well as numerous sub-divisions within the four main castes, a more complex system of subcastes and jatis is evident. The jatis have broken up into clans like Agarwal, Iyer, etc.

Mobility Across the Castes

The view of the caste system as "static and unchanging" has been disputed by many scholars. For instance, sociolgists such as Bernard Buber and Marriott McKim describe how the perception of the caste system as a static and textual stratification has given way to the perception of the caste system as a more processual, empirical and contextual stratification. Other sociologists such as Y.B Damle have applied theoretical models to explain mobility and flexibility in the caste system in India.. According to these scholars, groups of lower-caste individuals could seek to elevate the status of their caste by attempting to emulate the practices of higher castes.

Some scholars believe that the relative ranking of other castes was fluid or differed from one place to another prior to the arrival of the British. The distinctions, particularly between the Brahmans and the other castes, were in theory sharper, but in practice it now appears that social restrictions were not so rigid. Brahmans often lived off the land and founded dynasties. Most of the groups claiming Kshatriya status had only recently acquired it. The conscious reference to being Kshatriya, a characteristic among Rajputs, is a noticeable feature in post-Gupta politics. The fact that many of these dynasties were of obscure origin suggests some social mobility: a person of any caste, having once acquired political power, could also acquire a genealogy connecting him with the traditional lineages and conferring Kshatriya status. A number of new castes, such as the Kayasthas (scribes) and Khatris (traders), are mentioned in the sources of this period. According to the Brahmanic sources, they originated from intercaste marriages, but this is clearly an attempt at rationalizing their rank in the hierarchy. Many of these new castes played a major role in society. The hierarchy of castes did not have a uniform distribution throughout the country.

Flexibility in caste laws permitted very low-caste religious clerics such as Valmiki to compose the Ramayana, which became a central work of Hindu scripture. According to some psychologists, mobility across broad caste lines may have been "minimal", though sub-castes (jatis) may change their social status over the generations by fission, re-location, and adoption of new rituals.. Sociologist M. N. Srinivas has also debated the question of rigidity in Caste. In an ethnographic study of the Coorgs of Karnataka, he observed considerable flexibility and mobility in their caste hierarchies. He asserts that the caste system is far from a rigid system in which the position of each component caste is fixed for all time.

Movement has always been possible, and especially in the middle regions of the hierarchy. It was always possible for groups born into a lower caste to "rise to a higher position by adopting vegetarianism and teetotalism" i.e adopt the customs of the higher castes. While theoretically "forbidden", the process was not uncommon in practice. The concept of sanskritization, or the adoption of upper-caste norms by the lower castes, addressed the actual complexity and fluidity of caste relations. Historical examples of mobility in the Indian Caste System among Hindus have been researched. There is also precedent of certain Shudra families within the temples of the Shrivaishava sect in South India elevating their caste.

Historical Advantages of the Caste System

Historically, the caste system offered several advantages to the population of the Indian subcontinent. While Caste is nowadays seen by instances that render it anachronistic, in its original form the caste system served as an important instrument of order in a society in which mutual consent rather than compulsion ruled; where the ritual rights as well as the economic obligations of members of one caste or sub-caste were strictly circumscribed in relation to those of any other caste or sub-caste; where one was born into one's caste and retained one's station in society for life; where merit was inherited, where equality existed within the caste, but inter-caste relations were unequal and hierarchical.

A well-defined system of mutual interdependence through a division of labour created security within a community.

1. Preservation of order in society through the use of institutional stratification of social groups.
2. Integration of foreigners and invading forces into Indian culture by assigning a caste to them (a process that historian Jawaharlal Nehru referred to as "Indianization"): India has faced repeated invasions from outside the region, dating back to the Macedonian invasion by Alexander the Great. Most invaders were swiftly assimilated into ancient Indian society by assigning them specific castes. Examples include the Kambojas, believed to be of Indo-Scythian descent, who were retroactively assigned a social position in the Manusmriti.
3. The Varna system, with its normative interpretation as a division of labour, had and continues to have a heavy bias towards spiritual evolution. The deep religious proclivities and the urge for spiritual uplift had induced the people to search for simpler and effective ways to achieve the spiritual goal which led to innovations like the Bhakti movement which had a powerful impact on the socio-cultural-spiritual life of the people even at mass level without distinctions of caste or class or other social differences. It is these deeply run cultural roots which caused an abiding following for Hinduism even in the face of unrelenting assaults by other religions and had in fact continued to influence the lives of people even after their conversion to other faiths. Thus, the caste system can be said to have preserved ancient cultural values in Indian society.
4. The caste system played an influential role in shaping economic activities. The caste system functioned much like medieval European guilds, ensuring the division of labour, providing for the training of apprentices and, in

some cases, allowing manufacturers to achieve narrow specialisation. For instance, in certain regions, producing each variety of cloth was the speciality of a particular sub-caste.

5. Philosophers argue that the majority of people would be comfortable in stratified endogamous groups and have been in ancient times. Membership in a particular caste, with its associated narrative, history and genealogy would instill in its members a sense of group accomplishment and cultural pride. Such sentiments are routinely expressed by the Marathas, for instance.

BRITISH RULE

The caste system was first exposed to the modern Western world during the Portuguese occupation and rule of sections of India. The word 'caste' in this context is derived from the Portuguese, 'casta'. Later, other European empires, including the British, occupied parts of the subcontinent. The earliest use of caste as a basis for interpreting social and demographic data arose from British officials' concern to stamp out female infanticide. Later, the use of caste to classify the population formed a basis for British attempts at social engineering. According to certain British laws (such as the Criminal Tribes Act of 1871), many castes and tribes were described as habitually criminal, and adult male members of such groups forced to report weekly to the local police. The caste-based classification (moneylending, agricultural or martial) was also used for other purposes such as legislation controlling land transfers, the grant of proprietary rights, the regulation of rents, recruitment to the armed forces etc. British anthropologist Herbert Risley's *The Tribes and Castes of Bengal*, published in 1892, was one of the first works on the caste system in India written by a Western scholar.

The earliest forms of classification in the British censuses of India (1865, 1872 and 1881) were based on the varna system, with the population being divided into Brahmins, Kshatriyas, Vaishyas and Shudras. Denzil Ibbetson, in his introduction to the 1881 census of the Punjab, argued that the Indian caste system was more of a social than a religious institution, and that conversion from Hinduism to Islam had not necessarily the slightest effect upon caste. He stated that the varnas had "no present significance". The 1891 census was based primarily on castes as occupational guilds instead of the varnas. Some scholars state that the caste system was broken up greatly during British Raj in India. However, some other historians suggest that the impact of British reforms has been greatly exaggerated.

Initially, the British strengthened the caste system. They gave the Brahmins back special privileges the Muslim rulers had taken away. During the initial days of British East India Company's rules, caste privileges and customs were encouraged in the Bengal Army. But, British law courts disagreed with the discrimination against the lower castes. Many believe that the lack of British respect for sepoys' caste traditions was one of the reasons behind the Indian Rebellion of 1857. During British rule, the reservation of seats for the "Depressed Classes" was incorporated into the Government of India Act 1935, which went into force in 1937. The Act brought the term "Scheduled castes" into use, which was later clarified in The Government of India (Scheduled Castes) Order, 1936 which contained a list of scheduled castes.

British Census Officers determined caste hierarchy based on the principle, e.g. someone who accepts food and water from another person but the other person does not reciprocate the same way, then the other person is superior to the former. It was contested at many places (a notable example is that the Koeris of UP who said they won't accept water from Brahmins, and so should be placed higher than them). Because it was met with rampant controversies, arbitration was very common during those days. The most notable arbitration stories are:

1. Caste status of Kayastha
2. Caste status of Kurmi.

It raised more questions than it answered and subsequent census records varied radically, making it free for all, after some time.

Reform Movements

There have been cases of upper caste Hindus warming to the Dalits and Hindu priests, demoted to outcaste ranks, who continued practising the religion. An example of the latter was

Dnyaneshwar, who was excommunicated from society in the 13th century, but continued to compose the Dnyaneshwari, a Dharmic commentary on the Bhagavad Gita. Other excommunicated Brahmins, such as Eknath, fought for the rights of untouchables during the Bhakti period. Historical examples of Dalit priests include Chokhamela in the 14th Century, who was India's first recorded Dalit poet, Raidas, born into Dalit cobblers, and others.

The 15th century saint Ramananda also accepted all castes, including untouchables, into his fold. Most of these saints subscribed to the Bhakti movements in Hinduism during the medieval period that rejected casteism. Nandanar, a low-caste Hindu cleric, also rejected casteism and accepted Dalits. Many movements in Hinduism have welcomed Dalits into their fold, the foremost being the Bhakti movements of the medieval period. Early Dalit politics involved many Hindu reform movements which arose primarily as a reaction to the tactics of Christian Missionaries in India and their attempts to mass-convert Dalits to Christianity under the allure of escaping the caste system (unfortunately, there is Caste system among Indian Christians among large sections of Indian Christians).

In the 19th Century, the Brahmo Samaj under Raja Ram Mohan Roy, actively campaigned against untouchability. The Arya Samaj founded by Swami Dayanand also renounced discrimination against Dalits. Sri Ramakrishna Paramahamsa founded the Ramakrishna Mission that participated in the emancipation of Dalits. Upper caste Hindus, such as Mannathu Padmanabhan also participated in movements to abolish Untouchability against Dalits, opening his family temple for Dalits to worship.

While there always have been places for Dalits to worship, the first "upper-caste" temple to openly welcome Dalits into their fold was the Laxminarayan Temple in Wardha in the year 1928 (the move was spearheaded by reformer Jamnalal Bajaj). Also, the Satnami movement was founded by Guru Ghasidas a Dalit himself. Other reformers, such as Mahatma Jyotirao Phule also worked for the emancipation of Dalits. Another example of Dalit emancipation was the Temple Entry Proclamation issued by the last Maharaja of Travancore in the Indian state of Kerala in the year 1936. The Maharaja proclaimed that "outcastes should not be denied the consolations and the solace of the Hindu faith". Even today, the Sri Padmanabhaswamy temple that first welcomed Dalits in the state of Kerala is revered by the Dalit Hindu community. The 1930s saw key struggles between Mahatma Gandhi and B.R.

Ambedkar, most notably over whether Dalits would have separate electorates or joint electorates with reserved seats. The Indian National Congress was the only national organisation with a large Dalit following, but Gandhi failed to gain their commitment.

Ambedkar, a Dalit himself, developed a deeper analysis of Untouchability, but lacked a workable political strategy: his conversion to Buddhism in 1956, along with millions of followers, highlighted the failure of his political endeavours. India's first Prime Minister, Jawaharlal Nehru, based on his own relationship with Dalit reformer Ambedkar, also spread information about the dire need to eradicate untouchability for the benefit of the Dalit community.

In more contemporary times, India has had an elected Dalit president, K. R. Narayanan, who has stated that he was well-treated in his community of largely upper-caste Hindus (24 July 2002). Another popular Harijan includes Babaji Palwankar Baloo, who joined the Hindu Mahasabha and was both a politician and a cricketer. He was an independence fighter. In addition, other Hindu groups have reached out to the Dalit community in an effort to reconcile with them, with productive results. On August 2006, Dalit activist Namdeo Dhasal engaged in dialogue with the Rashtriya Swayamsevak Sangh in an attempt to "bury the hatchet".

Also, the "Pandaram" are an order of Dravidian Tamil Hindu priests (a task traditionally reserved for the Brahmins) based largely in Nepal and parts of South India. These Pandaram priests maintain the same tradition as the Brahmin priests, including using Sanskrit for the rituals.

They perform religious ceremonies from weddings to death rituals. They are highly respected within the Tamil community and are addressed reverentially. Also, Hindu temples are increasingly more receptive to Dalit priests, such as Suryavanshi Das, the Dalit priest of a notable temple in the midst of Patna, the capital of Bihar. Discrimination against Hindu Dalits is on a slow but steady decline. The results of Bhakti Movements are clearly visible. Numerous Hindu Dalits have achieved affluence in society, although vast still remain poor irrespective of caste. In urban India, discrimination against Dalits is largely disappeared, but rural Dalits are struggling to elevate themselves. Government organizations and NGO's work to emancipate them from discrimination, and many Hindu organizations have spoken in their favour..

2

Caste System and Social Mobility in India

CASTE SYSTEM

Caste meaning Varna or colour originated in Vedic period. Through this distinction Aryans claimed supremacy over the conquered (Dasas and Panis). It is a Portuguese word meaning clan. Aryans settled between the Indus and Gangetic regions around 1,000 B.C.; they mastered the art of cultivation with it emerged greater division of labour and hence need for different occupations. Once the Aryans settled as agriculturists the Aryan society developed into grouping what is known as the four-fold caste system.

Those who were fighting were known as Kshatriyas; those cultivating were known as Sudra; the priestly community elevated themselves to the status of Brahmins. Significantly, with the beginning of cultivation by the Aryans the earlier word "gavasthi" meaning search for cows came to mean 'to fight', because fights between the various tribes of Aryans for fertile land and herds of cattle were common. Soon, by 600 B.C. a new grouping emerged in the Aryan community, a group of people dealing with trade and commerce. This led to emergence of new class Vaishyas, the Sudra community moved up to form this new grouping, while the non-Aryans and mixed-Aryan became Sudras. The concept of pollution also figured during this time as those who undertook unclean occupations like cleaning of carcasses, fishing and other occupations came into existence.

From sixth century B.C. onwards the historical evidence reveal that the Sudras were primarily drawn from non-Aryans and mixed-Aryans. Ashoka enslaved one and-half lakh people after the Kalinga war and brought them to the Gangetic region to cut forests and cultivate land. The Mauryan Empire saw the establishment of caste system based on occupation. This period also saw Brahmanism growing obscurantist as well as repulsive because of its rituals and sacrifices. The Aryan rituals and festivals became more pronounced marked by elaborate ceremonies by the priestly class. Historical evidence shows that it was during the Aryan stay in the Saraswati region that the legend of Manu was created that all kings were adjudged as descendants of the ninth Manu, while Brahma created the first Manu. Here again Priestly class tried to assume power so that they were not neglected.

The emergence of 61 schools of religious thought saw two, Buddhism and Jainism surviving the Brahmanism. Confronted by these new faiths, Brahmanism lost ground. Vaishyas became Buddhist and Jainis since they were not accorded a respectable status in Aryan society. Royalty too patronized these new heterodox sects which tried to simplify life for the common people-Bimbisara, Chandragupta Maurya (probably a Jain) and Ashoka became Buddhist. The subsequent period see the emergence of more rigid form of caste system in which more communities were added as subjatis. The observations of Fahien in the fifth century A.D. clearly show that untouchability was institutionalized.

MAIN FEATURES OF CASTE SYSTEM

Caste system hierarchically divides the society. A sense of highness and lowness or superiority and inferiority is associated with this gradation or ranking. The Brahmins are placed at the top of the hierarchy and are regarded as pure or supreme. The degraded caste or the untouchables have occupied the other end of the hierarchy. The status of an individual is determined by his birth and not by selection nor by accomplishments. Each caste has its own customs, traditions practices and rituals. It has its own informal rules, regulations and procedures. The caste panchayats or the caste councils regulate the conduct of members. The caste system has imposed certain restrictions on the food habitats of the members these differ from caste to caste. In North India Brahmin would accept pakka food only from some castes lower than his own.

But he would not accept kachcha food prepared with the use of water at the hands of no other caste except his own. As a matter of rule and practice no individual would accept kachcha food prepared by an inferior casteman. The caste system put restriction on the range of social relations also. The idea of pollution means a touch of lower caste man would pollute or defile a man of higher caste. Even his shadow is considered enough to pollute a higher caste man.

The lower caste people suffered from certain socio-religious disabilities. The impure castes are made to live on the outskirts of the city and they are not allowed to draw water from the public wells. In earlier times entrance to temples and other places of religious importance were forbidden to them. Educational facilities, legal rights and political representation were denied to them for a very long time. If the lower castes suffer from certain disabilities some higher caste like the Brahmins enjoy certain privileges like conducting prayers in the temples etc. There is gradation of occupations also. Some occupations are considered superior and sacred while certain others degrading and inferior.

For a long time occupations were very much associated with the caste system. Each caste had its own specific occupations which were almost hereditary. There was no scope for individual talent, aptitude, enterprise or abilities. The caste system imposes restrictions on marriage also. Caste is an endogamous group. Each caste is subdivided into certain sub castes which are again endogamous. Intercaste marriages are still looked down upon in the traditional Indian society.

Functions of the Caste System

The caste system is credited to ensure the continuity of the traditional social organization of India. It has accommodated multiple communities including invading tribes in the Indian society. The knowledge and skills of the occupations have passed down from one generation to the next. Through subsystems like Jajmani system the caste system promoted interdependent interaction between various castes and communities with in a village. The rituals and traditions promoted cooperation and unity between members of the different castes.

The Dysfunctions

Caste system promoted untouchability and discrimination against certain members of the society. It hindered both horizontal and vertical social mobility forcing an individual to carry on the traditional occupation against his or her will and capacity. The status of women was affected and they were relegated to the background. The caste system divided the society into mutually hostile and conflicting groups and subgroups.

Dominant Caste

This concept given by M.N Srinivas holds that a caste is dominant when it is numerically higher than the other castes. In the Mysore village he described the peasant Okkalinga composed of nearly half of the population made up of nineteenth jati group. The Okkalinga were the biggest land owner. The chief criteria of domination of a caste are

1. Economic strength
2. Political power
3. Ritual purity
4. Numerical strength.

The dominant caste also wields economic and political power over the other caste groups. It also enjoys a high ritual status in the local caste hierarchy. The dominant caste may not be ritually high but enjoy high status because of wealth, political power and numerical strength. The presence of educated persons and high occupation rate also play an important role in deciding its dominance over other caste groupings.

Sometimes a single clan of dominant caste controls a number of villages in areas. The dominant caste settle dispute between persons belonging to their own and other jati. The power of the dominant caste is supported by a norm discouraging village from seeking justice from area, Govt. official, court or police located outside the village. The members of the dominant caste particularly those from the wealthy and powerful families are representative of this village in dealing with the officials.

ORTHO-GENETIC CHANGES AND SOCIAL MOBILITY

We stated earlier that the Indian society even in the past incorporated within it changes and mobility of one type or another. It, however, started undergoing changes in a more thoroughgoing fashion in the last century. Four specific trends of change evolved during *Pax Britannica,* the period between 1857 and 1947. The lead in bringing them about was taken by a number of enlightened Indians. The leaders who helped bring about such changes can be classified into four categories: the reformists, the nationalists, the reformist-nationalists, and the revolutionaries.

The reformists, believing in social reforms to be brought prior to national freedom, founded three schools of thought in the eastern, western and southern parts of the country respectively and had their roots in various 'Samajs' and 'Missions'. In some regions they adopted resolutions in favour of throwing schools and colleges open to women and lower caste children, and of abolition of sub-castes. Thus, in a broader sense, as has been discussed by Ambedkar, the reformists were the true nationalists, for they tried to purify the caste system and educate various segments of the population. However, the social reform measures adopted by them centered, by and large, around the Hindu religion and family. Consequently, they could not generate fully a sense of reorganisation and restructuring of the Hindu society or of the Indian society as a whole. "These efforts left the core of the traditional beliefs practically intact. The reformist movements, therefore, remained essentially as fringe-movements...". The second trend was generated and advanced by the nationalists, agglomerated from diverse social backgrounds. Their major concern was the transfer of political power, and the reform in society, in their strategy, was to be carried out later. Tilak, Gandhi and Nehru were pioneers of this trend of change.

The third trend was led by Ambedkar and his supporters, including the Maharaja of Kolhapur, who put both the issues of social reform and transfer of power together and laid major emphasis on the former. Though bitterly criticised by the nationalists, they fought for social reform as well as for a share of the deprived people in the existing power and pelf first and freedom from British imperialism afterwards. The fourth trend, i.e., of revolutionary activities, was led by those who believed in an overall change in the structure and functioning of Indian society to be brought about not through negotiations with but through revolts and violence against British imperialism. Its main concern was with the common problems of the exploited masses irrespective of their caste and communal background. But this trend was also opposed openly by the British rulers and even by those nationalists who adopted non-violent means to achieve political independence. Thus, the revolutionary activities, by and large, could not achieve as much success as they ought to have.

Both the recurrent and patterned changes mentioned above suggest that Indian society has undergone the process of social transformation since long. In fact, the people belonging to different castes and communities had witnessed mobility of one type or another in their social status in ancient and medieval times. During the latter half of British rule many lower castes and tribes made various efforts and claims for getting their ranks elevated in the local social hierarchies. They also got such claimed ranks recorded in a number of surveys and censuses. Their efforts and claims were made on the basis of their adoption of customs, traditions and styles of life of upper castes and improvements in their economic and political positions.

Most of the middle and lower level castes tried to enhance their status both in caste and class hierarchies and thus to achieve social mobility within such frameworks. Members of these castes, through the adoption of reference group behaviour, tried to achieve social mobility within the framework of caste ranking in a particular region. This was possible in terms of both the micro—and the macro-level consensus, establishing, firstly, correlation between caste rank and interaction, and between different contexts of ranking, and, secondly, consistency of rank criteria in historical as well as contemporary, and rural as well as urban perspectives. Various low castes sometimes achieved their claimed status, though such changes were resisted by the referent castes. The cultural adoptions by the lower castes occurred within the frame of the Brahman, Kshatriya, Vaisya and Shudra *varnas,* which might be treated as four models of social mobility. Finally, the lower castes adopted a number of mobility tactics for overcoming external opposition and maintaining internal cohesion.

Mobility in the class hierarchy occurred in the form of improving one's socio-economic position: one claimed, and sometimes also succeeded in getting a claim accepted, for an enhancement of one's initial class position to the subsequently higher one. Thus, mobility which occurred in the class hierarchy was in some context mobility between lower, middle and upper classes found in each caste (Beteille 1966), and in some other context across the sub-castes but within the caste system. In yet other context it consisted of bourgeois and proletarian classes based on economic interests (Patnaik 1972). In the first case, they certainly improved their class position but could not succeed in interacting on equalitarian basis with members of the same or similar class drawn from another caste. Similarly, in the case of mobility in the class structure of the second type the different sub-castes of a single caste came closer on the basis of their class position. Finally, over a period of time a type of class polarisation, exactly not identical to that envisaged in the Marxian frame of analysis, has emerged. This has caused, in certain ways, upward or downward mobility of people in the class hierarchy.

However, the dominant pattern of social stratification in India has been that of caste. The hierarchies of caste and class have not functioned, so far, in parallel direction. It seems the class structure is inclusive of caste structure and vice versa. Consequently, mobility of a person in the class structure has not always led to his mobility in the caste structure. This has happened more in the case of the lower and particularly the lowest castes who have suffered a lot from numerous social and religious disabilities in the past. Also, complete social mobility has occurred neither in the past nor is occurring at present—it is possible only through a vigorous political action evolving "a civic value-oriented social system instead of a family, caste, religion, region and language oriented one".

SOCIAL DISABILITIES OF THE SCHEDULED CASTES

We stated earlier that social change as well as mobility were present in Indian society, especially in the caste system, even in the past. There is, however, no denying the fact that in the traditional Hindu society numerous social, religious and legal disabilities had been imposed on the Scheduled Castes, previously known by different names (Ghurye 1969). They were considered untouchable and denied the rights of fetching water from public wells, admission to schools, and services of community priests, barbers and washermen. These castes endured humiliating restrictions even in the use of umbrellas and *dolls* (palanquins). Their women were not allowed to wear bangles and any clothes above the waist. They were prevented from taking out processions on occasions of weddings and festivals. "The social conception of theological contamination, *chhut,* which prevented the lower orders from association with the higher castes, and resulted in artificial ceremonies of purification, remained in force rigorously from the medieval periods".

The untouchables were segregated from habitations of the general population and required to reside mainly in thatched huts outside the village boundary. In most cases they were supposed to stay outside the city walls. Wherever they were allowed to live in cities and towns, they were confined to separate *mohallas* (neighbourhoods) which could be compared with modern slums. In some regions in South India certain measurements were in vogue for maintaining physical distance with the untouchables. The social and religious disabilities of the untouchables were at the climax during the Gupta period, the so-called golden era (around 400 A.D.) in Indian history, when their shadows and even sights carried pollution and defiled the higher caste people, and they were made to shout a warning to keep others away from their contaminating shadows.

The untouchables were engaged in hereditary menial (and also manual) occupations in the traditional economy. Though they were related to other caste people through the *jajmani* relations as mentioned earlier, they received occasional payments not in cash but in kind. They received patronage often of exploitative nature as they were not generally free to use their clientele in their occupational pursuits. A majority of them were landless labourers, engaged usually in agricultural pursuits on low payment. "Members of the low castes (especially untouchables), assigned to the most menial and compatible occupations, could never aspire to the status of peasants holding or cultivating land of their own". More than that, they had to consume coarse grains, and most of them were dependent on the *uchchistha* (unclean food materials left over by the other caste people), flesh of the canon, and *gobaraha* (coarse grains sorted out from animal dung) in some parts of the country.

The untouchables suffered a lot from religious disabilities, as no community Brahman *(purohit)* performed any ceremony for them, as stated earlier.

Being debarred from entry into temples they sought to propitiate local deities and demons by sacrificing 'unclean' animals (pig, cock, etc.). They believed in numerous superstitions. In principle, they were a part of the socio-political organisation at the village, town or city level and were governed under the same rules. But in practice, they were not allowed to use freely their conscience in decision-making an any issue and their views were presumed. On the whole, their low rank "...was derived from cumulative inequalities in the [social], economic, political and ritual systems" (Beteille 1969: 93) and they were condemned to permanent social degradation.

It is difficult to project empirically today a generalised picture of social disabilities of the scheduled castes due to various reasons. One, there are numerous castes and sub-castes among the scheduled castes spread in almost every village, town and city in different regions all over the country. In one legion a particular scheduled caste may be placed in a lower order, but in other regions the same may be assigned a comparatively higher rank.

Two, a scheduled caste in a certain region may be placed in a higher rank in the caste hierarchy but another caste of a similar social and economic standing may have a lower rank in the same region. Three, some scheduled castes related to the non-scheduled castes through the *jajmani* and other traditional roles defile the latter on certain occasions, but outside these roles their social intercourse with others is accepted. For example, a Chamar agricultural labourer in villages in eastern U.P. does not defile jaggery *(gur)* when he manufactures it for his master, but he defiles it if be touches it after the process is over.

Due to such situations there may not be unanimity about social disabilities of the scheduled castes. But if one looks carefully at the caste system, one may easily put forth arguments for such regional differences in social disabilities *qua* statuses and ranks of the scheduled castes in caste hierarchy. As mentioned earlier, the system itself, in principle, sanctions most or the disabilities of the scheduled castes, and the sanctions govern even today the course of interaction of all castes in certain situations.

In examining the aforesaid social disabilities of the scheduled castes one may argue about various forces and structural constraints which prevented these castes from revolting against the social system in the past. Moore, for instance, says: "Strikes of the modem sort, the Untouchables scarcely knew, partly because labourers were broken up into different castes... Another was the fact (especially in the agrarian sector) that higher castes often preferred small returns, with less trouble and supervision, to standing over workers and trying to compel them to improve their ways....".

He further argues: "The lower castes disciplined themselves...[as they] had to learn to accept their place in the social order. On this score, the leaders of the lower castes evidently had an important task to perform. For doing so they received quite concrete rewards. Sometimes they received commissions on the wages of labourers from their castes as well as fines for any transgressions of caste regulations".

At the doctrine level, the peasants and lower castes accepted the theory of reincarnation and responded accordingly. Attitude towards the monopolist of supernatural power seems to have been a mixture of admiration, fear and hostility. Although one may raise some doubts about the validity of Moore's arguments, especially about the higher castes' attitudes towards peasants and lower castes, yet one cannot deny his basic contention about the harsh and unequal treatment meted out to the untouchables. One can perhaps easily agree with Mencher (1974:473) who says "We have no idea how many unsuccessful (or may be occasionally successful) rebellions there were in the past by untouchables, but it is possible that when they thought they had a chance to succeed, they tried." Of course, there are examples of scattered revolts launched by lower castes including the untouchables (Gough 1973), some for economic betterment and some exclusively for raising their overall social status in caste hierarchy. But all such efforts lack systematic records perhaps due to the fact that they were scattered and tiny in their effect and, therefore, could not enjoy favour of the record makers usually hailing from the upper caste and upper class backgrounds.

GOVERNMENT MEASURES AND SOCIAL MOBILITY AMONG THE SCHEDULED CASTES

In the above mentioned situation of numerous religious and social disabilities of the untouchable castes and occurrence of both the recurrent and patterned changes in the past in the country, it is difficult to ascertain the number of mobile persons from amongst these castes and the degree to which they had adopted changes, especially before independence. Yet, one can agree with Moore's statement (1974: 369), "One may even hesitate to claim that their relation to their employers changed fundamentally during the British period." Ambedkar also blamed the British government for adopting a policy of non-interference in the indigenous traditions and beliefs of Indian people. This indirectly supported the dominance of upper castes and thereby the retention of the caste system. Thus, the British rule in India could not remove the social and religious disabilities of the untouchables as they, by and large, could not rise from their position of the earlier times.

All the above mentioned trends of change, however, prompted the British government, especially towards the end of its rule, to enact several laws, at both the provincial and the central levels, to remove social and legal disabilities of the untouchable or scheduled castes. At the provincial level, steps were taken, as 'welfare measures,' to provide the scheduled castes with various facilities, such as opening of schools and hostels, fee remissions, scholarships, boarding grants, and book allowances, to promote their studies and pursue industrial and technical training. Some reservation was also made in appointment of candidates belonging to these castes to government jobs. Central government issued circular to the effect "that no grants would be paid to any aided educational institution which refused admission to the children belonging to the depressed classes" (Ghurye 1969: 275).

Various state governments pledged, as 'protective' measures, to discontinue inhuman practices against the lower castes and delegated powers to the local administration to deal with offenders. They passed a number of laws throwing open public places, and prohibiting all restrictions on worship by the scheduled castes in temples controlled by the state. The Caste Disabilities Removal Act was passed at the national level as early as in 1850.

In spite of all such legislative measures no significant change occurred among the scheduled castes. For, there was lack of uniformity in laws at the national level, and implementation of these laws was slack and faulty. Similar was the case with efforts made by various voluntary associations, though the dynamic leadership of Mahatma Gandhi provided an case to what he called Harijans.

After independence more systematic attempts have been made by the government to deal with the problems of scheduled castes. They have been provided with special rights and privileges and their interests are safeguarded through various provisions made in the constitution. These provisions have been made in the form of (1) protective measures, such as prohibition of discrimination, of forced labour, and of untouchability, (2) welfare measures, guaranteeing representation in various categories of public services, in State Assemblies, and in Parliament, and (3) developmental measures, providing grants-in-aid and other facilities for social and economic development.

Several acts and regulations to remove legal and social disabilities and to improve socio-economic conditions of the scheduled castes were passed in several states in the first two decades after independence. The central government declared the practice of untouchability as an illegal and serious offence through adoption of the Untouchability (Offences) Act, 1955, under which an offender was subjected to imprisonment and a fine of upto Rs. 600. During the Emergency period, this act was amended as the Protection of Civil Rights Act (1976) with an extended duration of confinement and a fine amounting to Rs. 1,000 or more. A few acts were also passed at the central level to remove indebtedness and bonded labour.

The above mentioned constitutional provisions, acts and regulations safeguarding the interests of scheduled castes have been enacted with three broad *manifest* objectives: (1) to provide reservation to scheduled castes in education, employment, State Assemblies, and Parliament, (2) to give them protection from social injustices and from all forms of exploitation, and (3) to raise their overall standard and remove social disabilities from which they suffer. Besides, there is a *latent* objective, namely, improvement in their socio-economic conditions which could result in the transformation of the pattern of interaction between the scheduled and the non-scheduled castes from hierarchical to egalitarian.

Under a time bound scheme of protective discrimination, efforts are made to bring the scheduled castes, besides other weaker sections, to a level where they can compete with the general population in education, occupation, style of life, and political participation. Further, the constitutional safeguards intend to guarantee educational, occupational and political mobility which may facilitate the scheduled castes to achieve a better status in class structure. However, such safeguards do not guarantee fundamental improvement in their caste status. Moreover, "...no guidelines have been established for determining when this goal has been reached... The benefits obviously build a vested interest in their own perpetuation. To the extent that the correlation breaks down between caste membership and actual levels of income, education and power, the system which relies on such a correlation becomes less workable and more subject to criticism" (Dushkin 1972:169).

In the light of the above delineation of the latent and patent objectives of the constitutional safeguards and various acts and regulations adopted in favour of the scheduled castes, one can raise several basic questions about the success or failure of such provisions. Have the scheduled castes made any significant changes in their educational, economic and occupational conditions? Have the various laws promoted a new interaction pattern between them and the non-scheduled castes? To what extent have the social and ritual distances between the two receded? Whether the status of scheduled castes in caste hierarchy has been affected by their status, if improved at all, in class structure? Resulting from this, what are the levels of their status identification? With the adoption of various legal measures a number of social scientists in India and abroad have pursued research on some of the above raised issues relating to change and mobility among the scheduled castes. Some studies have focused on social disabilities of the scheduled castes, and highlighted their poor living conditions, with the view of inviting attention of the government as well as non-government agencies to deal with the problem. Others have noted the limited impact of various laws on social change among the scheduled castes, along with limited change in the attitudes of scheduled and non-scheduled castes towards each other.

No doubt, a certain amount of change and mobility has occurred among the scheduled castes over a span of time. Such change and mobility in religious, educational, economic and political spheres has been regarded as channels utilised by the scheduled castes to raise their status in caste hierarchy. Both upward and downward mobility of limited degree can be seen today among scheduled castes. Such mobility has both positive and negative consequences. Thus, recording positive consequences of upward mobility among these castes, it has been guessed that there will be no 'Harijan' problem in the coming two or more generations at least in urban Punjab. "To be sure, there will be poor Harijans but they will merge into the poor of all castes". But such a generalisation may be an overestimate of mobility taking place among the scheduled castes, because even a partial upward mobility among them generates two sorts of problems. One, the upwardly mobile scheduled castes find it very difficult to get fully assimilated in the subsequently higher castes or classes which often resent and condescend upon such effort. Two, they are, to some extent, cut off socially from the masses of the scheduled castes and are treated as alien by the people of both the categories. In fact, they have been considered to be in the state of 'semi-limbo'.

The negative consequences of social mobility among scheduled castes have placed them into a number of dilemmas which, together with their stigmatised ethnic (caste) identity (Berreman 1979), obstruct even their partial assimilation in the Hindu social system. The processes of industrialisation and urbanisation have not helped them much in escaping from stigmatised identity and in desegregating into the main social stream. "On net balance, social mobility among the scheduled castes is far from satisfactory" (Singh 1977: 31). I have mentioned elsewhere that even a limited amount of social mobility—mobility aspirations—among the scheduled castes is resented, on one pretext or another, by non-scheduled castes, resulting into conflict between them (Ram 1977). Hence, social mobility among the scheduled castes has been opposed by a number of educated and politically conscious members of these castes, who find this process not very helpful in getting their status in the caste system raised as equal to that of other castes (Moffatt 1975).

It is, thus, clear that prior to independence Indian society bad witnessed a certain type of social change and mobility, confined to certain groups of people, especially drawn from upper castes. The scheduled castes were subjected to various social disabilities. A number of efforts were made during this period to ameliorate their poor socio-economic condition, but with no appreciable gain. After independence, several more comprehensive and systematic measures have been adopted, under the policy of protective discrimination, for the socio-economic betterment of scheduled castes and for protecting them from various social and economic disabilities.

A latent objective of these measures is to enable the scheduled castes to compete with the general population in regard to socio-economic achievement and to contribute more positively to the social progress of the country. These measures have certainly helped them improve to some extent their socio-economic position but not much their caste status. On net balance, they have made a little dent in social mobility and faced its both negative and positive consequences. Social changes and mobility that have occurred among them also suffer from proper appreciation and objective evaluation in a given frame of time and space. We have seen in the preceding chapter that certain types of changes and social mobility have occurred, with limited and uneven pace and rate, among scheduled castes in the present time. Their social mobility has been mistaken either as abrupt change in their religious and social practices or as little improvement in their socio-economic condition. Most of the studies relating to scheduled castes lack empirical verification in proper theoretical and methodological perspectives. Their evaluation of social mobility among these castes is guided generally by a number of measures adopted under the policy of protective discrimination and not by proper assessment of benefits derived by the beneficiaries. The folly lies in grand generalisations about the adaptive and gradual changes taking place among these castes at both micro—and macro-levels.

THE PROBLEM

It is true that after independence a small number of persons belonging to scheduled castes have benefited from the policy of protective discrimination. These persons have now acquired probably a better socio-economic status than that in the earlier times and thereby achieved social mobility in the class structure. There is every likelihood that they are forging a new pattern of social interaction and relations with people in their workplace and elsewhere, irrespective of caste and community considerations. Thus, there are men in the lower castes who "......have either been upwardly mobile earlier, or are upwardly mobile now, or are getting equipped for upward mobility in the foreseeable future" (Saberwal 1972:114). People of the third type might have acquired 'psychic mobility', if not social mobility *per se,* due to non-availability of resources for them. However, the mobile scheduled caste persons are said to avail of maximum facilities meant for the whole community and, in the opinion of some sociologists and social anthropologists, they form a category of elite, or neo-Brahmans, or new middle class. They are, no doubt, socially mobile, hut the degree and direction of their mobility are not clear, as is evident from a number of studies mentioned. Thus, it becomes imperative to measure the precise degree of their social mobility in the class structure (i.e., changes in socioeconomic status).

With changes in their socio-economic status the mobile persons of the scheduled castes, or for that matter persons of any caste or community, develop a new interaction pattern with others of similar socio-economic status. Similarly, the pattern of their interaction with people of their own and other castes of relatively lower socio-economic status may also change. They may even perceive some changes in the behaviour pattern of individuals of other castes and communities towards them. Therefore, we are interested to find out the consequences of social mobility, i.e., the impact of their social mobility on their interactions and relations with their non-scheduled caste acquaintances, We also intend to know their interactions and relations with the people of their own caste and other scheduled castes who have not been able to avail of the opportunities provided by the government for their betterment. We, further, want to know their perception of changes in the behaviour of non-scheduled castes towards them, and changes in their own behaviour with people of their own and other scheduled castes who lag behind in social mobility.

We have said earlier that the constitutional measures help the scheduled castes achieve higher class status but do not guarantee any improvement in their caste status. The mobile scheduled castes might have achieved better class status due to changes in their social, economic, occupational and interaction positions. It is, however, unclear whether it facilitates to vigorously alter their caste status. It is thus important to examine the changes, if any, taking place in their caste status, the determining factors and indicators of such changes, and the congruity between their achieved (class) status and ascribed (caste) status.

The mobile persons from among the scheduled castes adopt the behaviour pattern of either certain individuals or groups and categories as a reference for their social mobility and identification (Mandelbaum 1972). They also try to associate themselves with their referents but at the same time find it difficult to merge their identity fully with that of the referents due to structural constraints and objective reality. Our intention in this study is to locate their positive and negative orientations to and adoption of reference individuals and groups for their social mobility and status identification. We also intend to find out the determinants of their selection of reference groups and individuals.

The benefits of protective discrimination bring the scheduled castes in a position where they are probably not able to get a socially accepted new place in caste hierarchy. Yet there may be four possible levels of their status identification: (1) they would identify themselves at their own caste level; (2) they would claim a status of superior caste by improving their class status; (3) they would be satisfied with their improved status in class structure without caring much for their status in caste structure; or (4) they would identify themselves at the non-caste-class level. More precisely, their status identification could be ethnocentric, in which they may or may not claim the superior rank of their own caste in caste hierarchy due to their improved status in class hierarchy, and identify themselves with their own caste fellows. Or, it may be 'contra-identification' where they may try to establish their identity contrary to the ethnocentric one. In contra-identification, they may identify themselves either with members of other, especially upper castes or classes, or outside of both the folds. In other words, they may not believe in any identification whatsoever in the stratification system and may have a frame of reference of non-stratificational identification. Therefore, we shall be interested in explicating the nature and level of their status identification.

In short, the following are the main objectives of this study

1. To identify the degrees and directions of social mobility among persons of scheduled castes.
2. To investigate patterns of their social interaction and relations with non-scheduled castes and with their parental stratum, and the level of ritual and social distance therein; their perception of changes in the behaviour of non-scheduled castes towards them, and their own behaviour towards the scheduled and non-scheduled castes.
3. To find out changes in their statuses both in caste and class structures, the determining factors and indicators of such changes, and congruity between achieved and ascribed statuses.
4. To explicate their positive and negative orientations to and adoption of reference groups and/or individuals; determinants of their selection of such referents; and cultural or structural contexts of reference group/individual behaviour in which they try to adjust themselves.
5. In the light of 3 and 4, to measure the nature and levels of their status identification.

The above mentioned objectives have been pursued in the light of a number of hypotheses relating to socio-economic background, social mobility in class and caste structures, social interaction and social relations, and status identification. A few hypotheses have been adopted from other studies of more or less similar nature. The hypotheses have been tested with support of data in appropriate contexts.

THE THEORETICAL FRAMEWORK

The framework of this study has been developed with the help of two sets of four inter-related theories: Lipset and Zetterberg's (1966) theory of social mobility; Homans' (1962) theory of status congruence; Merton's (Merton and Rossi 1968) theory of reference group behaviour; and Paranjpe's (1970:106-14) theory of ethnocentric and contra-identification. We have tried to analyse social mobility among scheduled castes within the frameworks of the first two theories. More specifically, social mobility in class structure has been measured through a multiple approach suggested in Lipset and Zetterberg's theory, with necessary modifications. We have relied on this approach because a comprehensive study of social mobility is possible through such an approach only and not through the single dimension approach, namely, the dimension of occupation. In the words of Heck (1956:132), "The multiple approach...wants, as fully as possible, to take the fact into account that society is characterised by multiple, overlapping, and even contradictory criteria of status." The above mentioned theory is based actually on certain assumptions directly related to the study of social mobility in a class based society. But a study of social mobility in India in general and among the scheduled castes in particular has to examine the mobility of status in caste structure besides that in class structure. We have, therefore, measured in this study a correlation of their mobility of statuses in class and caste structures and have called the extent of such correlation 'complete social mobility'. Further, a person might have achieved high status in class structure but been ascribed with low status in caste structure. So, as a consequence of social mobility, such discrepancy between the two types of statuses may create status anxiety for him. We have analysed status discrepancy and status anxiety of the mobile scheduled castes in the framework of Homans' theoretical formulation of status congruity and status anxiety. Although his model is also applicable to a society based on class structure, we have adopted it with necessary modifications in the specific context of India.

A person's status, besides its objective manifestation, is related to the self-image he projects to others. But he generally derives such self-image from others. In other words, a person internalises life styles and behaviour patterns of certain groups and/or individuals and projects them before others. Merton has called such internalisation 'anticipatory socialisation', based on values and styles of life of reference groups/individuals. Such an approach is applicable to the mobile persons of scheduled castes also. Therefore, derivation of their self-images has been analysed in Merton's frame of reference group/individual behaviour. A person may identify himself or his status in three ways, as stated earlier at the caste level, the class level, or beyond these two levels. If a socially mobile person identifies himself or his status at the level of his own caste, he may be proud of his caste background, as he believes in the demonstration effect of his achievement in relation to his caste background. Such identification is similar to ethnocentric identification. Or, if he is shy of his caste, he will try to 'pass' his caste background and identify at the other caste or class level or some other level, which is contrary to ethnocentric identification. The third type of identification occurs if he genuinely does not believe in any hierarchical system. Therefore, the level of identification has been measured in the light of Paranjpe's theory of ethnocentric and contra-identifications.

Properties of the Theoretical Framework

In their theory of social mobility Lipset and Zetterberg have underlined the dimensions of occupational and consumption rankings, social class, and power rankings, in addition to providing a methodological note. They have also pointed out causes and consequences of social mobility. According to them, social mobility of a group or individual is determined by the shift and ranking of occupations, consumptions, social power, and social class, "composed of individuals who accept each other as equals and qualified for intimate associations". Accepting occupation as the most common indicator of stratification, they have viewed that "occupational class is one of the major factors which differentiate people's beliefs, values, norms, customs, and occasionally some of their emotional expressions" *(op. cit.* 562). In their opinion, the recording of one's occupational class also needs the recording of the occupational setting, i.e., the kind of social structure in which the occupation under study is located. It is, however, not necessary that one's consumption position goes along with one's occupational and/or income position. "At the same occupational/income level, men will vary in the extent to which they are oriented towards acting out the behaviour pattern common to different social classes". One may change one's occupational class by changing one's job, but the real improvement in one's social class position is possible only if one is admitted to intimate relationships with members of the referred social class. Similarly, one's role relationship is considered in terms of one's authority (not political authority) exercised over others in the social system. Accepting such authority as one's social power, Lipset and Zetterberg have treated it as a separate dimension of social mobility.

Lipset and Zetterberg have accepted that there is a possibility of having a higher rate (and amount) of mobility in one dimension and lower in others. Therefore, the more qualified and accurate conclusions about mobility and stratification systems are possible only through a multi-dimensional approach in which one has to take all the possible dimensions together. Lipset and Zetterberg have suggested two sets of methodological approaches to the study of social mobility. In the first set, there are comparisons of (i) the present with the past, (ii) one area or country with another, and (iii) one model with another expressing equal opportunity. In the second set, there is the conventional operational method of ascertaining mobility by comparing father's and son's positions. In this method, Lipset and Zetterberg have suggested an enquiry into father's earlier occupation along with his last one (and the present, if still employed) and son's present as well as earlier occupations. Finally, they have suggested analysis of social mobility in terms of causes of (i) supply of vacant statuses, and (ii) interchangeability of ranks, followed by inquiry of political consequences. We have adopted in the present study only the multi-dimensional approach and the second set of the methodological portion of this theory. We have excluded the 'social class' dimension, because an inquiry into the willingness of the people of one social class to accept others as its members was beyond the perview of this study. However, we have included in our theoretical framework two more dimensions, those of education and income. We have done so because in a society like India, particularly in the case of the scheduled castes, education plays a pivotal role in social mobility. Moreover, mobility among the scheduled castes is a sponsored mobility (Schermerhorn 1978) where the government has been providing them with various educational facilities.

In Lipset and Zetterberg's view "a large number of families headed by men in low prestige (blue collar) occupations receive (net) higher incomes than many middle class families in which the wife does not work, and the children receive a prolonged education" (1966: 563). However, the lower prestige occupations, now often having incomes more or at par with the incomes of white collar occupations, affect one's style of life. But income is not considered a separate dimension of social mobility and is treated with the dimensions of occupation and consumption rankings. We have treated occupation, income, and consumption patterns as separate dimensions because there is every likelihood that one may be high in income and consumption rankings but low in occupational prestige, and vice versa. Similar may be the case with social power. Thus, we have included in our framework five dimensions: education, occupation, income, consumption pattern, and social power.

We have stated earlier that social mobility among the scheduled castes is a sponsored one. As regards causes of their social mobility, their supply to vacant statuses in the class structure and latently in the caste structure, and interchangeability of their ranks in such statuses, are facilitated, in principle, by the policy of preferential treatment accorded to them. However, it can be surmised that in most cases their social mobility, either sponsored or otherwise, is the result of their high aspiration and lofty motivation. Further, the scheduled caste government employees, for whom the present study is based, are not allowed, like other government employees, for active political participation, though they may have their distinct political views on certain issues. Therefore, we have not included various causes and political consequences, as suggested by Lipset and Zetterberg, in our theoretical framework.

We have mentioned that social mobility among scheduled castes is related to their status in both class and caste systems. For measuring this type of mobility we have also included in our theoretical framework Homans' theory of status congruence, as stated earlier. According to this theory, if there are persons who have their status factors in an organisation 'in line', they claim their status congruity, and those whose status factors are 'out of line', do not. In Homans' terminology, 'in-lineness' may be a condition of relative and distributive justice for such individuals, whereas 'out-lineness' may lead to status anxiety. We have adopted this theory for measuring the congruence of achieved and ascribed statuses of mobile persons of scheduled castes who may be in-line in their achieved status but out-of-line in the ascribed one, although their out-of-line status would mean here status within the line in the traditional status hierarchy. In such a case they might face a problem of status anxiety.

In the theory of reference group behaviour (and attitudes) and relative deprivation, Merton and his associates (Merton and Rossi 1968) have suggested that certain individuals or groups tend to adopt the behaviour (and attitudes) of other groups or individuals in order to achieve a similar social position. But if they fail in their achievement, they suffer from relative deprivation, because they find others belonging to their group achieving success in similar situations. Further, in the course of adoption of reference group/individual behaviour one also identifies oneself with the reference group/individual. Therefore, we have included in our framework an inquiry into the types of reference groups/individuals which the mobile scheduled castes may follow to achieve their respective social positions. We also wish to measure through this their relative deprivation.

The theory of ethnocentrism was propounded initially by Sumner (1965: 13-15) and developed later by a number of social psychologists. According to this theory, an individual or a group identifies with an ethnic group and claims ethnic superiority in comparison to other ethnic groups. In some cases, one hates and takes revenge on them. If in certain cases an individual or a group does not identify at the ethnocentric level, then identification may be at a level other than ethnocentric. Thus adopting the theory of ethnocentrism in the Indian situation, Paranjpe (1970) has stated that individuals may identify either with their ethnic (caste) group, or contrary to it. This may be true also in the case of status identification of the mobile scheduled castes, as stated earlier. In our framework we have adopted Paranjpe's (1970) theory of ethnocentric and contra-identification, adding the non-caste-class type of identification in the latter.

Integration of the Theoretical Framework

The above mentioned theories adopted in our framework have been linked up with one another. In the first set of framework the occurrence of complete social mobility can properly be examined only when the changes in one's caste status are taken into account along with changes in one's class status. If there is change in one's class status but no change in one's caste status, then one's status will be incongruent and social mobility incomplete. In such a situation one may suffer from status anxiety. Thus, there is sufficient ground to link Lipset and Zetterberg's theory of social mobility with Homans' theory of status congruence and status anxiety. Similarly, these theories can be linked with Paranjpe's analysis of status identification because, as stated earlier, the fully mobile persons of scheduled castes would prefer contra identification more than those who are not so mobile. There are two possibilities in Homans' theory of status congruence. If an individual finds his status incongruent, he will either develop status anxiety as mentioned above, or pay the cost of accepting his status inferiority. Through an exchange of social behaviour and face-to-face interaction he will learn the skills for achieving his status congruence. In this sense, his superiors become his reference group/individuals. Thus, the second possibility of status congruence may be related to the theory of reference group/individual behaviour adopted in our theoretical framework. Similarly, the theory of status congruence can be related to the theory of status identification, because those who have congruent status may prefer contra identification more than those whose status is incongruent, as mentioned above.

LOCALE OF THE PRESENT STUDY

There is 15% reservation granted to scheduled castes in various categories of jobs in the public or government sector. The private sector has not accepted the policy of reservation in jobs for scheduled castes will now. Since the job career of these castes is said to be safeguarded, in a way, in the public sector, the government departments and offices provide the best source of avenue for a study of social mobility among scheduled castes. The data for the present study has been collected from the scheduled caste government employees in Kanpur city, which is the eighth largest city in India and has a large number of government offices. The administrative machinery in the city is divided into the Municipal Corporation and the state and central governments. As the Kanpur Municipal Corporation has nominal representation of scheduled castes in its administration, we considered it desirable to cover administrative offices of the state and central governments which have a sizable number of employees of these castes at least in the non-administrative categories of jobs.

It is ironic that after a period of more than 35 years of reservation of seats in government offices no systematic and sufficient information is available regarding the number of scheduled caste employees in the public sector. To get the actual number of scheduled caste employees in each administrative office located in Kanpur city, we first approached the District Harijan and Social Welfare Office but with no result. Therefore, we made a survey of almost all the state and central government offices located in the city. The administrative heads of these offices were requested to provide names of scheduled caste employees in their offices. An informal technique was also adopted for the purpose, by seeking the help of some influential employees belonging to both the scheduled and non-scheduled castes in the respective offices. Thus, a comprehensive, but not exhaustive, list of 600 scheduled caste persons employed on permanent basis in the state and central government offices was prepared for the purpose of data collection.

It was proposed in the beginning to interview all the employees, in the list, but due to the time constraint the study was restricted to a sample of 40% (240) of them. The selection of respondents was based on stratified random sampling, where they were selected representatively from each category of jobs, ranging from sweeper (Class IV) to administrative (Class I) official, in both the state and central government offices.

NATURE AND ANALYSIS OF DATE: SOCIO-PERSONAL INFORMATION

In this set we collected from the respondents the following types of information (a) the respondents' caste, age, marital Status, number of male and female children, permanent habitation and socio-economic status of their family, their own educational qualification, and the extent to which they found education helpful in their career; (b) the nature of their present job, the reasons for their joining it, the difficulties they faced in getting it, their seniority in the job, and the length of their stay in Kanpur city; (c) their income, particularly their monthly salary, and emoluments from other sources; (d) their views regarding difficulties they were facing in a new social situation, the type of their neighbourhood, and reasons for moving and/ or not moving out of their neighbourhood.

Mobility Data

In this set we collected the following types of information: (a) the respondents' educational qualification, the cadre of job, their income, monthly expenditure of the current year and five years ago on essential and semi-essential items, and their social power in formal organisations and other associations; (b) social power enjoyed by their fathers in formal organisations (if they were employed therein) and in various other associations, or, in the case of fathers not employed in public sector jobs, their social power in the caste panchayat and similar other organisations; (c) educational qualifications and various jobs/ occupations of the respondents' fathers, starting from the first to the last job/occupation, and their monthly emoluments from it; (d) the respondents' shift, if any, from one job to another over a span of time.

Status Inquiry

We measured the respondents' statuses in caste and class structures on the basis of subjective and objective assessment. At the subjective level, we recorded their responses regarding their status as perceived by them and by their acquaintances in caste and class structures. Likewise, such statuses of their fathers, as perceived by others but reported by the respondents, were noted. Their caste status was measured by recording the types of their interaction with people of scheduled and non-scheduled castes. At the objective level, their status and that of their fathers in the class structure were computed on the basis of their educational, occupational, income, expenditure, and social power positions. However, in both the types of measurement, changes in the caste and class statuses of the respondents and of their fathers, the indicators and determining factors of such changes, and the congruity between their ascribed (caste) and achieved (class) statuses were recorded, mainly on the basis of their perception.

The change in their caste status and of their fathers was verified with the help of their knowledge of the perception of others about it. This was compared with their own perception of the ritual and social distances existing between them and non-scheduled castes. This was followed by the measurement of social status of the respondents and their fathers in an overall social stratification.

Status Identification

In the last set of information, an effort was made at two levels to know the nature of status identification of the respondents. At one level, they were asked about their interaction with people of the scheduled and non-scheduled castes. They were asked about their surnames, their disclosure of caste identity, and their general identification to a visitor. This was followed by an enquiry about their class identification. At the second level, the nature of their behaviour towards their own castes and the reference individuals and/or groups was inquired about. Finally, their perception of the status identification of their fathers, at both levels, was recorded.

Variables

In the first set of measurement of social mobility in the class structure, the items included in the background information about the respondents have been treated as independent variables, and social mobility as a dependent variable. In the second set, various dimensions or channels of social mobility in class structure have been viewed as independent variables, while consequences of social mobility in terms of changes in caste status have been treated as dependent variables. In the last set, status identification has been considered as a dependent variable, and socio-personal background and social mobility of the respondents as independent variables. Other variables have also been treated as dependent or independent according to the contexts in which they have been used.

Social Mobility Indices

For preciseness of measurement we have evolved a number of indices and scales. Social mobility in the class structure has been measured along five dimensions, as mentioned earlier. For this purpose, we have prepared a mobility index. For the dimension of education we have adopted partially the Kuppuswamy scale (Kuppuswamy 1959, 1962) with the following weightages assigned to the various levels of education: post-graduation/professional-7, graduation-6, intermediate/post-high school diploma-5, high school-4, junior high school-3, primary/literate-2, and illiterate-1.

We have assigned arbitrary weightages to other dimensions on the basis of validity of the 'face values' because of their specificity in our sample. Thus, we have given 1 to 8 weightages to different types/categories of occupations/jobs ranging from the caste occupation (in the case of father's occupation, if he was associated with it) to Class I government jobs. The justification for assigning higher weightages to the different categories of jobs is the social prestige attached to them and the people's higher preference for office employment. In other words, people attach more prestige, in varying degrees, to different categories of government jobs and to business than to cultivation, manual labour, and caste occupations.

We have given 1 to 9 weightages to the monthly emolument/salary/income ranging from Rs. 200 to 600+. Weightages 1 to 6 have been assigned separately to monthly expenditure, incurred on both essential and semi-essential items, ranging from Rs 100 to 400+. We have assigned 1 to 9 weightages to the different levels of social power acquired by the respondents and their fathers. We have aggregated these weightages, assigned to the different dimensions, with regard to the respondents and their fathers, and deducted the dimensional aggregated scores for the fathers from those for the respondents. Thus, we have tried to find the actual amount or degree of the respondents' social mobility in class structure, and interpreted it in terms of low, medium and high mobility. On the basis of aggregated scores of variations of multi-dimensions, we have constructed an 11-point index for measuring the directions of such social mobility among the respondents. The directions of social mobility have been measured horizontally and vertically. The extent of vertical mobility has been measured in terms of little, less, much, more, and most upward, and similarly, downward directions. However, the extent of the amount and direction of mobility among the respondents can neither be accepted as true projection of it nor as an absolute one, for want of an analysis of it in the case of non-scheduled castes of similar social background.

Socio-economic Status (SES) Scale

The socio-economic status of the respondents' families of procreation and of orientation has been measured by applying partially the aforesaid Kuppuswamy scale as developed, in an urban situation in India. As stated earlier, we have accepted his weightages assigned to education but have given arbitrary weightages to occupations/jobs and income on the basis of validity of the 'face value' because the occupation/job and income categories in our sample are different from those of Kuppuswamy's. The weightages assigned to occupations/jobs are: caste occupation-0, labour-1, non-sweeper, Class IV employment-2, cultivation-3, lower clerical/technical, Class III work-4, upper clerical/technical, Class III work-5, technical/non-technical, supervisory, Class III work-6, technical/non-technical, Class II officer-7, and technical/non-technical, Class I officer-8. Similarly, the weightages assigned, in ascending order, to the monthly emolument/salary/income are 1 to 9 for the range of Rs. 200 to 600+ at intervals of Rs. 50 each between two categories. Caste has been playing a significant role in determining socio-economic status even in cities, as is evident from a number of studies conducted in' this regard, while its importance is even greater in villages. We have measured socio-economic status of the respondents' family of procreation residing mostly in villages. We have taken caste of the respondents as a fourth dimension of their socio-economic status and that of their family of procreation, and assigned 1 to 8 weightages as given by 20 'judges' from among non-scheduled castes who either belonged to rural areas or were aware of the ritual and social status of the scheduled castes under reference. Thus, by aggregating weightages assigned to all the four dimensions we have measured socio-economic status of the respondents and of their family of procreation.

Caste Status Ranking (CSR) Scale

There are eight major scheduled castes *(jatis)* in Kanpur city: Chamar, Kori, Pasi, Balmiki, Khatik, Dhanuk, Dhobi, and Shilpkar (Stone-cutter) (Bhatnagar 1965: 62). All these castes are not' ranked equal in the caste hierarchy prevailing in the city. A caste is rated high or low on the basis of its ritual and secular services to other castes in a region. The material achievement of its members also contributes in this regard. It was difficult to measure the ranks of these castes (including the Dusadh with about 100 families in the District but thinly represented in the sample) on the basis of 'face values' of the respondents themselves, because all the scheduled castes, like the upper and intermediate castes, try to establish their status superiority over each other.

This problem was overcome by relying on the opinions of the 'judges', who ranked these castes by applying certain attributional/interactional criteria. The 'judges' considered power and wealth also of the members of the castes ranked by them. Thus, the ranks of these castes in a descending order are as follows: Kori/Tamta/Khokhar, Dhobi, Khatik, Dhanuk/Bahelia, Kanjar, Pasi, Jatav/Kureel/Chamar, Dusadh, and Balmiki.

Social Distance Scale (SDS)

The extent of behavioural social distance between the scheduled and non-scheduled castes has been measured through the modified version of Bogardus' (1967) social distance scale. Modification has been made by asking a question to the respondents: on what topics and how often they talked to members of non-scheduled castes. As regards probability level, we have provided three response categories: more freely, freely, and less freely; and assigned weightages to each category positively in terms of 2, 1, 0 and negatively 0, 1, 2. As regards ritual distance, we asked the respondents whether they were allowed to enter the kitchen, take meals/refreshments occasionally, and attend ceremonies in the house of their non-scheduled caste acquaintances. Their responses, recorded in terms of all, most, some, and none, have been assigned values of 3, 2, 1,0.

Collection and Tabulation of Data

An interview schedule consisting of structured as well as open-ended questions on various aspects of the problem was prepared. It was modified after its pretesting on 25 respondents drawn from all cadres of jobs in the state and central government offices. Beforehand, the respondents were taken into confidence by giving them a clear assurance that their information would be kept strictly confidential and utilised for the research purpose only. Rapport was established with them through their influential colleagues belonging to their respective castes, and a relatively friendly atmosphere was created during the interview period.

Most of the respondents were interviewed separately in their respective offices and a few at their residences. Some respondents preferred giving responses in public places like canteens and restaurants. In all cases, the respondent was put in an informal situation through gassipping, joking, etc. after each interview was over. The relevant information, apart from responses to the questions listed in the interview schedule, was extracted from them and recorded later. Thus, intensive data was collected in eight to twelve months. The data thus collected was computed in the form of frequency and bivariate tables. The associational relationships among different independent and dependent variables were obtained though Chi-Square test. Finally, a partial correlation was drawn to measure the extent of associational relationships among different variables.

RELEVANCE OF THE STUDY

The present study is relevant—from theoretical as well as applied points of view. Studies conducted on social mobility and status identification cover relatively open societies where mobility in one sphere is directly related to mobility in the others. But in societies where social stratification has been relatively rigid, mobility in one aspect does not lead necessarily to mobility in other aspects. Therefore, in a society like India a comprehensive understanding of social mobility is possible only through an examination of cumulative impact of a number of dimensions on a primordial structure like caste or other traditional social organisations. So is the case with status identification. Therefore, an examination of related independent and dependent variables is likely to provide an insight into the dynamics of social mobility and status identification, which in turn may provide a theoretical understanding of social mobility in a less developed society like India.

At the applied level, the present study may help identify the aspirations and expectations of the 'mobile scheduled castes'. In other words, it may provide an indicator for measuring desires and efforts of the scheduled castes for elevation of their status in the caste or the class structure or both. It may also help recognise the built-in constraints in the constitutional and legal measures and the limitations of administrative actions in fulfilling the expectations of the scheduled castes. If we find that the scheduled castes primarily expect rise in their caste status through rise in their class status, and that the constitutional measures cannot help them in this endeavour, the study may suggest to limit their expectations in accordance with the reality of the situation. Or, the society may also adopt non-legal measures to help them realise their expectations.

This study may pinpoint the unwanted widening gap between the mobile scheduled caste persons/groups who are said to extract frequently the benefits of the privileges and facilities meant for the scheduled castes as a whole and those persons/groups who lag behind in this regard and are less mobile or even immobile. It may highlight the traditional social and ritual distances and the barriers of some types lying between the scheduled and non-scheduled castes and suggest some alternative measures that may slash such barriers. A far reaching consequence of the derivations of this study may be a turn towards the establishment of an egalitarian interaction pattern between the scheduled and non-scheduled castes, which may facilitate generation of the holistic form of social change, mobility and development in the country.

3

Varna System in Hindu Religion

The Hindus have Varna System. It is not at all caste-equivalent. It simply indicates a social division based on Gunas There exists all over the world one sort of division or the other in a society, which is so inevitable for social growth and prosperity. Each individual is possessed of a particular ability by nature. One may well perform a physical labour, another may be more of a thinker and some may be artistic some inclined to technology, music. Medicine, trade, industry or any other material or spiritual activity. The Lord speaking on action and inaction in Geeta (IV-13) says,'the four Varnas have been created by Him according to differentiation of Gunas and Karmas.' These Varnas are 1-Brahman; 2-Kshatriya; 3-Vaishya; and 4-Sudra. Varna means different shades of texture or colour. They represent mental temper. There are three Gunas—Sattva, Rajas and Tamas. Sattva is white, Rajas red and Tamas black. These in combination of various proportions constitute the group or class of people all over the world with temperamental differences.

The above classification is based on this assumption. In continuation, Veda Vyasa says in the same couplet, 'by the differentiation of the mental quality and physical action of the people.' It is clear that the type of ones action, the quality of ego, the colour of knowledge, the texture of ones understanding, the temper of fortitude and the brilliance of ones happiness defines ones Varna. Not by birth a man becomes Brahman but by cultivating noble thoughts and good intentions of service alone, one can ever aspire to Brahman hood. The Brahman is generally Sattvik. Sama and Dama are his valuable assets. He is serene and self-controlled and is possessed of the quality of austerity. (Tapas) He has purity, uprightness and forbearance. He has a will to acquire knowledge (Jnan), Vigyan (Wisdom) and faith.

The Kshatriya is a warrior class, powerful of physique and might. They are possessed of more of Rajas Guna with base of Sattva. They have a duty to protect the Dharma and the people. They are bold, alert and full of fortitude, generosity. discipline and modesty along with masterly behaviour mingled with Ishvar Bhava (Love of God). The Vaishya class is a trader class and prefers business of all kinds. It is possessed of Raj Guna mixed with Tamas. They deal with wealth and gold and strive for material prosperity of the self as well as of the people in general. The Sudras are working class people, artisans and craftsmen. They are physically strong and hard working. They are possessed of Tamas with a base of Rajas. Really speaking, Sudra class is indispensable to society as they are like a spiral chord on which rests the social structure.

Thus it is clear that the whole Varna System stood on the basis of Gunas and karmas of the individual. It has nothing to do with birth. To quote Mahabharata, the serpent god asked Yudhisthir to tell him the virtues of the caste. He says that those Brahmans who were fond of personal pleasures, prone to violence, had forsaken their duties and were red limbo, fell into the category of Kshatriya. Those Brahmans who derived their livelihood from kine, who were yellow and sub-divided by agriculture and who neglected to practice their duties, fell into the category of Vaishyas.

Those Brahmans who were addicted to mischief and falsehood and were covetous, lived by all kinds of works and fell from purity and were black went to the condition of Sudra. As a conclusion, the serpent god says that the man in which the marks of a Sudra are not found is no Sudra, whereas while a Brahman who acts so is not a Brahman and may be called a Sudra. It is clear that the world being the projection of Brahma is therefore Brahma-roopa and these castes came up later as a creation of man in society. Therefore it stands for modification and change according to times.

The Intent of Varna System

The various stratification of Varna system was meant to settle the Hindu life and regulate the society for a united action. Every society in the world has some form of groups that works for the common cause of social progress and general prosperity. In the various spheres of life, cultural, spiritual, religious, economic, political and social, medical, science and technology and even unskilled workers, there are groups united differently to work for the social cause of all the people. In Hinduism, this division is called Varna System. Each Varna has its social purpose, its own code, norms of behaviour and keeps its independent identity. Still each part remains an integral part of the whole. The whole is always present in the part and the part is ever a part of the whole. This is the spirit behind the creation of Varna System. The four Varnas represented the people of wisdom, of action, of compassion and loving feelings, and of service to people. It was not intended to be hereditary and connected with birth. and therefore free interchange and intermixing was liberally permitted.

It is indeed unfortunate that the Varna System came to be connected with the Caste System. We can not know how and why and when it so happened. It grew up with a sort of spiritual monopoly of a certain group bent upon its material prosperity. It established the class of Brahman by birth to safeguard their posterity. It is they who created and developed the ideas of inferiority and superiority among the people. This led to discrimination and distinction between various groups of occupations and the degradation of society began and reached so low as there came out people such as untouchables and pariahs. Thus the Varna turned Caste System brought about social degradation and downfall dividing people as low and high and the lowest. The Varna System, so sound and healthy and perfect came to such a pitiable state. It needs a reconstitution at this stage.

India is a developing nation. It has a responsibility to safeguard the rights of people as enshrined in the Constitution, irrespective of considerations of caste, creed, colour or sex. It is the need of the day that the Hindu scriptures be thrown open to all people of caste and sex so that they may have right understanding of their faith It may lead to the fall of the man-made Caste System like a sand hill. When the boundaries of the world are vanishing and there is open mixing of people and ideas, there has to be a ready flow of crossovers among the people as in the past. The watertight compartments only stink. The Hindu society has to be wellknit for the good of the world. It is a fact that the Buddhists discarded the Vedas to preach against Caste System; Kabir followed the same path of denouncing the Hindu scriptures while opposing the Casts System. A proper understanding of scriptures can remove the ignorance and illusion. Gandhi and Aurobindo favoured Varna System though opposed Caste System. Swami Dayananda with authority on Vedas declared that Vedas do not mention about Caste System and opposed caste system tooth and nail while defending the scriptures. There is nothing in the scriptures to justify the caste division, only the Varna System exists as an integral part of the whole society. It is not the Caste System at all.

There are people in large majority who realise that the most oppressed people today called as Sudra were really a great adherent of Hinduism. In the Buddhist dominated era, they did not change their religion though the call was in their favour. During the terror rule of Islam for conversion, they did not convert and suffered from the rulers as well as from their own people who called them by many abusive names such as Sudra, Chamar. Bhangi. Harijan. Achuta or untouchables and even today remain bracketed in schedule caste and schedule tribes. They had opportunity to convert and be saved from humiliations and insults but they preferred to stay as Hindus and suffer as Hindus.

It is high time we get rid of such abuses and grant same and equal rights to these religious heroes as are enjoyed by the others in the Hindu society. Are they not a part of the whole and is the whole an invalid one? No, we have to restore their dignity as in the Vedic days. We have to treat them as a part of either Brahman class or as Kshatriya class to which they really belong. The ancestors of Raiyadas were Chanvar Kshatriyas and so are others. Restore them to their past glory and while doing so do not forget to undo what we have done by granting them the prevalent privileges intact for their growth without any restriction. We have to do it. No one else can do it. Do it now and here for unity of Hindu life and religion as we have a duty to rescue the present world from terror, chaos. disbelief and confusion. It is only the Hindu philosophy of unity in Diversity that can bring relief to the confused masses of humanity today.

Indian Caste System

A Graver intellectual confusion than that caused by the non-translation of the word Caste there has seldom been. The assumed impossibility of finding an equivalent for the idea in English has led to the belief that there is something mysterious and unprecedented in the institution. People become bewildered as to whether it is a religious or a social obligation. Every one demands of the reformer a conflict with it. The whole question grows obscure and irritating. Yet all this time we have had an exact synonym for the word, and the parallel is the closer since our word connotes the same debatable borderland between morals and good taste. Caste ought to stand translated as honour. With Oriental quaintness, it is true, India has given a certain rigidity to this idea, but her analysis of the thing itself is as profound as it is acute.

Our conduct is commonly governed far more by social habit than by considerations of right and wrong. When the tide of the ethical struggle has once set in over some matter, we may regard ourselves as already half-lost. Why are my friend's open letters absolutely safe in my presence, though I am longing for the information they convey? Why can money given for one purpose not be used for another, when all the canons of common sense and expediency urge that it should? Who will confess to an effort in speaking the truth at any cost whatever? Why, when I am annoyed, do I not express myself in the language of Billingsgate? To each of which questions one would reply, somewhat haughtily, that the point was one of honour, or, that such happened to be the custom of one's class. Yet if we examine into the sanction which honour can invoke there is nothing beyond a rare exercise of the power of ostracism. The Church excommunicates, the law imprisons, but society merely "cuts" the offender in the street. Yet which of these three inflicts the deepest wound? It is as true of London as of Benaras that caste-law is the last and finest that controls a man. For it comes into operation at that precise point where tribunals fail. It takes cognisance of offences for which no judge could inflict penalties. It raises standards and demands virtues that every man will interpret according to the stringency of his pride, and yet that no one can feel himself to have wholly fulfilled. And it does all this without once permitting the sensation of merit. Having done all, one remains an unprofitable servant. For no one would count the punctual discharge of debts (all debts are debts of honour), the hauteur that brooks no stain upon the name, and the self-respect that builds the whole ethical code upon itself, as religious observances. These things were due, we say, to our birth or blood, or position before men.

It is true that their non-fulfillment would leave a stain upon the conscience, and it is also true that the attempt to work out the obligations of honour must be the immediate test of the sincerity of one who proposes to lead a life of greater devotion and earnestness than common. Still, caste is not the same thing as personal piety and perhaps for this reason complete renunciation of its claims and benefits is essential in India to the monastic life. There is another point about our Western conception of noblesse oblige. Few as the persons may be who could formulate their sentiment; the fact pervades the whole of the social area. Each class has its own honour. If honourable employers feel compelled to think of the comfort of their workers, honourable servants feel equally compelled to keep their lips shut on their masters' affairs, and either responds to an appeal in the name of his ideal. The priest may find the honour of his profession in conflict with that of the detective, but all the world will uphold the faithfulness of both.

The efficient realisation of his ideals by the schoolmaster will involve an occasional pardon, even of a grave offence, if he conceives forgiveness to be the best formative influence which at the moment he can command. The very same effort in the merchant will require a distribution of punishment that is rigorous and just, since order, integrity, and unfailing promptitude—not the development of human character—are his ends. Thus every man, in every critical act of his life, calls silently for the judgment of his peers and refuses all other.

The weaknesses of caste everywhere are manifold. For society, like the individual, is always apt to insist upon the tithing of mint and rue, and to neglect the weightier matters of the law. But it is not usually the martyr who marks its worst failure. He is the white dove cast forth by crows, that is, a member of a higher tried by consensus of the lower castes. We have here a case of government usurping the functions of society, much as if the headmaster should exercise authority in a dispute among boys.

For it is essential to the very idea of honour that every caste should be autonomous. The true failure of caste occurs whenever it establishes such an ascendancy of social opinion over the individual's conscience that his power of advance is impeded and he becomes less of a man, or less really beneficent socially, by remaining more of a gentleman—a state of things which is not uncommon among ourselves. For we may postulate that all ideals are helpful only in so far as they subserve a man's manhood and freedom, and destructive the instant they render him less able to express his own inmost will. It is he; therefore, who ought to have been a martyr and chose ease who is the true caste victim, not the hero of an auto-da-fe.

That this is a real danger we all know. What Protestant has never exalted the creed of his sect over freedom of thought? What Catholic has never put comfort above spirituality? What politician has not preferred party above principle? What student of science has never been prejudiced against new truth? And if we look without, where do we not see the mere breaker of conventionality treated as outside brotherhood? Where do we not find persons conforming to usages that displease them, merely because they would be inconvenient to dispute?

A certain sweeping justification of such facts may be urged, inasmuch as there are circumstances under which the cohesion of the group is well worth the sacrifice of the liberty of a few individuals. And the habitual outrage of custom without reason is perhaps rightly held to be as anti-social as any felony. In the last resort, however, social pressure must be held in bounds, for nothing should interfere with a man's right to try himself, or sap the roots of his independence. And society is a vague and irresponsible magistrate, with so little illumination as to his own purposes and tendencies that he frequently mistakes the pioneers of his march for deserters and orders the stoning of prophets, whose sepulchers and monuments will be erected by his children.

The question of the inner trend or intention of the social movement must form the law in whose name all doubtful cases are tried. And, while it is never easy to determine the point accurately for one's own people, in the case of the Hindu race the supreme purpose of their past evolution is quite apparent. Even a cursory reading of the Laws of Manu displays Indian society as united in a great cooperation for the preservation of the ancient race-treasure of Sanskrit literature. The feeling must have grown up when the Vedas alone required conserving, and the families entrusted with various portions were encouraged to become in all ways dependent on the community, that every energy might be devoted to the task in hand. This is the real meaning of prostration at the feet of Brahmans, of the great merit acquired by feeding them, and of the terror of the crime of killing one. It is not the man; it is race-culture that is destroyed by such an act. As ages went on and the Upanishads and other things were added to the store, that which was hitherto memorised became entrusted to writing. The Vedas became Scriptures—and now the method, of psychology, of astronomy, of mathematics, made themselves felt as integral parts of the Aryan treasure, in common with Sanskrit literature. This widened the conception of culture without liberalising the social bearings of the question, and the Brahman caste continued to be recognised as the natural guardians of all learning, the old religious compositions being still regarded as the type. If we ask how it happened that the Aryan folk became so early conscious of their responsibility in the matter of Sanskrit letters, there can be only one answer. They found themselves in the presence of other and unlearned races. This point brings us to the question of the origin of strongly differentiated castes in general. In its nature caste is, as we have seen, honour; that is to say, an ideal sentiment by whose means society spontaneously protects itself from some danger against which it is otherwise defenceless.

For instance, life in Texas having been for many years dependent on the possession of horses, and safeguards against the horse-thief being few and difficult, he came to be the object of unprecedented social abhorrence. Horse-stealing was the last crime a lost soul would stoop to. In a similar way, as some think, may have grown up the Indian feeling about cow-killing. If the cattle, in time of stress, were killed for food, agriculture would be unable to take a new start, and so a people accustomed to eat beef grasped the situation perhaps, and renounced the practice. But since these two sentiments pervade whole nations, they are not exactly what we are accustomed to think of as caste, inasmuch as in the latter there is a distinct gradation of rank connected with the sentiment. In the term "blackleg" applied by trade unionists to competing forms of labour, we have an instance of the kind we want. Here we have an occupational group giving birth immediately to the ideal which is necessary to its safety. Throughout the worlds of love, of war, and of work, indeed, honour is an instinct of the very greatest potency. How few men, after all, desert to an enemy as spies! How strong is the feeling of class-obligation amongst servants and working men! This element is very evident in the Indian industrial castes, which are often simply hereditary trade-unions. No Englishman is so powerful, nor is any Hindu so hungry, that one man could be bribed to take up the trade of another. Nothing would induce the dairyman, for instance, to take charge of a horse, or a laundryman to assist the household.

But the very strongest, and perhaps also ugliest, of all possible roots of caste is the sense of race, the caste of blood. We have an instance of this in the animosity that divides white men from negroes in the United States, and we have other instances, less talked of, all up and down our vast British possessions. There is probably no other emotion so inhuman which receives such universal sympathy as this. For it is fundamentally the physical instinct of a vigorous type to protect itself from fusion. And both sides participate in the revulsion. Here we have the secret of rigid caste, for the only rigid caste is hereditary, and of hereditary caste the essential characteristic is the refusal of intermarriage.

Granting, then, what could not well be denied, that the Aryan forefathers found themselves in India face to face with inferior and aboriginal races, what may we gather, from the nature of the caste system today, to have been the elements of the problem, as they more or less clearly perceived it? Those elements we may infer to have been four in number:

1. They desired above all things to preserve the honour of their daughters from marriage with lower and savage peoples. Exclusion from marriage with any but one's own caste became the rigorous rule, the penalty fell on the father and the family that permitted a woman to go unguarded on this head. To this day, if a son marry beneath caste he degrades himself; but if a daughter be wrongly given, the whole family becomes out-casted.
2. They seem to have desired to preserve the aboriginal races, on the one hand from extermination, and on the other from slavery of the person two solutions which seemed later the only alternatives to Aryan persons in a similar position! Those aborigines, therefore, who became dependent on the Aryan population, had their definite place assigned them in the scale of labour, and their occupations were secured to them by the contempt of the superior race.

   We must not forget, in the apparent harshness of this convention, its large factor of hygienic caution. The aborigines were often carrion-eaters, and always uncleanly in comparison with their neighbours. It was natural enough, therefore, that there should be a refusal to drink the same water, and so on.

   On the other hand, it is one of the mistakes of caste everywhere, that it institutionalises and perpetuates an inequality which might have been minimised. But we must not forget, in the case of the Indian system, the two greater evils which were avoided altogether.
3. The Aryans realised very clearly that it was not only their race but also their civilization that must be maintained in its purity. The word Aryan implies one acquainted with the processes of agriculture, an earer of the ground, to use an Elizabethan word—accustomed therefore to a fixed and industrialised mode of living, evidently in contrast to others who were not.

   Fire and the processes of cooking and eating food are easily distinguished as the core of the Personal life and establishment in a climate where habits can at any time be made so simple as in India. It is these that can never be dispensed with, though they may be arranged for to-night in a palace, and tomorrow in the jungle under a tree.

In view, then, of the necessity of safeguarding the system of manners grew up the restrictions against eating with those of lower caste, or allowing them to touch the food and wants of their betters. The fact that the Aryan could eat food cooked by Aryan hands alone implied that the strictest preliminaries of bathing had been complied with.

By a continuous crystallisation, all caste laws—from being the enunciation of broad canons of refinement as between Aryan and non-Aryan—came to be the regular caste-barriers between one class and another of the same race. In this way they lost their invidious character.

It is undeniable that this caste of the kitchen, so wittily named "don't touchism" by a modern Hindu leader, lends itself to abuse and becomes an instrument of petty persecution more readily than the intermarriage laws. Some of the saddest instances of caste-failure have occurred here. Nevertheless, the original intention remains clear and true, and is by no means completely obscured, even with the lapse of ages.

4. It was, however, in their perception of the fourth element of the problem that the early Aryans triumphantly solved the riddle of Humanity. They seem to have seen clearly that amongst the aborigines of India themselves were many degrees of social development already existent, and that these must be preserved and encouraged to progress.

From such a comprehension of the situation sprang the long and still growing graduation of non-Aryan castes, some of which have established themselves in the course of ages within the Aryan pale. Marriage, for instance, is an elabourate and expensive social function in the highest classes. But as we descend it becomes easier, till amongst the Baghdis, Bauris, and other aboriginal castes, almost any connection is ratified by the recognition of women and children. This is a point in which Eastern scores over Western development; for in Europe the Church has caused to be reckoned as immoral what might, with more philosophy, have been treated as the lingering customs of sub-organised race-strata.

As is the nature of caste, mere social prestige constitutes a perpetual stimulus and invitation to rise, which means in this case to increase the number of daily baths and the cleanliness of cooking, and to restrict to purer and finer kinds the materials used for food, approximating continually toward the Brahman standard. For is it not true that noblesse oblige? This fact it is that makes Hinduism always the vigorous living banyan, driving civilization deeper and wider as it grows, and not the fossilised antiquity superficial observers have supposed.

Such, then, is the historic picture of the rise of caste. The society thus originated fell into four main groups:

(1) Priests and learned men—the Brahmans;

(2) The royal and military caste;

(3) Professional men and merchants—the middle-class or bourgeoisie, as we say in Europe; and

(4) The working people, or sudras, in all their divisions.

(Of the second group only the Rajput branch remains now stable. For the military caste, finding itself leaderless under the Maurya dynasty, is said to have become literary, and is certainly now absorbed in the bourgeoisie.)

This functional grouping, however, is traversed in all directions nowadays by the lines of caste. In the mountains it is no uncommon thing to find the Brahman acting as a labourer, impressed as a coolie, or working as a farmer, and in the cities he belongs largely to the professional ranks. Many of India's most learned and active sons, on the other hand, belong to the third and even fourth divisions. And the new castes, which are of constant growth, are less easy than the old to classify.

Every new community means a new caste in India. Thus we have the Mohammedan, the Christian, and the modern reform castes—of all of which one peculiarity is non-belief in the caste principle!—as well as others. And who shall determine, for instance, to which of the four main grades Islamism, with its inclusion of peasant, citizen, and prince, belongs?

The fact is, if a man's mode of life be acceptable to his own caste-fellows, the rest of Indian society has no quarrel with it.

And this autonomy of castes it is which is the real essential for social flexibility and fundamental equality. As bearing on this point, few utterances have ever been so misquoted as the great dictum of Buddha, that "he who attains to God is the true Brahman." For this is misquoted whenever it is made to imply that the Brahman holds in any sense a monopoly in religion. No possible statement could be more foreign to the genius of Hinduism. When we read that shortest and greatest of India's gospels, the "Bhagavad Gita" (a poem composed by Brahmans, preserved by Brahmans, and distributed through the length and breadth of the country, always by Brahmans), we find ourselves in the presence of the most comprehensive mind that ever contemplated Hindu life.

The compassion of Buddha, perhaps, looms greater across the centuries, but in dealing with social problems his very tenderness and spiritual fire make him second to Krishna, who was always calm, broad, and consistently national in his outlook. We must accept the Gita as an authoritative pronouncement on Hindu society. And the Gita rings with the constantly reiterated implication that "he who attains to God is the true man," while it interprets all life and responsibility as a means to this end. Thus, "Better one's own duty, though imperfect, than the duty of another well discharged. Better death in one's own duty; the duty of another brings on danger." We have to remember, too, that the Gita is made up of the very best of the Vedas and Upanishads, and was specially written for the benefit of women and the working classes, who, as destitute of classical learning, had little chance of studying these great scriptures.

But its contents were to depend upon Brahman effort for promulgation. Another witness to the fact that spirituality has always been regarded in India as the common human possession lies in the Hindu word for religion itself—dharma, or the manness of man. This is very striking. The whole weight, of the conception is shifted away from creed, much more from caste or race, to that which is universal and permanent in each and every human being. And, last of all, we may remember that the greatest historical teachers of Hinduism—Rama, Krishna, and Buddha, besides many of the Upanishadic period—were men of the second, or military, caste. No, the Brahman was never in any sense the privileged monopolist of religion: he was a common channel of religious lore, because his actual function was Sanskrit culture, and Sanskrit happens to be the vehicle of the most perfect religious thought that the world ever produced, but "realisation" itself has always been recognised as a very different matter from this, and, Brahman or non-Brahman, has been accepted wherever it appeared. The advantage that the priestly caste did undoubtedly enjoy, however, lay in the fact that in their case the etiquette of rank led directly to the highest inspiration, as the scholar's life, even in its routine, will be nearest to that of the saint.

One peculiarity of the place of the religious life in the Indian system is that it is an inclusive term for all forms of higher individuation. Theoretically, to the Hindu mind, all genius is inspiration, the perception of unity; and the mathematics of Euclid or the sculpture of Michael Angelo would be as authentic an expression of the religious consciousness as the sainthood of Francis. Only the result of this method of interpretation is that sainthood takes precedence of all others as the commonest form of greatness. Scientific research, as in the astronomy of Bhashkar Acharya and the psychology of Patanjali, has not had sufficient opportunity of securing defined and independent scope. And literature has been yoked to the car of mythology as much as the art of medieval Italy.

Nevertheless, India is too well acquainted with genius to forget that the caste of the spirit is beyond human limitation, often beyond recognition. It is held that the best lower men can do for that brotherhood which asserts itself in the consciousness of greatness is to give it freedom. Hence a man can always be released from social obligations if he desire to live the life of ideas, of the soul. Only, it is held that if he will not fulfil the law, neither shall he add to the burdens of the community. So he who claims to be one of the great spiritual beyond-castes must renounce family and property, relying upon the charity of men for his daily bread, and knowing well that for any work of scholarship—such as the observatories at Benaras and Jeypore—a Hindu government at least would provide him ample means. It is only as long as one avails oneself of the benefits of the social structure that it is held not unreasonable to require conformity to its usages. This renunciation is Sannyas, the Indian form of monasticism, and Sannyas, theories to the contrary notwithstanding, has always been open to all castes. Indeed, it is held that when the responsibilities of life are over, a man's duty is to leave the world and spend the remainder of his days in that state; and in some parts of Northern India one meets with "Tyagi Mehtars," or monastics who were by birth the lowest of the low.

Theoretically, the monk is caste-fellow of the whole world, prepared to eat with any one; and where, by sheer dint of spirituality and self-discipline, such a feeling is realised; every Hindu in India considers the broken bread of this lover of mankind as sacramental food. It is usual, too, to eat from the hands of holy men without inquiry as to their standing when in the world. One of the most interesting points in all this to a Western mind is the difference implied and established between the caste of priests or chaplains on the one hand, and the fact of spiritual realisation, outside all caste, on the other. Nothing in the Indian thought about life can be more striking than this. The family chaplain in Bengal may be the official teacher, but every man and woman discards his authority silently the instant they find some soul (in the world or out of it; it may be husband or child, or the holy man living in his garden; usually it is an ascetic), with a quickening spiritual touch upon their own. He or she then becomes the guru, or teacher, and this relationship is made the central fact of life. The appearance of this new teacher, when he is powerful enough to be an important social phenomenon, is the historic origin of almost all new castes. The Sikh nation was formed in this way by a succession of gurus. Chaitanya welcomed all castes to Vaishnavism and made it possible for them to rise thereby. The scavengers, too low to venture to claim either Hinduism or Islamism as their own, were raised in consideration and self-respect by Guru Nanak and Lal Begi Mehtar—the last a saint of their own degree.

The preacher arises and proclaims the new idea. He gathers about him men of all classes: the educated won to the service of his thought, the ignorant swept in by the radiance of his personality. Amongst his disciples distinctions of caste break down. The whole group is stamped with his character and prestige. Eventually, if it contain a preponderance of Brahman elements, it may take rank with the best, carrying certain individuals up with it. But if it be composed chiefly of the scum of society, it will remain little considered; and yet, in the strength of its religious and intellectual significance may certainly claim to have progressed beyond its original point. Such is likely to be the fate of the present Christian converts. Those who are recruited from the lowest pariahs may acquire a certain prestige from their new faith and take a better place in the social scale, consequently, in centuries to come. At the same time we must not forget that forty or fifty years ago, conversions were made that undoubtedly involved great sacrifices, and the descendants of these Christians may lose rather than gain in the long run.

Taking the history of Hinduism as a whole, we observe a great systole and diastole of caste, the Buddhist and the present Christian periods ranking as well-marked eras of fusion, while the intervening centuries are characterised by progressive definition, broken every now and then by a wave of reform which thought itself a movement towards caste abolition, but ended simply in the formation of a new group. For this is the fact in which all would-be reformations in India find at once their opportunity and their limit. It may now be taken as proved that in order to affect caste widely the agitator would need to aim deeper than the external phenomena, at underlying spiritual impulses.

If this theory of caste be valid, then, we find that the word signifies not so much mere rank in society as the standard of honour which is associated with rank. And as the private's conduct may be governed as much as his officer's by enlightened self-respect, we have seen that honour is something which applies to the whole of society equally. Even Tennyson, it will be remembered, pictures the country youth as outvaunting Lady Clara Vere de Vere in her pride of birth. The word caste, therefore, is by no means that antithesis of democracy which has been so commonly assumed.

Neither, amongst a people familiar with the process of self-organisation, would it prove any barrier to efficient cooperation. For the one essential to this power is an established habit of ignoring all points of mutual difference not germane to the matter in hand. What we call good-breeding, or what India calls caste, ought to make this easier. For any group of men met together for a common purpose find their individual rights secured to them in this way, and are free, by age-long acceptance, from any suspicion of another's desire to interfere with them. This is a basis of strength and not of weakness; so that it seems, if Indian men and women are not at present capable of combined action to any great degree, it is a matter of their own neglect of the habit, and not a necessary consequence of their institutions. We need not too readily accept the statement of such weakness, either, as infallible. My own observation has been that the Hindu people are capable enough of vigorous cooperation along the lines natural to them, those of the undivided family, the village community, and others. That inability which Europeans would show to face these tests, they may be expected to display before ours

To be absolutely just, however, we must admit that the observance of caste law has entailed many foolish and irritating losses upon society during the last fifty years. We have seen that there are definite reasons, not wanting in cogency, why a man of good birth should not eat in all companies, or of food cooked by hands supposed less cleanly. Such rules, however, cannot be kept by those who, for any reason, cross the seas to Europe. This fact, more than any other detail, makes it a matter of out-casting to take the journey and persecutions have sometimes ensued which are shocking to contemplate. A man may care little about the loss of station for his own sake, but the shoe pinches when he finds himself unable to make worthy marriages for his daughters; hence he will often submit to a heavy fine in order to buy back his position.

This rouses the cupidity of ignorant and conventional persons who happen to have authority with the stay-at-home community, and such are apt to be unscrupulous in bringing about the ruin or recantation of any who resist their power. This is a series of events which does occur occasionally; but it need not be supposed that every Europe-returning Hindu who is kept at arm's length is a martyr. There is an element of distrust for the moral results of a visit to the West in the situation; and this is not altogether unreasonable. It is chiefly with regard to possibilities of political, practical, or technical education that caste deterrence is to be regretted, and it is obvious that as communities progress in the power of estimating modern conditions, they must recognise the suicidal nature of such an attitude.

Yet it is curious to note here how caste may become thus a very real instrument of equality, for the power of the individual to advance is by this means kept strictly in ratio to the thinking of the society in which he lives. This fact is characteristic. The good of caste, of race, of family stands first and only second that of the individual man or woman in India. To take another plane. Let a man of the lower castes become wealthy, and he is compelled to educate men of his own rank to marry his daughters. Thus the group to which he owes birth, vigour, and development receives from him again the benefits of his life's work. This is the exact opposite of the European device, where the upper class absorbs money, talent, and beauty from the lower, while that is continually recruited by the failures from above.

The fact that every human force is polar in its moral activity needs little demonstration in the case of social pride. Every day we see this working on the one hand for the highest idealism, on the other for revolting egotism. Social exclusiveness may be condoned, it may even robbed of its sting but, especially when coupled with personal exultation, it can never be made anything but vulgar-looking to the disinterested outsider. It is not to be supposed that Indian caste forms any exception to this rule of double effect. Nevertheless, it is well to understand the conditions of the sentiment, perceiving how inevitably this very thing repeats itself wherever two physically-distinguishable races are found side by side.

And it cannot be denied that great benefits as well as great evils have accrued from caste. It is an institution that makes Hindu society the most eclectic with regard to ideas in the world. In India all religions have taken refuge the Parsi before the tide of Muslim conquest; the Christians of Syria; the Jews. And they have received more than shelter—they have had the hospitality of a world that had nothing to fear from the foreigner who came in the name of freedom of conscience. Caste made this possible, for in one sense it is the social formulation of defence minus all elements of aggression. Again, surely it is something that in a country conquered for a thousand years the doorkeeper of a viceroy's palace would feel his race too good to share a cup of water with the ruler of all India. We do not easily measure the moral strength that is here involved, for the habit of guarding the treasure of his birth for an unborn posterity feeds a deep, undying faith in destiny in the Hindu heart.

"Today here, tomorrow gone," says the most ignorant sotto voce as he looks at the foreigner, and the unspoken refrain of his thought is, "I and mine abide for ever." Caste is race-continuity; it is the historic sense; it is the dignity of tradition and of purpose for the future. It is even more: it is the familiarity of a whole people in all its grades with the one supreme human motive—the notion of noblesse oblige. For though it is true that all men are influenced by this principle, it is also probably true that only the privileged are very conscious of the fact. Is caste, then, simply a burden, to be thrown off lightly, as a thing irksome and of little moment? And yet, if India is ever to regain national efficiency, this old device of the forefathers must be modified in the process,—exactly how, the Indian people themselves can alone determine. For India today has lost national efficiency. This fact there is no gainsaying. Her needs now are not what they were yesterday. The Brahmans lose distinctiveness in these days of cheap printing and widespread literacy. But this only means that the country requires multiplied methods of self-expression as the goal and summit of her national endeavour.

She wants a greater flexibility, perhaps, a readier power of self-adjustment than she has ever had. But it ought to come in an influx of consciousness of those great spiritual tides on whose surface all questions of caste and non-caste can be lifted into new and higher inter-relations. Chief among all her needs is that of a passionate drawing together amongst her people themselves. The cry of home, of country, of place is yet to be heard by the soul of every Indian man and woman in Hindustan and following hard upon it must sound the overtones of labour and of race. Then the question of whether to walk or not in the ways of the forefathers will be lost in the knowledge of the abundant power to hew out new roads, as those fathers did before them. Has India the possibilities still left in her own nature which can bring to her such an epoch?

There are some who believe that there is no task beyond the ultimate power of the Hindu peoples to perform. The nation that has stood so persistently for righteousness through untold ages has conserved such vast springs of vigour in itself, as must ultimately enable her to command Destiny. The farseeing wisdom and gentleness of her old constitution may unfit her for the modern world, but they are a sure proof, nevertheless, of her possession of sufficient sense of affairs to guide her to a full development once more.

For, after all, who were these old forefathers, with their marvelous cunning? What inspired them so to construct the social framework that every act of rebellion and invasion should end henceforth only in contributing a new morsel of colour to fit into the old mosaic? Ah, who were they indeed? We may well ask, for have we not all this time been calling by their name one far greater than they, one infinitely more deserving of our reverence—the Communal Consciousness, namely, of a mighty patient people, toiling on and on through the ages up the paths of knowledge, destroying never, assimilating always, what they gain of truth and science, and hesitating only a little before fresh developments, because they are so preoccupied with the problems of the past that they do not realise that stage is done, and that the sun is risen today on a new landscape, confronting them with fresh perils and unthought-of difficulties?

DEGENERATION OF THE VARNA SYSTEM

The Varna system was started as analogous to professional guilds, but as a result of exploitation by some priests, and socioeconomic elements of society, this system became hereditary and degenerated over the centuries. The ancient culture of India was based upon a system of social diversification according to spiritual development. Four orders of society were recognized based upon the four main goals of human beings and established society accordingly. These four groups were the Brahmins, the priests or spiritual class; the Kshatriya, the nobility or ruling class; the Vaishya, the merchants and farmers; and the Shudras or servants. These four orders of society were called "varna", which has two meanings; first it means "colour" and second it means a "veil". As colour it does not refer to the colour of the skin of people, but to the qualities or energies of human nature. As a veil it shows the four different ways in which the Divine Self is hidden in human beings.

In ancient India, these divisions were not based on birth but based on qualifications. According to the Bhagavad Gita this Aryan family system broke down in India over three thousand years ago at the time of Krishna. Hence after three thousand years this system of determining natural aptitude has degenerated into the caste system which resembles it now only in form. As the Varna system became increasingly rigid and based on inheritance, it was enveloped by another system known as the caste system. Thus, this varna system determined the social structure of ancient Hindu society. The caste system could not have been part of Hindu religious philosophy, since it violates fundamental Hindu doctrine, according to which there is no absolute distinction between individuals, since the atman dwells in the hearts of all beings. There is no religious sanction whatsoever to the concept of the caste system in Hinduism.

Swami Sivananda (The Divine Life Society, Rishikesh), in his commentary on Gita, Ch.18, verses 41, and 45 says: "Mankind is organized into the four castes and each man's life is divided into four stages, according to the nature of the Gunas (traits) and the degree of growth or evolution. This is the division of labour for which each caste is fitted according to its own nature. The duty prescribed is your sole support, each devoted to his own duty in accordance with his own nature or caste, and the highest service you can render to the Supreme is to carry it out wholeheartedly, without expectation of fruits, with the attitude of dedication to the Lord. The caste system is, indeed, a splendid thing. It is quite flawless. But the defect came in from somewhere else. The classes gradually neglected their duties. The test of ability and character slowly vanished. Birth became the chief consideration in determining castes. All castes fell from their ideals and forgot all about their duties."

VARNA-NOT RACIAL COLOUR

Varna was conferred on the basis of the intrinsic nature of an individual, which is a combination of the three gunas. The term, 'Varna', has nothing to do with racial colour. It is related to the three 'gunas' or traits-white (sattva or sagacity), red (rajas or aggressiveness), and dark (tamas or ignorance) which all men and also all living beings possess, albeit in different proportions-varying from species to species, from man to man and even from sibling to sibling.

Alain Danielou has said: "That abusive caste practices were introduced when the administrative power ceased to be in Hindu hands, thus making the repression of abuses legally impossible. Such abuses as there are have been greatly exaggerated in order to justify Western domination and are normally quite local. In most of India, the caste system functions today as it always has; as a harmonious whole in which each is satisfied with his social lot, in which the freedom of each tribe, and religious group to live according to its customs, traditions, and convictions is respected as it is in no other country and no other form of society.

Manu Smrti: Not a Religious Book:

"The Seniority of Brahmans is from Sacred Knowledge, that of Kshatriyas from valour, that of Vaishyas from wealth in grain, but that of Sudras is from age alone." (Manu Smriti II, 155)

"Manu has declared that those Brahmans who are thieves, outcasts, eunuchs, or atheists are unworthy to partake of oblations offered to gods and ancestors." (Manu Smriti III, 150)

" A Brahmin who departs from the Rule of Noble Conduct, does not gain the fruit described in the Veda, but he who duly follows the Rule of Noble Conduct, will obtain the full reward." (Manu Smriti I,109)

" He who possesses faith may receive pure learning even from a man of lower caste, the highest law even from the lowest, and an excellent wife even from a base family." (Manu Smriti II, 238)

Manu Smriti which outlines the scheme of the four varnas (socioeconomic classes) and four ashramas (stages of life of the individual) refuses a provide for the fifth varna. The four classes are adequate to cover all the sections of the society. Manu Smriti is a sociological treatise and not a religious or theological work. It has never been held on par with the Vedas and has never been claimed to be a Holy Book whose authority is unquestionable. Manu Smriti does not deal with the Absolute, a field specialized in by the Upanishads. Manu Smriti is as this-worldly as the Arthashastra is. Manu was also only a Codifier (Documenter of the then-existing codes) of the Caste System and was not to be interpreted as the creator of the Caste System.

"Only the British administrators and jurists who dominated the scene since 1757 found it expedient for their purposes to present it as a religious code binding all the Hindus. The original text of Manu Smriti has been tampered with is acknowledged by Sir William Jones who introduced it as the law book of the Hindus, as he agrees that ' it is accommodated to the improvements of a commercial age'. The extant text of Manu Smriti is a doctored version, doctored to benefit the commercial class of Britain which had sponsored the East India Company, the company for which he was serving as a judge at Calcutta."

Varnashrama Dharma, said to be the mainstay of the Hindu Social Order has no sanction in the Vedas. In ancient India, these divisions were not based on birth but based on qualifications. According to the Bhagavad Gita this Aryan family system broke down in India over three thousand years ago at the time of Krishna. Hence after three thousand years this system of determining natural aptitude has degenerated into the caste system which resembles it now only in form.

Manu made it clear that superiority is not by birth but by Conduct. This Principle was further emphasized later by Maharishi Veda Vyasa in Mahabharata. Manu himself says that if there is anything in his Smriti which is not acceptable to the conscience of any person, that person should reject it and act according to his/her own conscience.

> *"For choosing your course of conduct at any time and place, keep in view the instructions given first in Sruti (Vedas), then in Smritis, Itihaas (History of great personalities) and finally you act according to your conscience." (Manu Smriti, 11, 6).*

> *"Just as a wooden toy elephant cannot be real elephant, and a stuffed deer cannot be a real deer, so, without studying scriptures and the Vedas and the development of intellect, a Brahmin by birth cannot be considered a Brahmin. " (Manu Smriti 11-157).*

Louis Francois Jacolliot (1837-1890), who worked in French India as a government official and was at one time President of the Court in Chandranagar, translated numerous Vedic hymns, the Manusmriti, and the Tamil work, Kural. His masterpiece, La Bible dans l'Inde, stirred a storm of controversy.

Manu-Hindu Law: The Hindu law were codified by Manu more than 3,000 years before the Christian era, copied by entire antiquity and notably by Rome, which alone has left us a written law-the code of Justanian, which has been adopted as the base of all modern legislations.

Jurisprudence: "Observe, enpassant, this striking coincidence with French law, that the Hindu wife, in default of her husband's authority may release from her incapacity, by authority of justice. " "The contract made by a man who is drunk, foolish, imbecile or grievously disordered in his mental condition...." Manu further adds, "What is held under comprehension-held by force is declared null."

Would not this be thought a mere commentary on the Code of Napoleon? Of 4-5,000 years after "How far is all this from those barbarous customs of first ages, when every question was solved by violence and force, and what admiration should we feel for a people who, at the epoch at which Biblical fall would date the world's creation, had already reached the extraordinary degree of civilization indicated by laws so simple and so practical."

CASTE SYSTEM AND CODE OF MANU

The Hindus have been an intensely practical people. The magnificence of daring glimpses into the cosmos as their meditations or scientific investigations revealed to them, convinced them beyond doubt that the complexity of earthly existence could be reduced to some order and the march of human progress subjected to some form of control. They embraced in their researches such subjects as astronomy, physics, chemistry, biology, medicine, ethics, logic, psychology, aesthetics, politics, economics, sociology, and metaphysics. Indeed, in sociology alone, they have left us over twenty treatises; and the Code of Manu, the subject of the present study, is only one of them. Manu, Manas, manava, all have the same philological root, man, to think. Manu's Code, therefore, is a treatise of social relations for human beings. It lays emphasis on reason, the thinking faculty (manas), in the ordering of man's social relations. It stands for a planned society. Manu's social theory is an art of life; it is a technique, not mere congeries of consistent concepts.

An individual's life is divided into four parts—1. studentship, 2. householding 3. partial retirement or hermitage, 4. and complete retirement. Correspondingly, there are four groups: 1. the manual worker, 2. the merchant, 3. the warrior, and 4. the teacher. A unity of function ties each stage of individual life to the corresponding group. This unity, which lays emphasis on harmonious relations, is the dharma, or the ethics of Manu. There are thus presented four social institutions: 1. the educational, 2. the family-economic, 3. the political, 4. and the religious.

STABLE HUMAN SOCIETIES

Alain Danielou says: "The Hindus assert that their social formula meets the requirements of man's individual and collective nature. The fact that the Hindu civilization has been able to survive over thousand of years, despite disorders caused by invasions, schisms, and internal wars, and has been capable of constant renewal, as demonstrated by one brilliant period after another, merits all our attention in the study of a social system whose longevity is unique in history."

ARYAN INVASION THEORY AND CASTE SYSTEM

Guy Sorman visiting scholar at Hoover Institution at Stanford and the leader of new liberalism in France, writes: "The Invasion theory has today become the standard explanation for the caste system, though it came up only in the 19th century. Besides, all we have to attest the Aryan invasion is a specious interpretation of the Mahabharata, which is like searching the origins of European aristocracy in the works of Homer! In any case, it is doubtful whether a single invasion, which was more likely a slow infiltration of the North, could have succeeded in structuring so perfectly Indian society along ethnic lines for over three thousand years. Finally, in South India the caste system among the dark, skinned Dravidians is as rigid as it is in the North, though the Aryans in all probability never reached there.

The racial origin of caste hypothesis tells us little about India but it does tell us a great deal about the 19th century Westerners who invented the Aryan invasion theory. It was at the same time that Sieyes and Augustin Thierry claimed that the French nobility was of Germanic stock, whereas the lower classes were of Gallic origin; so the 1789 Revolution was a race war rather than a class war! It was also in the 19th century that appeared the myth of the Indo-Europeans being at the source of all Western civilization and for this we have to thank British authors who were taken up with evolutionist theory. Indian historians trained in Europe have fallen victim to this myth but that does not make it any more authentic. Later on, at the beginning of the 20th century, it became fashionable to support the Marxist theory which replaced race with class, though its premises were just as shaky."

VARNASRAMA SOCIAL SYSTEM

There is a natural system of social organization which can bring about a peaceful society where everyone is happy. This system is described in the timeless Vedic literature of India and it is called Varnasrama dharma. The purpose of the Varnasrama social system is to provide a structure which allows people to work according to their natural tendencies and to organize society so that everyone, regardless of their position, makes spiritual advancement.

People can only work with a cooperative spirit if there is a central point. Over the years proponents of many different political ideologies have tried to unite society by providing such a central point, however, these attempts have all ultimately failed. Generally people work for their own pleasure and this is sometimes extended to working for the family, the nation or even the whole world. Because the aims and aspirations of the members of society are so varied it is practically impossible to achieve a peaceful situation as everyone is working to fulfil his own personal goals. The only universal central point around which everyone can work is God. He provides an absolute, eternal centre for all our activities. If we try to make something else the central point the resulting society is doomed to fail. The Varnasrama system recognizes there are many different types of people who may not be spiritually inclined. The society is organized under the direction of qualified Brahmans and is divided into four occupational and four spiritual divisions in such a way that everyone is serving God simply by performing their occupational duties. As the entire society is arranged to please God, anyone working within the society also pleases God.

The Structure of Varnasrama Society: The practical application of the Varnasrama system is to divide the society according to four occupational and four spiritual orders of life. The Varnasrama system recognizes the natural talents and abilities of each person and provides work according to a persons qualities. There are four qualities of work, the Brahmans are the intellectual and priestly class, the Kshatriyas are the government, the military and the administrative classes, the Vaishyas are farmers and businessmen, and the sudras are workers. There are also four spiritual divisions, brahmacary, student life, grhastha, married life, vanaprasta, retired life and sunnyasa, renounced life. If this system is properly implemented under the direction of qualified Brahmans the result will be peace and prosperity throughout the world.

The Corrupt Indian "Caste" System: The Varnasrama social divisions are based on qualities and work. If someone has the qualities of a brahmana and if they work as a brahmana they are accepted as a qualified brahmana. This system should not be confused with the corrupt "caste" system of India. In India people claim to be Brahmans simply because they are born in a brahmana family even though they do not possess the qualifications or qualities of a brahmana and in most cases they are not working as Brahmans either.

The result of the corruption of the original system has been the destruction of the entire social structure in India and the "caste" system is now being used by the rich to exploit and oppress the poor.

Divisions According to Qualification: In Varnasrama society all members are equally important. An analogy comparing the social body to the human body is given to explain this. The Brahmans are the head of the body as they possess the intelligence and give directions to the other parts of the body. The Kshatriyas are likened to the arms of the body as their business as administrators and the military is to protect the social body from threats from outside (attacks from enemies) and disruption from within. (Thieves and rogues). The Vaishyas are likened to the stomach. The stomach provides energy to the body. The Vaishyas, as the productive class, are the farmers and businessman who produce and distribute food to the social body. The Vaishyas are also responsible for protecting the cows.

The sudras are likened to the legs as they provide the manual labour required by the social body. We look after our whole body. It is not that we attend to problems affecting the head and neglect problems in the legs. The body works as a coordinated unit and a problem anywhere in the body causes a disruption to the proper functioning of the whole body and is therefore immediately attended to.

The social body should work as a coordinated unit with different members of the society acting in their respective positions as Brahmans, Kshatriyas, Vaishyas and sudras according to their qualities. The result will be a happy, peaceful and efficient society.

The Brahmans: Although all members of the social body are important, as the Brahmans are the intelligent class directing society by giving guidance and advice to the king or government (Kshatriyas), it is vital that they be properly qualified. If the head of society is not functioning properly the whole social body is in trouble. All over the world we are seeing misguided governments make the lives of their citizens hell, simply because they have no qualified Brahmans to give them advice. The whole planet has become very unfortunate and disturbed due to such unqualified leadership.

The brahmana's position is that of an unpaid adviser to the king or government. The business of the brahmana is to understand the Vedic Scriptures and be expert in applying them in different places and at different times. The Vedic system doesn't require the creation of any new rules or legislation The perfect laws have been given by Manu, the father of mankind in the Manu Samhita, and the qualified brahmana simply implements these timeless laws. There is no need for imperfect man made laws. The qualities of a brahmana are given in the Bhagawad Gita as peacefulness, self control, austerity, purity, tolerance, honesty, knowledge, wisdom and religiousness and all of these qualities must be actually manifest before someone can be accepted as a brahmana.

Giving Charity to the Brahmans: On special days such as the birth of a child, marriage and other auspicious occasions it is customary for the Kshatriyas and Vaishyas to give in charity to the Brahmans. The Kshatriya king is wealthy because in return for giving the citizens protection he levies taxes. The Vaishya farmers and businessmen are wealthy because of their farming and trading activity.

The brahmana takes whatever small amount is required to maintain himself and his family and he distributes the rest of the charity he receives for the benefit of the people in general. Because the brahmana is intelligent and an expert in spiritual matters he can understand how best to distribute charity. It is for this reason in Vedic society charity is given to the Brahmans. It is not very intelligent to give charity to unqualified persons, for they will simply squander it. For example if you give a drunkard money, it will be used for purchasing alcohol, not food. Such charity is charity in the mode of ignorance and is not very auspicious.

The Kshatriyas: The Kshatriyas take the positions of king or politicians and the military. They administer society according to the directions and advice of the Brahmans. Their qualities are given in the Bhagawad Gita as heroism, power, determination, resourcefulness, courage in battle, generosity and leadership.

The Perfect King: A good Kshatriya king is strong and just, he acts according to the advice of the Brahmans, he is loved by the law abiding citizens and feared as death personified by the thieves and rogues. In a country ruled by a qualified Kshatriya king the citizens are protected and thus they develop good qualities and are peaceful and happy. Because the king is strong and honest the citizens have no fear of being disturbed by thieves and rogues or by attacks from invading armies. They also have no fear of being plundered by unfair or exorbitant taxation or dishonest government officers, as such a strong king will quickly correct any corruption within his own ministry.

The lives of many saintly kings are described in Srimad Bhagavatam and we recommend those interested m hearing more about the qualities and activities of such great souls study the Srimad Bhagavatam.

The Problem With Modern Government: In modern governments we find many politicians and government officers who are simply interested in a good salary and a comfortable life. They achieve this for themselves and their colleagues by levying exorbitant taxes and creating an ineffectual and bureaucratic top heavy government.

The citizens under the rule of such an unqualified government are most unfortunate. They are not protected from thieves and rogues from within the country. Instead they are exploited by the governments taxation system. Excessive taxation is levied to maintain the ineffectual top heavy bureaucratic system. No one can be happy in such a difficult position

Selection of Members of the Government: Unless a person has the qualities of a Kshatriya he should not be given the position of king, president, Prime Minister, minister or a military man. If the men in these positions do not have the qualities of a Kshatriya (heroism, power, determination, resourcefulness, courage in battle, generosity and leadership) then the government becomes unworkable and the society suffers due to lack of protection. Currently, all over the world, the people in general are suffering because the governments of the world are full of unqualified persons who have no idea of the process of creating a fair society and maintaining law and order.

The Vaishyas: The Vaishyas are responsible principally for the production food and the protection of the cows. It is the duty of the Brahmans to understand the Vedic Scriptures and give guidance to the Kshatriya government and military who, in turn give directions to the Vaishyas and the sudras. The qualities of a Vaishya are given in the Bhagawad Gita as farming, cow protection and business and they work to provide the society with the required food, clothing and other goods.

The Sudras: The sudras have little intelligence and must therefore be engaged in the service of one of the other three classes. Their occupation is to perform manual labour, give service and to engage in arts and craftsmanship. The sudras are unable to support themselves independently therefore they must take shelter of an employer who can direct and provide for them.

It is described in this age of Kali almost everyone is a Shudra. We can actually see society is now so degraded that practically everyone must work as a Shudra by serving an employer. Only the sudras take such employment, the Brahmans simply depend on God and this way they get everything required. They receive charity from members of the other divisions of society. The Kshatriya has some land and collects taxes from the citizens and the Vaishya makes some money by trading farm produce and doing business. Only the sudras depend on someone else for their maintenance. If proper education is provided then the sudras who have the capacity to learn can be elevated to higher positions in the social structure. A society of sudras means a society of chaos as sudras don't have the intelligence to organize society, therefore, there is great need to train qualified Brahmans to re-establish the "head" of the social body. If this is done there is certainly hope for the future.

4

Natural Inequalities of Caste and Class

Caste is the most contentious issue that has fascinated and divided scholars who have wished to study this system of stratified social-hierarchy in India. There is an enormous body of academic writing and political polemic on the issue. These are basically the part of debate on the transformation of Indian society under the impact of colonialism and its administrative mechanisms. Some argue for the continuities of pre-colonial social-structures including caste. Others stress the basic qualitative changes introduced by the colonial rulers. Louis Dumont, the French scholar and writer of a famous book on caste, *Homo-Hierarchicus*, constructed a textually-informed image of caste.

In this image, two opposing conceptual categories of purity and pollution are the core elements of caste-structure. These unique core principles of caste-hierarchy, according to Dumont, are observed in scriptural formulation as well as the every-day life of all Hindus. In other words, these values separate Indians culturally from the Western civilisation, making India a land of static, unchangeable, 'oriental' Brahmanical values. This notion of caste has been challenged by Nicholas Dirks and others. Dumont's notion was criticised as it failed to explain the social change, dynamism and individualistic strivings even within the traditional Indian society. Gerald Berreman pointed out that the principle of Brahmanical hierarchy was not uniformly followed by all Hindus. He also criticised the Dumontian notion that power and economic factors are distinct and epiphenomenal to caste. It has been pointed out by others that caste hierarchy is not a fixed hierarchy; rather it is context-specific and fluid and contains seeds of contestation among various castes.

Nicholas Dirks cites ethnographic and textual evidence to demonstrate that Brahmins and their texts were not so central to the social fabric of Indian life. According to this view, powerrelations and command over men and resources were more important. Brahmins were merely ritual specialists, often subordinate to powerful ruling families. The caste-based scriptural or Brahmanical model of traditional India was an invention of the British Orientalists and ethnographers, according to this view. However, caste played a very critical role in the Indian social-reformers' and nationalists' perception of caste. It was certainly not a mere product of British imagination.

INVENTION OF COLONIAL MODERNITY

As we hinted above, two opposing viewpoints see caste differently. Some view it as an unchanged survival of Brahmanical traditions of India. According to this view, Brahmanism represents a core civilisational value and caste is the central symbol of this value. It is the basic expression of the pre-colonial traditions of India. Contrary to this view, Nicolas Dirks, in his *Castes of Mind* (2001), argues that caste is a product of colonial modernity. By this he does not mean that caste did not exist before the advent of British. He is simply suggesting that caste became a single, unique category under the British rule that expressed and provided the sole index of understanding India. Earlier there were diverse forms of social-identity and community in India.

The British reduced everything to a single explanatory category of caste. It was the colonial state and its administrators who made caste into a uniform, all-encompassing and ideologically consistent organism. They made caste a measure of all things and the most important emblem of traditions. Colonialism reconstructed cultural forms and social-institutions like caste to create a line of difference and demarcation between themselves as European modern and the colonised Asian traditional subjects. In other words, British colonialism played a critical role in both the identification and production of Indian 'tradition'.

The colonial modernity devalued the so called Indian traditions. Simultaneously, it also transformed them. Caste was recast as the spiritual essence of India that regulated and mediated the private domain. Caste-ridden Indian society was different from the European civil society because caste was opposed to the basic premises of individualism as well as the collective identity of a nation. The salience of this pre-colonial identity and sense of loyalty could easily be used to justify the rule by the colonial modern administrators. So, according to Dirks, it was the colonial rule of India that organised the 'social difference and deference' solely in terms of caste.

The attempts to downplay or dismiss the significance of Brahmins and Brahmanical order is not in accordance with familiar historical records and persistence of caste-identities even in the contemporary Indian social life. Caste-terms and principles were certainly not in universal use in pre-colonial periods. Caste in its various manifestations and forms was also not an immutable entity. However, starting from the *Vedas* and the Great Epics, from Manu and other *dharmasastras*, from *puranas*, from ritual practices, the penal system of Peshwa rulers who punished culprits according to caste-principles, to the denunciations of anti-Brahmanical 'reformers' of all ages, everything points towards the legacy of pre-colonial times. It is true that there were also non-caste affiliations and identities such as networks of settlements connected by matrimonial alliances, trade, commerce and state service in the pre-colonial times. However, caste was also a characteristic marker of identity and a prevailing socialmetaphor.

Caste was not merely a fabrication of British rulers designed to demean and subjugate Indians. It did serve the colonial interests by condemning the 'Brahmanical tyranny', colonial administration could easily justify their codes to 'civilise' and 'improve' the 'fallen people'. Moreover, strengthening of the caste-hierarchy could also act as a bulwark against anarchy.

NATURE OF CLASS INEQUALITY

Class societies are characterised by the horizontal division of society into strata. In Marxist terms, classes are defined by their differential access to the means of production. The dominant classes appropriate the 'surplus' produced by other classes through their control of means of production, and thus exploit their labour. The actual configuration of social classes varies from one society to another. The rise and growth of Indian social classes was organically linked to the basic structure of colonialism and bore the imprint of that association. What constitutes the dominant proprietary class in the urban-areas is marked by plurality and heterogeneity in its composition. A clear-cut demarcation along the lines of merchant, industrial and finance capital is not possible in case of India. The Indian business classes exhibit a complex intertwining of functions. Under the colonial rule, the Indian businessmen were initially relegated to small private trade, money lending and acted as agents of foreign British Capital.

The British capitalists and merchants controlled the upper layer of Indian economy represented by the big joint stock companies, managing houses, banking and insurance and major exportimport firms. Despite obstacles and constraints, the Indian capitalist class grew slowly and steadily and breached white 'collective monopoly'. With all structural constraints, colonialism also guaranteed the security of private property and sanctity of contract, the basic legal elements required for a market-led growth. The expansion of foreign trade and commercialisation eased the capital shortage and accelerated the growth of sectors where cost of raw-materials was low such as cotton textiles, sugar, leather, cement, tobacco and steel. Certain groups of Parsis, Marwaris, the Khojas, the Bhatias and Gujarati traders benefited from their collaboration with the European companies and pumped their resources into the manufacturing sector. This Indian capitalist class grew, diversified to some extent and acquired important position by 1940s. This class thrived during Independence under the government's policy of importsubstitution and quantitative controls. The 'Public-Sector' units provided the infrastructure and the intermediate and capital goods to this 'protected' class while the public lending institutions provided it with cheap sources of finances. The assets of the biggest 20 industrial houses increased from Rs. 500 crores in 1851 to Rs 23,200 crores in 1986. This was the result of benefits derived from state-developed infrastructural facilities, subsidised energy inputs, cheap capital goods and long-term finance made available to these by big monopoly industrial houses under the planning. On the other hand, almost 70% of the people exist on merely subsistence level and 76.6 million agricultural labourers earn only one-tenth of what an organised sector worker in the city earns. In the 1980s, unemployment reached about 10% of total active population. In the urban centres, the bulk of labourers are working in unorganised informal sectors. The vast army of pavement vendors, domestic servants, porters and street hawkers represent a kind of disguised urban unemployment.

The class-composition in the rural areas also bears the stamp of colonialism. The older group of rural gentry, although its wings were clipped away by the British colonial regime, was retained and transformed into a kind of rentier class of landlords invested with newly defined property rights on land. This was especially true of permanently settled Zamindari areas of Bengal and Taluqdari areas of Awadh. This landlord-rentier class generally emerged from the pre-existing groups' of Zamindars and Taluqdars who had enjoyed the rights of revenuecollection under the pre-British regimes. They exercised "extra-economic' feudal coercion over their small marginal share-croppers. Since the Congress Party favoured a bureaucratic rather than mobilisational form for carrying out a gradual social transformation after Independence, the power and privileges of these semi-feudal agrarian magnates remained intact in some areas. These classes now managed the new democratic polity. The failure to implement radical agrarian reforms meant that the availability of resources and accessibility to spaces within the new polity to the socially marginal groups remained limited.

The rich farmers, however, are numerically the most important proprietary class in the rural areas. In areas outside Zamindari settled areas of Bengal, the colonial state settled land revenue with dominant cultivating groups. A class of rich farmers emerged from these groups. They took advantage of the expanding market networks under the colonial economy and they had resources like sufficient arable land, livestock, implements and better access to credit. They also became less dependent on money lenders and they took to usury themselves.

The Jat peasants of Punjab and the Upper Doab, the Vellalas in Tamilnadu, the Kanbi-Patidars of South Gujarat, the Lingayats of Karnataka and the Kamma-Reddy farmers of Andhra constituted this group. The tenancy legislation under colonialism and after Independence initiated the process of transfer of landed resources from non-cultivating, absentee landlords to the enterprising rich farmers. Some older groups of rentier landlords also converted themselves into this class. The political clout of this class grew as it drew encouragement from state's policy of providing price-supports to agricultural produce and from liberal provisions of subsidised inputs such as water, power, fertilizers, diesel, credit and agricultural machinery. This class is easily identifiable by the ownership of landed and other agricultural resources. In 1970s, about 20% households of the rich farmers owned about 63% of rural assets such as land, livestock, building, and implements. This disproportionate access to rural assets is combined by its control over wage labour which is used to produce a sizeable marketable surplus by this class. The other pole of rural social-structure is the world of semi-proletariat having little or no control over productive resources. The agricultural labourers are a predominant group with little or no guarantee of a regular employment, often burdened by coercive domination of rich farmers. The bureaucratic-managerial elite also constitute a significant class in India as the relatively weak capitalist class at the time of India's Independence was not in a position to completely subordinate the highly developed administrative state apparatus. The growth of non-market mechanisms and planning in the allocation of resources and economic patronage also resulted in the expansion of bureaucracy. This class expanded in the post-colonial phase with the spreading out of education and need for professional and white-collar jobs involving new skills and expertise. This is not merely an auxiliary class of bourgeois as there are conflicts of interests between the public sector professionals and private capital. The command over knowledge, skills, tastes and networks of relationships are notable features of this class.

INTERRELATION OF CASTE AND CLASS HIERARCHIES

Caste and class point towards inequality and hierarchy. In both the cases, however, the principle of organisation differs.

The core features of caste are: endogamy or marriage within caste, occupational differentiation and hereditary specialisation of occupations, notion of pollution and a ritual hierarchy in which Brahmins are generally at the top. Classes, on the other hand, broadly refer to economic basis of ownership or non-ownership relation to the means of production. But how does caste and class correlate to each other? Classes are sub-divided in terms of types of ownership and control of economic resources and the type of services contributed to the process of production. The Brahmanical ritual hierarchy of the caste is also not universally applicable and upheld by all. In many cases, ritual hierarchy is only contextual. The prosperous Jats in North India enjoy social and political dominance without equivalent ritual status. In most popular renditions of caste, hierarchy alone is emphasised and that too from Brahmanical point of view. Sometimes, however, caste works as a discrete community, without hierarchical relationship to other segments of society. Our conceptual categories do not always recapture the existing social reality. For instance, a conceptual distinction is often made between sharecroppers and agricultural labourers. In actual life, however, there is a high degree of overlap and they do not constitute discrete entities. Similar overlap is found in the rentier-landlord and cultivator-owner categories. The picture becomes hazier when we turn to caste-class configuration.

Caste and class resemble each other in certain respects and differ in others. Castes constitute the status groups or communities that can be defined in terms of ownership of property, occupation and style of life. Social honour is closely linked to ritual values in this closed system. Class positions also tend to be associated with social honour; however, they are defined more in terms of ownership or non-ownership of means of production. The classes are much more open and fluid and have scope of individual upward social mobility. In caste system, only an entire segment can move upward, and hence, the mobility is much slower. Although there is considerable divergence between the hierarchy of caste and that of class, the top and bottom segments of the class system are largely subsumed under the caste structure. The upper castes own means of production (land in rural areas) and act as rentiers. The landless agrarian proletarian coincides with the lower castes or dalits who provide labour services for the rentier upper caste people as well as rich prosperous farmers of intermediate level. At the intermediate level, articulation of class-identities is more complex. The process of differentiation of communities dislocates class-relations from the caste-structure. If caste and class show a fair degree of overlap at the top and bottom level and in some cases appear almost co-terminus, the picture is quite ambiguous at the intermediate level of caste hierarchy. Similarly, the processes of modernisation especially urbanisation, acquisition of education and new skills act as the forces of dislocation that puncture the forces of social inertia and modify caste-rigidity.

SOCIAL INEQUALITIES, DEVELOPMENT AND PARTICIPATORY POLITICS

If social inequalities are so deeply entrenched, then how do they affect the developmental process and participation of deprived sections of society in a democratic polity? This key question has been answered in different ways. Kothari, while analysing the intrusions of caste into politics and politics into caste, distinguishes three stages in the progression of political modernisation after Independence. In the first stage, he says the struggle for political power was limited to the entrenched and the ascendant castes. In the second phase, competitions within these castes for power led to factionalism and in the third stage, lower castes have been mobilised and are asserting themselves in the political domain. In his words "It is not-politics that gets caste-ridden; it is the caste that gets politicised". With the extension of franchise in the post-colonial India, each social group and sub-group got mobilised for a share in the developmental process and competed for positions in the state-bureaucracy. The Indian polity is, thus, governed both by vertical mobilisation by the dominant castes and horisontal alliances in the name of *jati* and *varna*. The political parties exacerbate the existing cleavages in a developing society like India. The salience of primordial ties of kinship, caste and community play significant role in hindering the establishment of civil society. Moreover, there is never a set chronology of mobilisation and political modernisation, especially any pre-ordained and unconditional progression along a set path. In the rural hinterlands, cleavages of caste and community and articulation of kinship and territorial affinities work against implementation of a piece of redistributive land-reforms. The rich prosperous farmers use the existing social networks in the multi-class agrarian mobilisation in the electoral arena to mobilise and harness marginal and small farmers for their own economic interests such as lower taxes, higher prices for agricultural produce, better subsidies and cheaper credit facilities.

So, despite the egalitarian ideal of post-colonial Indian state, there are still disproportionate access to resources, power and entitlements between different social classes and castes. The relationships between the upper and lower castes in the rural areas are still governed by the ideology of caste. According to Andre Beteille, professionalisation and specialisation of modern service sector in the post-colonial Indian society has increased the role of formal education, technical skills and training; 'family' and not caste plays critical role in the social reproduction of inequality, especially in urban areas. However, it is still a debatable point whether the increasing bureaucratisation of professional activities per se enhances the chances of social mobility and equality of opportunities. Although, there may be no legal barriers to entry into new occupation, the unequal distribution of life chances, status and power on the grounds of birth determine the social and political trajectories that accord positions, ranks and power to the individuals.

The establishment of a formal democracy in itself is no guarantee that all citizens will enjoy equal access and participation in the political processes. Political privileges are retained and ingrained in many non-elective institutions, the civil bureaucracy and the police in particular. They protect the interests of the dominant proprietary classes and the upper castes. The lower castes and classes are not yet sufficiently empowered to shape and mould the political processes or the state's social and economic policies. The powerful landed magnates of upper castes in the countryside and the industrial and business classes of urban rich make use of authoritarian streak inherent in the non-elective institutions to deny genuine democratisation of polity. The apparent assertion of their rights and mobilising capacity by the backwards and scheduled castes is used by the crafty politicians to augment their power and wealth. Such mobilisations, thus serve the interests of a spoils system and a thoroughly corrupt and inefficient bureaucracy instead of articulating a programme of equitable development and social empowerment. Apart from other institutional constraints, the failure of democracy to grant substantive democratic rights and deliver the promise of redistributive justice is rooted in the class and caste-based inequalities in India. Dreze found evidence of subtle forms of deprivation in the rural areas of the Eastern U.P. in terms of accessibility of the disadvantaged groups to schooling, health services and exclusion of marginal sections of population from effective participation in the political processes.

THE MEANING OF THE TERM 'CASTE'

The two main ideas denoted by a caste are a community or persons following a common occupation, and a community whose members marry only among themselves. A third distinctive feature is that the members of a caste do not as a rule eat with outsiders with the exception of other Hindu castes of a much higher social position than their own. None of these will, however, serve as a definition of a caste. In a number of castes the majority of members have abandoned their traditional occupation and taken to others. Less than a fifth of the Brahmans of the Central Provinces are performing any priestly or religious functions, and the remaining four-fifths are landholders or engaged in Government service as magistrates, clerks of public offices, constables and orderlies, or in railway service in different grades, or in the professions as barristers and pleaders, doctors, engineers and so on. The Rajputs and Marathas were originally soldiers, but only an infinitely small proportion belong to the Indian Army, and the remainder are ruling chiefs, landholders, cultivators, labourers or in the various grades of Government service and the police. Of the Telis or oil-pressers only 9 per cent are engaged in their traditional occupation, and the remainder are landholders, cultivators and shopkeepers. Of the Ahîrs or graziers only 20 per cent tend and breed cattle. Only 12 per cent of the Chamars are supported by the tanning industry, and so on. The Bahnas or cotton-cleaners have entirely lost their occupation, as cotton is now cleaned in factories; they are cartmen or cultivators, but retain their caste name and organisation. Since the introduction of machine-made cloth has reduced the profits of hand-loom weaving, large numbers of the weaving castes have been reduced to manual labour as a means of subsistence. The abandonment of the traditional occupation has become a most marked feature of Hindu society as a result of the equal opportunity and freedom in the choice of occupations afforded by the British Government, coupled with the rapid progress of industry and the spread of education. So far it has had no very markedly disintegrating effect on the caste system, and the status of a caste is still mainly fixed by its traditional occupation; but signs are not wanting of a coming change. Again, several castes have the same traditional occupation; about forty of the castes of the Central Provinces are classified as agriculturists, eleven as weavers, seven as fishermen, and so on. Distinctions of occupation therefore are not a sufficient basis for a classification of castes. Nor can a caste be simply defined as a body of persons who marry only among themselves, or, as it is termed, an endogamous group; for almost every important caste is divided into a number of subcastes which do not marry and frequently do not eat with each other. But it is a distinctive and peculiar feature of caste as a social institution that it splits up the people into a multitude of these divisions and bars their intermarriage; and the real unit of the system and the basis of the fabric of Indian society is this endogamous group or subcaste.

The Subcaste

The subcastes, however, connote no real difference of status or occupation. They are little known except within the caste itself, and they consist of groups within the caste which marry among themselves, and attend the communal feasts held on the occasions of marriages, funerals and meetings of the caste *panchayat* or committee for the judgment of offences against the caste rules and their expiation by a penalty feast; to these feasts all male adults of the community, within a certain area, are invited. In the Central Provinces the 250 groups which have been classified as castes contain perhaps 2000 subcastes. Except in some cases other Hindus do not know a man's subcaste, though they always know his caste; among the ignorant lower castes men may often be found who do not know whether their caste contains any subcastes or whether they themselves belong to one. That is, they will eat and marry with all the members of their caste within a circle of villages, but know nothing about the caste outside those villages, or even whether it exists elsewhere. One subdivision of a caste may look down upon another on the ground of some difference of occupation, of origin, or of abstaining from or partaking of some article of food, but these distinctions are usually confined to their internal relations and seldom recognised by outsiders. For social purposes the caste consisting of a number of these endogamous groups generally occupies the same position, determined roughly according to the respectability of its traditional occupation or extraction.

Confusion of Nomenclature

No adequate definition of caste can thus be obtained from community of occupation or intermarriage; nor would it be accurate to say that every one must know his own caste and that all the different names returned at the census may be taken as distinct. In the Central Provinces about 900 caste-names were returned at the census of 1901, and these were reduced in classification to about 250 proper castes. In some cases synonyms are commonly used. The caste of *pan* or betel-vine growers and sellers is known indifferently as Barai, Pansari or Tamboli. The great caste of Ahîrs or herdsmen has several synonyms—as Gaoli in the Northern Districts, Rawat or Gahra in Chhattîsgarh, Gaur among the Uriyas, and Golkar among Telugus. Lohars are also called Khati and Kammari; Masons are called Larhia, Raj and Beldar.

The more distinctly occupational castes usually have different names in different parts of the country, as Dhobi, Warthi, Baretha, Chakla and Parit for washermen; Basor, Burud, Kandra and Dhulia for bamboo-workers, and so on. Such names may show that the subdivisions to which they are applied have immigrated from different parts of India, but the distinction is generally not now maintained, and many persons will return one or other of them indifferently. No object is gained, therefore, by distinguishing them in classification, as they correspond to no differences of status or occupation, and at most denote groups which do not intermarry, and which may therefore more properly be considered as subcastes. Titles or names of offices are also not infrequently given as caste names.

Members of the lowest or impure castes employed in the office of Kotwar or village watchmen prefer to call themselves by this name, as they thus obtain a certain rise in status, or at least they think so. In some localities the Kotwars or village watchmen have begun to marry among themselves and try to form a separate caste. Chamars (tanners) or Mahars (weavers) employed as grooms will call themselves Sais and consider themselves superior to the rest of their caste.

The Thethwar Rawats or Ahîrs will not clean household cooking-vessels, and therefore look down on the rest of the caste and prefer to call themselves by this designation, as 'Theth' means 'exact' or 'pure,' and Thethwar is one who has not degenerated from the ancestral calling. Salewars are a subcaste of Koshtis (weavers), who work only in silk and hence consider themselves as superior to the other Koshtis and a separate caste. The Rathor subcaste of Telis in Mandla have abandoned the hereditary occupation of oil-pressing and become landed proprietors. They now wish to drop their own caste and to be known only as Rathor, the name of one of the leading Rajput clans, in the hope that in time it will be forgotten that they ever were Telis, and they will be admitted into the community of Rajputs. It occurred to them that the census would be a good opportunity of advancing a step towards the desired end, and accordingly they telegraphed to the Commissioner of Jubbulpore before the enumeration, and petitioned the Chief Commissioner after it had been taken, to the effect that they might be recorded and classified only as Rathor and not as Teli; this method of obtaining recognition of their claims being, as remarked by Sir Bampfylde Fuller, a great deal cheaper than being weighed against gold. On the other hand, a common occupation may sometimes amalgamate castes originally distinct into one. The sweeper's calling is well-defined and under the generific term of Mehtar are included members of two or three distinct castes, as Dom, Bhangi and Chuhra; the word Mehtar means a prince or headman, and it is believed that its application to the sweeper by the other servants is ironical. It has now, however, been generally adopted as a caste name. Similarly, Darzi, a tailor, was held by Sir D. Ibbetson to be simply the name of a profession and not that of a caste; but it is certainly a true caste in the Central Provinces, though probably of comparatively late origin. A change of occupation may transfer a whole body of persons from one caste to another. A large section of the Banjara caste of carriers, who have taken to cultivation, have become included in the Kunbi caste in Berar and are known as Wanjari Kunbi. Another subcaste of the Kunbis called Manwa is derived from the Mana tribe. Telis or oilmen, who have taken to vending liquor, now form a subcaste of the Kalar caste called Teli-Kalar; those who have become shopkeepers are called Teli-Bania and may in time become an inferior section of the Bania caste. Other similar subcastes are the Ahîr-Sunars or herdsmen-goldsmiths, the Kayasth-Darzis or tailors, the Kori-Chamars or weaver-tanners, the Gondi Lohars and Barhais, being Gonds who have become carpenters and blacksmiths and been admitted to these castes; the Mahar Mhalis or barbers, and so on.

Tests of what a Caste Is

It would appear, then, that no precise definition of a caste can well be formulated to meet all difficulties. In classification, each doubtful case must be taken by itself, and it must be determined, on the information available, whether any body of persons, consisting of one or more endogamous groups, and distinguished by one or more separate names, can be recognised as holding, either on account of its traditional occupation or descent, such a distinctive position in the social system, that it should be classified as a caste. But not even the condition of endogamy can be accepted as of universal application; for Vidurs, who are considered to be descended from Brahman fathers and women of other castes, will, though marrying among themselves, still receive the offspring of such mixed alliances into the community; in the case of Gosains and Bairagis, who, from being religious orders, have become castes, admission is obtained by initiation as well as by birth, and the same is the case with several other orders; some of the lower castes will freely admit outsiders; and in parts of Chhattîsgarh social ties are of the laxest description, and the intermarriage of Gonds, Chamars and other low castes are by no means infrequent. But notwithstanding these instances, the principle of the restriction of marriage to members of the caste is so nearly universal as to be capable of being adopted as a definition.

THE FOUR TRADITIONAL CASTES

The well-known traditional theory of caste is that the Aryans were divided from the beginning of time into four castes: Brahmans or priests, Kshatriyas or warriors, Vaishyas or merchants and cultivators, and Sudras or menials and labourers, all of whom had a divine origin, being born from the body of Brahma—the Brahmans from his mouth, the Kshatriyas from his arms, the Vaishyas from his thighs, and the Sudras from his feet. Intermarriage between the four castes was not at first entirely prohibited, and a man of any of the three higher ones, provided that for his first wife he took a woman of his own caste, could subsequently marry others of the divisions beneath his own. In this manner the other castes originated. Thus the Kaivarttas or Kewats were the offspring of a Kshatriya father and Vaishya mother, and so on. Mixed marriages in the opposite direction, of a woman of a higher caste with a man of a lower one, were reprobated as strongly as possible, and the offspring of these were relegated to the lowest position in society; thus the Chandals, or descendants of a Sudra father and Brahman mother, were of all men the most base. It has been recognised that this genealogy, though in substance the formation of a number of new castes through mixed descent may have been correct, is, as regards the details, an attempt made by a priestly law-giver to account, on the lines of orthodox tradition, for a state of society which had ceased to correspond to them.

Occupational Theory of Caste

In the ethnographic description of the people of the Punjab, which forms the Caste chapter of Sir Denzil Ibbetson's *Census Report* of 1881, it was pointed out that occupation was the chief basis of the division of castes, and there is no doubt that this is true. Every separate occupation has produced a distinct caste, and the status of the caste depends now mainly or almost entirely on its occupation. The fact that there may be several castes practising such important callings as agriculture or weaving does not invalidate this in any way, and instances of the manner in which such castes have been developed will be given subsequently. If a caste changes its occupation it may, in the course of time, alter its status in a corresponding degree. The important Kayasth and Gurao castes furnish instances of this. Castes, in fact, tend to rise or fall in social position with the acquisition of land or other forms of wealth or dignity much in the same manner as individuals do nowadays in European countries. Hitherto in India it has not been the individual who has undergone the process; he inherits the social position of the caste in which he is born, and, as a rule, retains it through life without the power of altering it. It is the caste, as a whole, or at least one of its important sections or subcastes, which gradually rises or falls in social position, and the process may extend over generations or even centuries.

AN ATTEMPT TO DEFINE CLASS AND SOCIAL CLASS

The word *class* and especially the term *social class* have been and remain a source of great confusion in social science. It is the intention of this chapter to contribute to social theory by systematically analysing these terms in a more comprehensive manner than has been heretofore attempted. A full understanding of social class is prerequisite to an extended discussion of social class rigidity and mobility. Sombart believes the time has come for social scientists to come to an understanding as to the meaning of class (*Glierdun nach Ständen*). The present confusion may be attributed to the many meanings of the word and to the fact that this has never been recognized, he says.

Some economists have been reluctant to use the descriptive terms "economic classes" and "occupational classes" and have preferred to refer to such divisions as "social classes." This has been one source of confusion.

Economic Aspects of Definition of Class and Social Class

People speak of propertied and property-less classes, of productive and unproductive classes, and of the working class. Mombert states that such general terms leave the word *class* quite empty of meaning. Simkhovitch defines classes as groups with similar sources of income. They are conscious of similar or identical economic interests. A social class is, for him, an organized body of individuals whole economic interests coincide. This formulation is quite Marxian, and it considers the class as a pressure group. L. Von Stein divides the classes of society into ownership classes, legal classes, and honorific classes. It is this last-mentioned category which many modern authorities would identify with social classes.

Although this is not his conclusive explanation, Ginsberg at one point states: *The primary determinants of social stratification are without doubt largely economic in character. Economic conditions determine an individual's occupation, and this in turn is generally a fair index of his mode of life and educational attainments, from which again may usually be inferred the sort of people whom he would meet on equal terms, the range of individuals from among whom he would normally choose his partner in marriage, and so forth.*

A discerning critic might re-phrase the foregoing in these words: *The key to a person's economic condition is best found in the social class into which he was born. His social position determines the occupation for which he fits himself or which he has a chance of entering after training. The social class condition in which he is reared is an index to his mode of life and to his educational training. From it we infer, certainly, the sort of people whom he meets on equal terms; and it is his background, not his present economic condition, which is most likely to limit his choice of mate, etc.*

This debate runs through the literature on social classes, in one form or another, and the reader will have to decide which argument has the more cogency, the economic or the socio-psychological explanation of causation. Gumplowicz takes his place alongside the economic determinists in saying that "a man's behaviour is determined immediately by his economic status, which constrains him to follow a certain mode of life and awakens the corresponding mental conditions within him." Marshall divides class from social class by associating the former with production and the latter with consumption. Veblen's well known theory of modern hierarchies of prestige is in terms of conspicuous consumption rather than in terms of "relationship to the instruments of production," the Marxian formula. A recent textbook in sociology, however, states that a "social class is an economic group whose members are alike in their relations to the process of getting a living." Few social theorists still hold this view; Mombert, Speier, Ginsberg,

MacIver, Mess, Vablen, and many others have directly or indirectly refuted it. Max Weber synthesizes the economic aspect and the socio-psychological factors in the making of status groups. He lists: "(1) the possession of economic means, (2) the external standard of living, (3) cultural and recreational possibilities." As a matter of descending importance, the order should perhaps be reversed. Social contracts might come first, conspicuous consumption second, and the possession of wealth third.

Occupational and social hierarchies. Since Many writers have used the terms occupational hierarchy and social hierarchy synonymously, there must be a relationship between the two hierarchies. Complete identicalness has been discredited by theorists, and although an adequate formula of the exact relationship is difficult to invent, attempt is made here to do so.

Bücher discerned the close relationship between the status of the individual and his choice of an occupation. The inference here is that the status determines the vocation of one's choice quite as much as the vocation determines the status of the individual later in life.

He states: In so far as our propertied classes are also social classes according to occupation, they are not such because their occupation creates property, but rather because property determines the selection of a vocation....

Every vocation under our industrial organization yields an income; and only the propertied person is in a situation to seek out for himself the more lucrative positions...while the unpropertied person must be content with the inferior positions.

Given a broader interpretation, but in the same spirit, this could read: Members of the higher social classes will enter a given field according to the amount of esteem, prestige, and money which the occupation represents. It is not so much that the occupation gives the person prestige — rather it is a case of the person lending his social dignity, or lack of it, to the occupation he enters. Persons of high standing are likely, more often than not, to aspire to reputable positions with real chance of success. If the work desired requires both social and technical training, those of the higher and middle classes have the social background and the necessary time, patience, persistence, and money to obtain that technical training.

Men with such advantages have tended to monopolize political and colonial offices in the British Empire, for instance. From such groups were the army officers of the *Kaiserreich* (the first German Reich) chosen. They had the background and social contacts which gave them high status; they prepared themselves by university training and special education for the positions awaiting them.

In an extended debate with Bücher Schmoller argued that the social classes were a product of the division of labour and the accumulation of property. But Bücher answered that "the differences in property and income are not a consequence of the division of labour, rather they are its chief cause." In attempting to prove this, Bücher points out that persons on certain social levels intermarry and have close social ties. As a part of this regular association with each other they tend to hold for each other positions comparable to their social rank. Although their vocations often change from one generation to the next, the rank is likely to remain the same.

Thus Bücher rejects Schmeller's theory that the work makes the man and chooses to believe that the different social classes choose the various vocations, leaving the least desirable occupation to those with the greatest immediate need or with the least training and conditioning in restrain and in long-term planning. Bougle attributes to socialist theory, in particular, the doctrine that "the division of labour gave rise to the classes and that social specialization is a result of technical specialization." Marshall affirms Bücher: "In all societies Social Class is concerned with the selection of occupations... the conventional view for a man of a given station to occupy himself." Landtman says that "the rich and powerful prefer to leave every kind of industrial employment to others, whereby divisions of occupations is brought about."

The economic interpretation of causation in this sphere of is championed by Fahlbeck. It is his opinion that in this age persons are not bound to the class of their birth.

The work of an individual "determines his final position in the social sense." Nothaas agrees with Fahlbeck: "... occupation has become the basis of class identification... occupation more than anything else determines class membership in modern society..." No intimation is given here, as is strongly stated by Bücher and Marshall, that status determines occupational choices and chances.

Fairchild lists occupation as one of the free choices of the individual. A full expression of this theory would probably reveal that the average person may have a wide range of choices with regard to type of calling but not with regard to the rank of the occupation chosen.

Indeed, the occupational opportunities of the average person are severely limited by his class standing. His parents may neglect him; they may exploit him; they may want to see him at an early age independent of their support. (Study and observation reveal these to be the habits of the lowest classes generally.) They lack the foresight, the moral stamina (inhibitions), and the means to give their children the home life, education, poise, and connections which might improve their lot. The opposite is true of the entrenched middle and upper classes, in general. The social class interpretation of occupational choice in contradiction to the economic interpretation is stated succinctly by Bougle: "... instead of belonging to a particular class because one has entered a particular vocation, one enters a particular vocation because one belongs to a particular class. Social standing governs the distribution of functions."

The simplest analysis of modern society reveals that occupational categories do not correspond to hierarchies of social prestige, privilege, honour, and power. A "lawyer" is a person who has passed the Bar examination. He may be highly esteemed, or he may blush when his friends refer to him as a lawyer, because he may be finishing his fourth year with the Works Progress Administration.

A person's "position in the occupation," as stressed by Mombert, reveals much more. In the case of an employee of a university, it may indicate that he is an instructor in rank. Superficially considered, one instructor is the equal of every other. As has been shown, there are writers who build their theory of the social class structure on this premise. Observation demonstrates, however, that the theory of equal social status for equal professional rank cannot be applied with satisfaction to cases one confronts day after day.

Some instructors are young men marked to rise, with fine family backgrounds, who have married ultra-fashionable women. The faculty directory of New York University, for instance, shows that some of them live at conspicuous addresses. Other instructors are older men, with feelings of failure, who wrestle monthly with the family budget. Certainly here is abundant evidence of social heterogeneity in the presence of occupational homogeneity. Men work side by side who do not, in their leisure time, have enough in common, strictly from the social class point of view, to enable them to fraternize with one another.

Whatever occupational category is mentioned, observation quickly shows it not to be homogeneous in the social class sense. There are, within any given community, many social divisions among farmers. Even the term "farm-owner" does not describe the social position and circle of friends of the person thus designated. The same is true of the category "tenant." In referring to social classes many of the more careful writers avoid direct reference to occupations. MacIver states categorically: "Class distinctions rest in the last resort not on function but on *status*." Mombert rules out occupational groups from his category of social class, which he identifies with class.

It can be safely stated that the weight of authority is now on the side of those who differentiate between occupational categories and social status groups. Rene Worms makes the empathic statement: "One must not confuse classes with professions. A profession includes all men whose activity produces a given result, whatever their rank on the social ladder." Tawney repudiates the theory of parallelism between the social functions and the social classes in these words: "The class system takes off its overalls and office coat and wears a costume appropriate to the hours of ease." Slowly, this position is coming to be accepted in social science.

Wealth and social status. The relationship between economic factors and social class is further complicated by the question of the relationship between wealth and social standing. Do great and medium wealth determine high and medium class standing, respectively; or do high and middle class status determine the distribution of great and medium wealth?

Throughout human history it has not been characteristic of social classes to be strictly plutocratic. Rome, for instance, definitely rejected the plutocratic theory of status. Precedence, social esteem, and social prestige have rarely if ever been computed in purely non-personal, material terms. Sumner and Keller observe: "Plutocracy has been held in check by aristocracy of birth, though aristocrats do not normally renounce their opportunity of becoming rich." Social class usually breathes the atmosphere of aristocracy, i.e. exclusiveness based on social antecedents. This has been generally true of the craft artisans, the middle classes, and the upper classes of all societies alike. Furthermore, social class uses social advantage to reap economic rewards.

In how far does this theory hold? It is true that a family is not socially rated according to its economic means? Is it possible that status produces and distributes wealth even more frequently and effectively than wealth produces status? Should the slogan, "A man's social position depends upon his economic power," be preceded by the statement: "Usually a man's wealth depends upon the social class in which he was reared." "Among primitive peoples," we are told, "wealth is perhaps more likely to be a result of power than power of wealth." For modern times Mombert would reverse this emphasis.

He holds that the social factors of class determination may formerly have been predominant, but that with the growth of capitalism the economic factors have been ascendant. If wealth had been equally accessible to all classes, Mombert's theory would unquestionably be true, but such approximate equality did not exist. Wealth became relatively more independent of the social class system, but never completely free of its controls.

Discussions pertaining to the relationship between economic and social factors in this regard frequently mention the theoretical ease with which a wealthy person in England, for instance, can be arranged to be knighted. This is given as evidence of the power of wealth to acquire status. The converse argument is that the nobility can recover its fortune at any time by marrying into the wealthier non-noble families. It may be argued with reason that all rich men did not become knights or nobles, but almost all titled families have remained affluent up to the present era. Gonnard states: "The conquest of wealth is a consequence, rather than a cause, of class formation. Classes arise, first of all, from differences of origin..."

Gurewitsch belongs to the same school of thought: "Social power is, at the same time, economic power and gives the higher classes a relatively higher economic position." If it is true that the possessing classes tened to become the dominating ones, then it follows that the dominating classes tend to become the posessing ones.

A young man usually acquires from his parents, if they belong to the middle or upper classes, something of economic value far beyond whatever financial provision they make for him. The intangibles handed down from parents to children include social contacts, technical skills, attitudes, values, and desires: all of which may be of considerable economic significance. Such assets can more easily be turned into economic goods by these classes than can a person without means and status first acquire the means and then "purchase" the status. Social class continuously translates itself into wealth, great or small.

With wisdom it can be said that the king is rich because he is king; he is not king because he is rich. A careful survey of the literature on this subject has revealed that the chief point of emphasis of writers in this field has been reversed in the past half-century. When Sir Henry Maine surveyed the theories regarding the origin of aristocracies, he found that the emphasis was placed on kingly favour. He then set about to show that some noble lines were founded by rich cattlemen, that the heroes of the Nibelungenlied were "not only noble but rich." The inference here is that these nobles and warriors became such by virtue of their means, but the evidence is lacking to prove that wealth actually produced the first upper classes. They could have acquired wealth as a consequence of their power.

Max Weber, in describing how wealth became concentrated, shows the priority of social position over economic power. He writes: *The differentiation in wealth... has different sources. One is chieftainship, whether in the chieftain of a clan or a military group. The division of the land among the members of the clan was in the hands of the clan chieftain. This traditional right often developed into seignioral power which became hereditary.* Classes are not always made or unmade by economic trends, as the theory of economic determinism would teach; on the contrary, the king or tyrant sometimes undermines old aristocracies and exclusive groups and builds up different ones in their place.

Personal factors, most frequently of a social class character, often pave the way for the distribution of the economic surplus among persons. The workings of the social upon the economic factors in the life of colonial America are delineated by Adams:... access to official society was a prerequisite to the securing of this influence [ability to obtain land grants] and as the society was comparatively limited, intermarriage among its members became increasingly frequent...

The financial standing of their members thus increasingly also enabled them to strengthen their position as merchants. In all the colonies, the councils were almost wholly made up of the members of these aristocracies... By means of their large landholdings, their possession of a considerable portion of the cash capital of America, their position as merchant creditors of the smaller people, their control of the councils, and their priviledged situation with regard to the dispensers of patronage and favours, as well as the more intangible influences always appertaining to a distinguished social position, the aristocrats by 1700 were fastening a firm grip both upon the political management and commercial exploitation of the New World.

There is one great difference between the generalization that new wealth purchases new status and the idea that old status is a source of wealth, both new and old. The latter is always an active process. Century after century it functions smoothly. The former statement is true only in certain times and places. The present period in the United States, at least the period from 1860 to the present, has perhaps seen more of the economic influence on social classes than human history has ever before experienced. The upper classes, in other words, have been temporarily unable to monopolize wealth and therefore hold their ranks firm. However, the amount of social class continuity has far outweighed the amount of social class percolation. Social class produces wealth, each station more or less according to its place on the scale. Social class in America has not formed its structure each generation out of "new men" characteristically. That is, the upper and middle classes have not neglected their economic opportunities to the extent that any overwhelming amount of wealth has been allowed to fall into the hands of persons of lower class standing, with which they could overcome and outrank those persons of respectable and reputable percentage.

In order to demonstrate that families of high social standing tend to monopolize opportunity in the economic realm. There one finds that, although application was made by many fine families of Scotland to be allowed to take up, early in the seventeenth century, the newly subjugated lands of North Ireland, when the final list of those accepted was issued, the larger tracts were generally distributed among persons of higher rank. The typical manner in which middle class families went bond for each other, the degree to which they were prepared, if given the chance, to further entrench their own economic position. But many were destined to disappointment. Their superiors came before them. *The uses to which wealth is put.* Plainly, a miser is without significant social status. Once one has obtained wealth, whether by inheritance or through the careful training and education provided by one's parents, or through one's own efforts or good fortune, there is always the problem of putting it to use.

Some persons, although they have money, do not obtain social status from its use because of the way they choose to spend (or not spend) it. While it is true that "the only practicable means of impressing one's pecuniary ability on these unsympathetic observers of one's everyday life is an unremitting demonstration of ability to pay," as Veblen says, yet it does not follow that people are wise in choosing between different items of expenditure — if it is social status they wish to obtain, or as is more often the case, to retain. Although it is probable that only a very small fraction of the population of any land is iconoclastic, many who acquire riches never learn how to put them to social class uses. The familiar theory that if a family is newly rich it can, given time, acquire polish, manners, and contacts, which make up for high social standing," should, perhaps, be qualified somewhat. The necessary quantity of wealth requisite to entrace into classes considerably higher than one's own (such as might come to a miner who make a big strike or to a farmer who becomes rich from oil) is subject to dissipation even before the end of one lifetime. Furthermore, the necessary self-discipline, such as is required in turning over the children to trained governesses, is frequently lacking.

Research has shown that successful and wealthy men in Virginia send their children either to private schools and colleges, or, if self-made, they sometimes let them take business courses in the local high school and do as their fathers did: start at the bottom. One son is given associative contacts; the other is assured that industry will suffice for success. Fathers of traditional social status, choosing the former approach, are generally more practiced in the arts of winning and keeping social status than are fathers, themselves self-made, who start their sons where they started. However, the wiser men of new success ape the habits of families of long high social standing. Their material success becomes incorporated, then, into the social class system.

Social status, even the retention of social status, is never purchased outright. It is earned. Time, effort, patience, careful planning, and money are the price. Mere pride, *hauteur*, never suffices to obtain social prestige. The real cost is unending contact: seeing, greeting, meeting people. Social life is a treadmill from which there is no rest; the people are really hard at work carrying out its obligations. "A leisure class always gives great attention to the arts of social intercourse," says Ross. But the classes who spend their days in active work are also attentive to their social obligations. Clubs, committees, teas, drinking parties, all consume precious leisure hours. Workers' wives, too, rise early and clean the house; for when visitors come, there must be a neat place in which to sit. And the hostess, even on such an informal occasion, has thought of her personal appearance.

Wealth and social status resolve themselves, in so far as they are allied to each other, then, into the following interrelationships: (1) New wealth is more accessible to families of high and middle class standing than to families of low status. (2) Families of low standing which succeed in acquiring great of medium wealth may, sometimes, with great care and good luck, move into classes much higher than their former position. When this has been accomplished, their wealth belongs henceforth to that higher social class. However, this can happen only when (a) property and riches are not carefully controlled and monopolized by the middle and upper middle class families, and (b) where the social class structure condescends to admit shifting of status through the display of pecuniary strength.

POLITICAL ASPECTS OF DEFINITION OF CLASS AND SOCIAL CLASS

In addition to purely economic criteria frequently used to define class or social class, there comes in second place the question of how status is affected by politics. Do Republicans constitute one social class, Democrats another, and Socialists still a third? If a section of the population is unable to exercise the franchise, does it, therefore, constitute a "class"? Only in some communities does it occur to people *directly* to identify one's social status with one's political party, as between the two major parties of this country. Limited social discrimination is, however, frequently exercised in some circles against a person because he is a member of the Republican or Democratic party.

But the problem of the radical or workers' party or parties offers much more difficulty. Is not the workers' party, whatever its name, a class party? Does not everyone who votes and works for this party consider himself to be a member of the working class? Is a radical intellectual socially as well as politically a member of the struggling lower orders of society?

Social Status and the class struggle. Is there a direct connection between the social classes and the class struggle? Recently a sociological textbook identified the two. Here the classes are defined as the two competitive groups, capitalists and labourers, in a struggle for economic goods. The authors state:

Although we are not quite clear what we mean when we call someone a capitalist and another a worker, yet if J.P. Morgan and John, the ditch digger, were brought together we would have little difficulty in distinguishing the two, not only by their appearance, but, more important for the sociologist, by their attitudes, their stereotyped notions about each other, their prejudices, antipathies, and loyalties. The "working class" man is a part of a culture complex. His place in the economic struggle gives him common interests with others of low income and with others who work in factories and are dependent upon wages paid by the boss. If they are conscious of these common interests and do something about it, such as supporting each other's strikes, they show signs of becoming "class conscious."

Here we are confronted with organizations (whether strictly on the political front or in the field of industrial warfare in this instance being of no consequence), with a community of interests. The differences between organizations, according to Sorokin, create a basis for what is nowadays called class-differentiation, with its class antagonisms and class friction.

Observation and reflection lead to the conclusion that the class struggle, which is a descriptive term used to apply to the industrial conflicts and to some of the parliamentary struggles of the last century, is a struggle between pressure groups and parties. It is hardly a term applicable to the jealousies, disloyalties, yet social cohesion, of social groups which make up the social classes.

The class struggle is something definite and exact, fixed by usage. The word *class* here, as in the case of the occupational classes, is correctly used, if by it is meant definite organizations which act as political parties or pressure groups, only so long as it is not confused with social strata or social classes, whose purposes are of another kind, whose loyalties are different, whose existence continues even after political parties, labour unions, and the class struggle have been abolished or made meaningless. There is, then, a working class which is composed of all those who vote the labour ticket, and in this case it does not include the doorman who always votes Tory. But there is another working class, as Marshall insists, which is a "real sphere of social intercourse" and which remains a social class, even though the "working class organization... occupied entirely in the defence of its interests against capital, belongs rather to the category of party."

Almost all revolutionary parties of working class orientation have intellectual leaders drawn largely from the middle and upper social classes. These parties seek to capture the state, and as such are parties. Many workers refuse to cooperate with them. Schumpeter, using class in the sense of social class, points out this fact:

For each individual his class membership is a given fact which is independent of his will. But he does not always confirm it by his actions. Persons are known to function, especially politically, with and for a social class to which they do not belong. In practical life these cases are well known, and we speak of them as fellow-travelers, renegades, etc.

In either its revolutionary or is institutionalized form the class struggle, except for some slave and serf uprisings, has not characterized the history of man except during the past two centuries. To function, it must have as its base the right of free assembly, free speech, and a free press, or their equivalent. Social classes, on the contrary, have always existed, at least among civilized men.

Usage has been of assistance in one respect. Professor Nathan, following usage, distinguishes between the proletariat and the proletarians. In the one case he lectures of class consciousness in the class struggle sense; in the other case he is referring to those whose way of life and non-militancy characterize their social class attitudes.

Class consciousness and social class consciousness. What, then, is class consciousness? Obviously, there must be two kinds. Class consciousness in the Marxian sense of intense loyalty, solidarity, and enmity is familiar to everyone who has read in social science. It is a feeling of unity against all who will not accede to the wishes of the "latent masses." Like the class struggle, class consciousness of this type "did not really show itself until the nineteenth century..."

Capitalists and their lackeys, typified by commuters on certain railway lines, are also known for their feelings of politico-industrial class consciousness. Their position is merely the other pole of the same axis, in so far as the kind of consciousness is concerned. They may, as may leading trade unionists, also be highly class conscious in the social class sense, however. In this case they and the trade union leaders might be equals and therefore on the "same side of the tracks." John L. Lewis has a son in Princeton. Ginsberg rejects the organizational approach to the word *class*. To him the classes are not associational (British usage) and "they cannot be defined by their ends or purposes." He identifies social class consciousness with consciousness of kind, feelings of equality and harmony, and feelings of superiority.

This carries the discussion to another plane, into another world. This is not the socialist formula for winning the class war; this is a description of the social class structure. *This is another kind of class and another kind of class consciousness.*

Here a man is not a loyal fighter. On the contrary, he lets lesser friends go by the board, while he cultivates new and superior acquaintances. He deserts his middle class and apes the one just above. Dawson and Gettys show how many middle class families give much attention to the ways of *la haute societe* because they hope someday to break into its ranks. Marshall states specifically that "Social Class is based rather on *similarity of attitudes* than on *identity of interests*... Class consciousness may, therefore, be combined with an ambition to rise, or to enable one's children to rise. This has led to the assertion that disloyalty is a characteristic feature of Social Class." There are those who do not seek to climb. They are to be found in all ages and all kinds. In general, they are more characteristic of the social classes than are those who discontentedly strive to rise. Their class-consciousness is expressed in acceptance, deference, respect for position, for rank, for superior status. Gurewitsch believes that people enjoy paying deference to those higher on the social scale, because these contacts give one a feeling of power. At the same time on may wish to be in their place.

Sumner holds that the "masses" are the core of the social structure, conservative, living on by tradition and habit, filled with inertia. They are inclined to accept their lot; they are not characteristically restive and desirous of climbing up the social ladder.

The social class structure, then, is a part of society that endures political upheavals — it does not produce them. Other forces produce political convulsions, political strife, and class conflict.

In fact, most of the political revolutions of history, before 1917, were not greatly significant to the social class structure. Those families that had been prominent, powerful, and recognized before the upheaval have been seen to persist in influence and affluence after the first phase of the revolution has spent itself. Ogg states that, "The mob which stormed the Bastille in 1789 was composed largely of landless, hand-to-mouth people, but before the Revolution had far progressed, the fortunes of the movement had fallen completely under the guidance of men who were economically and socially of a higher rank..."

There is, of course, a relationship between the class struggle and class consciousness in the politico-industrial sense and the social class consciousness of family competition, accommodation, and cooperation. Sometimes rapidly, but usually slowly, political upheavals will change even the personal and family relationships and stations within a village or a great city. The present war era [WWII] is one that undermines the social status, even the actual lives, of many families in high social positions.

The organizations of worker, of retailers, of taxpayers, of teachers, of employers, also tend to group people socially as well as politically. This fact was more apparent and outstanding in times and places where the political, economic, and social activities of groups tended to coincide more closely than they do today — as, for instance, during the better days of the craft and merchant guilds.

SIGNIFICANCE FOR SOCIAL CLASS

What has achievement and fame to do with social class standing? The distinction can perhaps be made that an individual is notorious or famous, but a family belongs to a social class as a unit. Prestige of class belongs to a child even before he has a chance to show his worth to society. Children of very famous persons are frequently at a disadvantage — those of high class, rarely. The personal achievements of one individual sometimes have a definitive bearing upon the social status of his family and the generations that follow. For instance, if the achievement is in a field that can be taught to the offspring, as dramatics, those bearing that name (Booth,

Barrymore) have a chance to capitalize upon the prestige of the forebear. If the achievement results in the accumulation of a fortune (as in the case of Cornelius Vanderbilt), the effect may be quite lasting upon later generations. The family to which a famous person belongs only slowly, and usually only after one or two additional generations of achievement, enters into a class position equivalent to the greatness of the achievement-reputation. Lincoln, although a famous President, did not associate with the "best people" socially; his son did. Charles Edison is beginning to convert his father's reputation, and his own achievements, into social class. His children will be much sought after.

Notoriety is scarcely at all significant for social class. People are notorious for all kinds of things; for swallowing goldfish and eating phonograph records, for being Public Enemy No. 1, for hitting a baseball 467 feet. Many famous men, renowned for their achievements, have had no appreciable influence upon the social class hierarchy, because they have left no descendants. Their careers are often at the expense of family obligations; there is no perpetuation of status. They are flashlight bulbs, illuminating their corner of the stage briefly but well. Achievement, followed by achievement, followed by achievement, will make up for social contacts and status commensurate with the achievement. This is the story told by the Adams family, the Byrds, the Lodges, the Cabots, the Roosevelts. In the case of the Johnson family, the famous member was a president, the offspring unknown, their offspring unknown; achievement did not translate itself into status. It is possible that a whole definition of class could be built around the word *achievement*. Such a definition would read: Any family whose line shows consistent non-achievement for three generations in terms of anything worthy of praise by its neighbors (such as cleanliness, industriousness, morality, or other socially approved values) is very low indeed. The social case records of charity organizations of long standing show many such families.

Any family whose history of achievement shows a consistent record of planning, of doing the most with all available means, of keeping up its morals, of being seen and heard at the right time and place, of teaching and preparing each generation for its tasks, of wasting little time and little money, of remaining relatively sober, and of watching for favorable connections — that record would be recognized and would give the family at least middle-class status, quite apart from any temporary financial condition. Keeping a family line consistent and intact is itself an achievement. Noble families 700 to 1000 years old win additional respect among aristocrats for this achievement. Craftsmen, in older countries, pride themselves on the consistency of their lines.

Tentatively, one may offer the following formula for dealing with achievement, notoriety, and leadership on the one hand, and social class on the other. The financial page of a large newspaper gives the names of business leaders. The regular news pages give the names of prominent politicians. Tabloids contain the photographs of all notorious persons, especially those of great popularity and those involved in scandals. But if one wishes to know the names of the socially most acceptable families, it is wise to watch news items pertaining to weddings, parties, and resorts. Here one does not find the complete social hierarchy, but the space given to such kinds of news, especially in a local paper, indicates how important certain families are considered to be, and (by omission) how unimportant others are. Society editors actually rank the people in their districts, in fact.

Legal Classes and Social Classes

There are noblemen, slaves, freedmen, redemptionists, burghers, aliens, citizens, voters, and criminals: are these social classes? A former president of France, presiding over a banquet of the Association for the Defence of the Middle Class, reproached the organization for its name, saying: "*Depuis 1789, Dieu merci, il n'y a plus de classes en France...*"

Because, under feudalism, there were once feudal status groups, fixed by law, are there now no status groups? And were those legal divisions social class divisions? Perhaps it would be correct to perceive two kinds of status, one legal and one social. There is and was legal status; there is and was social status. Perhaps only occasionally in human history have these categories exactly coincided, more probably never. Social status, if defined in terms of mutually exclusive groups whose positions are fixed in normal social contacts by consensus, has always found ways of getting around legal restrictions. It is inconceivable that anywhere or at any time have *all* the families in any society had identical legal and social status. In fact, any large number of families within any legal category is likely to be divided into strata of a social class nature. This has always been true of noblemen, criminals, citizens, etc. Slaves, chained together in gangs, are slaves in the legal sense and lowest on the social scale in the class sense. But what of the slaves in the royal households (where slave pimps have been known to outrank free officials), slaves who were prominent physicians, slaves who sometimes acted as ghostwriters for Cicero and others?

Social ranks among criminals. There seems to be little reason today for confusing social classes with degrees of criminality, true as it is that the different social classes tend to be guilty in different degrees of the same crimes. The obvious fact remains that there are Whitneys, Hineses, and poor unfortunate Jackson whites in the state and federal prisons. Sutherland has described in detail the kinds of criminality more common to certain of the social classes, even by persons "socially accepted and approved, looked up to."

Histories tell, and correctly so, of criminals being brought to the shores of Colonial America. Lack of space, however, prevents a full explanation her of what kinds of people these criminals were. One might, especially if not given to reading extensively in this field, get the impression that there was some kind of social uniformity among those thus labeled.

The story is related of a lawyer convicted of stealing books at Cambridge who was exiled to America. "Though it was customary for the commoner sort of prisoners to be conducted on foot... this barrister and four other prisoners, including an attorney, a butcher, and a member of a noble family, were allowed to ride in hackney coaches with their keepers... they were treated on board ship with the marks of respect and distinction." It is generally agreed that an appreciable proportion of the so-called criminal labourers were political prisoners taken in the rebellious seventeenth century. These men frequently represented the best elements in England and were a source of strength rather than weakness to the colonies.

Social differences among slaves. There is abundant evidence that status groups in the true sense of the actual social position do not conform to legal categories. Lowie shows this is the case of slaves:

The slaves of course occupy the status of inferiors, but here some discrimination must be exercised. There were indeed captives enslaved in war who could be sold like cattle and executed at their master's will. But there was another class of native slaves pawned for debt and these enjoyed far milder treatment, suffering no particular loss of prestige since their servitude was often undergone to rescue and impoverished kinsman. Wundt saw many of the factors entering into the status of persons in bondage. Both to the free and the enslaved parts of the society it makes a difference, he says, whether the enslaved are related to the tribe or are strangers. There is also a difference according to the personal relationship between master and slave.

Wundt's first principle is illustrated in the case of the first blacks brought to Virginia. They are reputed to have been indented to white masters, but only a part of the first group and none of the later ones were released. They were black; they were held in perpetual slavery. Wundt's second qualification is illustrated especially in Roman slavery, where the high degree of culture on the part of many Greek slaves made it easy for them to make a favorable personal adjustment in their relations with their Roman masters.

The inability of law to regulate social intercourse, to set up barriers over which people cannot climb, becomes quite evident when analyzed. Where persons live in close and personal proximity, they will form their own social groups, in spite of legal regulations to the contrary. The *lex Julia* forbade the marriage of freedmen with daughters of senatorial houses. "Yet we know of several such marriages in the first century... Felix, the brother of Pallas, had married in succession three ladies of royal blood, one of them the granddaughter of Cleopatra."

The term "servile origin" means something definite in the legal sense, but it does not always have even similar significance socially. In Rome there were many kinds of slaves whose native languages prevented them from being of any importance in Roman society, but not so the Greeks. But even the Greek slaves were of many kinds. "Cicero... mentions that well-born children had been carried off from Misenum under the very eyes of a Roman praetor.

The term *freedman* falls into the same category. It is of more value in law than in sociology. "Freedmen also entered the professions — teaching, medicine, painting... or, by iron of circumstances, slave-dealers." It is probable that writers use the words servile origin, nobility, merchant class, indentured servant, and so forth, in describing what they also term social classes, because these names are convenient handles to take hold of. They are definite and concrete, whereas the terms upper class, middle class, lower class are much more abstract. It is hard for "lowest classes" to compete with "slaves," even though the former is a more exact term for referring to persons and families of very low status. The latter is only a legal term and actually indicates only a legal condition.

Redemptionists of varied social status. Indented servants did not make up a single social class. Wertenbaker writes:

Some [indentured servants] were persons of culture, and, on rare occasions, of means... There are many instances of gentle blood becoming indentured servants to lawyers or physicians, in order to acquire a knowledge of those professions... Tutors were sometimes brought over from England under terms of indenture to instruct the children of wealthy planters in courses higher than those offered by local schools.

Greene states that "many white servants were of the better sort," and some of them, besides being teachers, were skilled workmen, "the best of whom subsequently acquired land for themselves."

Carman summarizes in these words: *Not all indentured worked out their terms of servitude on farm or plantation. In ability they varied greatly. The vast majority were ordinary labourers; a few were skilled workmen, and some were skilled artisans, tradesmen, or persons trained in the professions.*

Social classes among the nobility. Under feudalism noblemen had status and rank within the framework of the legal structure. Many of the formal aspects of status were governed by law.

Without attempting here, as will be done later, to trace the development of social class during the period of feudalism, it will suffice to state, with See: *The nobility did not form a homogenous class. There were privileged lords and others. In the first place, there were those who had been presented to the king and queen... The presentation was not only an honour. It conferred considerable advantages, especially in the army... The greatest privileges and most lucrative offices and pensions went to the court nobility.*

In contrast to the splendor of the court and those admitted to it, one reads of the poor nobility. They were numerous, lived in wretched circumstances, appealed to the king for funds to educate their children, farmed their own small plots, allowed their daughters to work in the barnyards and fields. "Accordingly it is easy to understand the hostility felt by the poor, petty nobility toward the court nobility of 1789, for the latter garnered all the favours..." What was true of the French nobility before the Revolution was true of the grades and kinds of noblemen in England, in Poland, in Italy, in Germany. There were gradations among the nobility as there are now among the bourgeoisie. It does not clarify social class theory to refer to legal categories as classes or as social classes.

The foregoing material has dealt with the objective criteria of social classes: economic, political, religious, racial, cultural, and legal. Each has proved to be related to and influential upon the social class structure, but none alone explains or determines social class; nor does an arbitrary mixture of any two, three, or more of these aspects, as can be quickly seen from reading in Sorokin's *Social Nobility* Social class also requires a socio-psychological and subjective interpretation.

SUBJECTIVE DEFINITIONS OF SOCIAL CLASS

Those who read in the literature of social class wish, from time to time, that the use of terms were more consistent, so confusing are the many distinctions. But there is little agreement. Each writer seems to go out into his social world with his categories and to divide the people into classes. Hence there are hundreds of formulations and many distinct approaches. In social theory there might be more progress were more attention given to concepts. Geiger, the one authority on the subject of classes who surveys the various definitions for the reader before announcing his own, points out that sections of the populations (Bevölkerungsmassen) are not classes or status groups. "Which persons go to make up a stratum is determined by *themselves*. The concept of stratum must be achieved autogenetically, not subsumptively." This definition, if not complete, is beyond doubt a good starting point toward a deep understanding of the concept *social class*. Max Graf Solms aus Assenheim finds within a class the congenial atmosphere, "whereas occupation, income, and so forth, vary."

Common ways and common ideals. A synthetic definition, including many factors of a subjective nature, would include many of the following ideas: Classes are inevitable in every complex society. They are a result of intellectual, moral, and economic differentiation. In its present form a social class is a group of persons conscious of having a common way of life, of having similar needs and aspirations and similar ideals and possess a comparable degree of culture. The individuals in the group judge by the same scale the values of life, and therefore tend to have the same moral ideals and to be the same social type, the same idea of honour, and consequently with a certain feeling of solidarity toward similar groups of other nations as well.

Max Weber distinguishes between class as category and social class. He emphasizes the personal choice element in the formation and maintenance of social classes: "There are ownership classes and occupational classes and social classes: social classes are determined by the totality of those class positions between which a personal exchange is easily possible and, generation after generation, is found typically to take place." This definition intimates that the social classes are made up of families, not of individuals, that a certain amount of social class rigidity or continuity is necessary to the formation of a true social class, and that social class rests upon a foundation of exclusiveness based upon the standard of values of the participants themselves. Traditional personal exchange, then, becomes the hallmark of social class.

Social class standing a birthright. Schumpeter states definitely: "We said that for the individual his membership in a definite class is a given fact — he is born into a certain class position." This emphasis upon the conditions of birth is to be commended, for obviously the secret of achieving a particular class standing with the greatest chance of success list most dependably in making a judicious choice of parents — not from the biological standpoint, but from the standpoint of the end desired, social standing. Social classes are based on human intercourse and association, and it is very much to anyone's advantage to find himself early in life among the right people.

A full and adequate definition of social class, in fact, will take this into consideration. As Ross says: "Social strata there will no be unless there is some kind of *inheritance* — of occupation, of prestige, of office, of authority, of property on the one hand; of lowly calling, of unfreedom, of disability on the other." This interpretation differs from those who confuse social classes with mere occupational or political hierarchies of individuals. If civilization is to have classes, inevitably, it will no be because someone has to work and someone else has to give orders. It will be because parents strive to place their children in positions equivalent to or higher than their own. Social strata are characterized by their time span (Dauer).

Landtman makes the traditional or hereditary factor in social class fundamental to the definition. He states: "Inequality in standing and influence may exist without these advantages being necessarily hereditary, but in such cases the difference depends upon individual conditions and does not create classes." True social classes exist only where the conditions of life are relatively constant from generation to generation, where people know each other's families and where they belong together through contact and similar ways of living. According to this formula political or economic power can be referred to as frequently belonging to certain social classes, sometimes to individuals or political parties. Hitler, from this definition, would be considered a ruler and a member of a party; the Kaiser was a ruler and a member of a ruling social class.

Thomas and Znaniecki make a sharp distinction between a person's social position or prestige and his individual or personal prestige:

Superiority of social position is a source of prestige even independently of any actual power which the superior class may or may not possess... Moreover, when the leader relies on the prestige of his profession or class, he is forced to keep the traditions and to hold the esprit de corps by which this profession or class tries to maintain its prestige, and this evidently limits his initiative... Jackowski or Wawrzyniak can hardly be characterized as priests or noblemen, but simply as individuals, each as a unique personality.

The individualistic interpretation persists, however. Sorokin makes it the fundamental basis of his volume on social classes. According to his interpretation, it could be said that a Sunday School class is "stratified" if it had a rotating chairman. And it is Sorokin's belief that these "strata" of leaders make up the social classes. Panunzio also defines class as "a horizontal division of society embracing persons of same or similar economic rank, religious or political status, or possessing common cultural characteristics." Here one finds nothing concerning class formation which results from the coming together of such families as find themselves congenial to each other — and nothing pertaining to the attainment of social position through social transmission. A substitute definition, so stated as to bring out the contrast, would read: A social class is a horizontal division of society, embracing families whose social backgrounds and training are sufficiently similar to permit free and unrestrained social contacts, families which belong to the same circle, with relatively equal rank in the community.

Refined definitions of social class. To found a whole hierarchy of social classes upon fine and subtle distinctions of exclusiveness— upon backgrounds, manners, ways of living, may seem at first glance like building a house upon the sands. Yet it can and is being done by modern students of social class. Ferre observes, for instance:

Between the high and the middle bourgeoisie, as between the nobility and the high bourgeoisie, we find only subtle differences in their social life, their standard of living, and their manners....

The solid rocks of political office and cold cash in the bank seem much more real than exclusiveness arising from feelings of superiority and inferiority. But the sinews out of which the tough fabric of the social class structure is woven and repaired consist of powerful mechanisms of social super-ordination and subordination. Nor are the divisions abrupt. The colors and shades merge like those of the rainbow. And, to change the figure again, some individuals are like jacks running wild throughout the deck. These latter, of course, attract most of the attention. They are the exceptions, not the rule.

The subjective approach to social classes is found in the writings of Hans Speier, one of the most competent and careful students of this subject. He writes:

The concept of class compatible with this theory of honour cannot be found in Marx; rather its formulation must follow the line suggested by Eugene Dupreel: "A social class is a group placed in a hierarchy in a position above or below that of another group comparable to it, another class. The inequality of two classes or their hierarchical order does not result directly from any advantage or prerogative of either of them, such as wealth. It results only indirectly: it is necessary that one of the two classes be recognized by itself and by the other class, as advantageous and superior. This recognition is explicit or implicit."

Honour, implicitly or explicitly paid, is a basic phenomenon of man's social experience. One of the most expert formulations of social class, as it can be seen to be after careful comparison with others, is that of Ginsberg: *Classes in modern societies may be described as groups of individuals who, through common descent, similarity of occupation, wealth and education, have come to have a similar mode of life, a similar stock of ideas, feelings, attitudes and forms of behaviour and who, on any or all these grounds, meet one another on equal terms and regard themselves, although with varying degrees of explicitness, as belonging to one group.*

The psychological basis of social class distinctions is well expressed by MacIver: "The sentiment of class is above all a sentiment of disparity. It does indeed unite those who feel distinct from other classes, but it unites them primarily because they feel distinct. Above all, it unites the 'superior' against the 'inferior.'"

Exclusiveness, that is, social exclusiveness, is the cornerstone of all social structures. The upper classes are protected, or, more properly, they protect themselves, from intimate contact with the classes below them.

Human beings are very sensitive to those different from themselves, and social class differences are doubly significant because they immediately call into play attitudes of deference, subordination, or condescension. Until one knows who the other is, in the social class sense, one is likely to remain aloof and to feel ill at ease. Thus the importance of correct social introductions. When one knows the class to which another belongs, one knows how to behave towards him.

Another short and lucid definition of social class reads: "The class is a group (ensemble) of individuals socially assimilated to each other, excluding distinctions caused by age, sex, and occupation." That is to say, the assimilation does not have to be complete. Room is left for such heterogeneity as springs from age, sex, and occupation. It is a bold, but commendable, step to disassociate the term occupation from that of social class. Dawson and Gettys have listed the non-material stuff out of which social class is made: hauteur, snobbishness, titles, specialization in certain forms of etiquette, speech, etc.

It would seem to be the wiser course to refer to families, not individuals, as the elemental units of social classes. Descriptively, the behaviour that makes for the formation and maintenance of social classes reads something like this: *Every family has, also, to keep up a "front" and to gain acceptance within some group of families. It becomes identified with a social class, or with a "social set" in which it plays a rôle. This rôle requires effort and conscious thought on the part of some members of the family. The family income will be budgeted among the various kinds of expenditure according to the conception the family has of itself... Each separate family has to maintain, by conscious effort, its place among the other families.*

Is it not probable that this is the basis upon which the social class structure rests: the ceaseless activities of families finding their places in the different communities throughout the land? Lippmann also makes much of the idea of social sets. His remarks could well be labeled one of the understanding definitions of social class. He writes: Usually the distinguishing mark of a social set is the presumption that the children intermarry. To marry outside the set involves, at the very least, a moment of doubt before the engagement can be approved. Each social set has a fairly clear picture of its relative position in the hierarchy of social sets... *Whatever the tests of admission, the social set when formed is not a mere economic class, but something more nearly resembling a biologic clan. Membership is intimately connected with love, marriage and children, or, to speak more exactly, with the attitudes and desires that are involved. In the social set, therefore, opinions encounter the canons of Family Tradition, Respectability, Propriety, Dignity, Taste and Form, which make up the social set's picture of itself, a picture assiduously implanted in the children.*

Since each community is made up of a hierarchy of social sets, it is logical to refer to a social class as the sum total of all the like social sets within the cultural area. A family, in moving to another part of the United States or Canada, for instance, would, after the initial stage of social introductions and of getting acquainted, find itself in the social circle most like the one from which it came, still within the same social class, however.

With Schumpeter, it may be concluded that the "family, not the physical person, is the true unit of class theory." In conclusion, too, the importance of social class considerations in all human relationships cannot be overemphasized. Social class enters into every handclasp, every greeting, every appointment. As one eminent sociologist has stated:

The legal and economic order supposedly makes no distinction between the gentleman and the lady on one hand and "hoi polloi" on the other, but in ordinary affairs this distinction is much more important than are other varieties... the clumsy divisions of the political or economic order are of no help. Even professional or occupational groupings do not afford a secure basis for differentiation.

5

Transformation of Caste System

The caste system has been traditionally analysed as based on the notion of ritual purity. In this view, its holistic character-to use the terminology of Louis Dumont-implies that the dominant values that of the Brahmins, are regarded by the whole society as providing universal references, role models. Hence the central role played by Sanskritisation, a practice that M.N. Srinivas has defined as 'the process in which a "low" Hindu caste, or tribal or other group, changes its customs, ritual, ideology and way of life in the direction of a high, and frequently, "twice-born' caste" that is the Brahmins, but also the Kshatriyas or even the Vaishyas.

Low castes may for instance adopt the most prestigious features of the Brahmins' diet and therefore emulate vegetarianism. Such a process reflects a special coherence in society, all the groups admitting the values of the upper castes as the legitimate value system. Such coherence is not synonymous with cohesion. In fact, sanskritisation itself bears witness of an aspiration to social mobility and therefore tensions: Low castes constantly try to improve their social status by imitating the high castes and contest the position, which has been assigned to them in the system. Moreover, the myths of origin of the low castes are always centered around the idea of an initial decline: even Untouchable castes claim to descend from Brahmin castes and that they have fallen from this rank often because of the malicious intent of upper caste people. The myth of origin of the Chamars is very telling in this aspect:

their original ancestor was the youngest of four Brahmans brethren who went to bathe in a river and found a cow struggling in a quicksand. They sent the youngest brother in to rescue the animal, but before he could get to the spot it had been drowned. He was compelled therefore by his brothers to remove the carcass and after he had done this they turned him out of their caste and gave him the name of Chamar. The four brothers epitomise in this narrative the Brahmins, the Kshatriyas, the Vaishyas and the Shudras.

Robert Deliege points out that such a myth is very similar to that of another Untouchable caste, the Paraiyar of Tamil Nadu. In Fact, according to him, 'the untouchable myths are quite distinct from those of higher and even middle_range castes', so much so that one can speak of an 'intouchable myth of origin'. However these myths do not reflect the existence of a separate, untouchable identity: 'they take caste for granted, and by stressing their brotherhood with Brahmans, they acknowledge the superiority of the latter'. This is pure sanskritisation. For Srinivas, the mobility associated with Sanskritization results only in positional changes in the system and does not lead to any structural change. That is, a caste moves up above its neighbours and another comes down, but all this takes place in an essentially stable hierarchical order.

The system itself does not change'. Indeed, the values sustaining the social system remain the same. While the Brahmins are the main objects of imitation, Srinivas points out that the sanskritisation process does not refer to them only. The Kshatriyas are often chosen as role models too. D.F. Pocock even suggests that there is a 'Kingly model of Hindu society'. However this style of self_promotion did not simply rely on the imitation of the superior. In fact the second varna has been one of the main avenues for social mobility because the Shudras could conquer power and replace Kshatriyas as rulers on the basis of their mere strength and because Brahmins then legitimised their rise by evolving the needed genealogies. Srinivas indeed points out that 'the Kshatriya category was the most open one in the caste system'. While this openness is a very important element in the promotion of the low castes, it does not question the system either since it has to be sanctioned by Brahmins who retain their paramount importance and whose values remain supreme. Historically, low caste groups have also explored avenues for upward mobility through the bhakti movements and the sectarian model. Since the Buddha, gurus have recurrently questioned the caste system on behalf of the fundamental equality of men before god. Their disciples who were initiated into monastic orders forgot about their caste to form new fraternities. Srinivas emphasised that the 'protest sects' in a way 'offered opportunities for mobility to members of the so-called low castes'. However, this equality was otherworldly: it did not affect the social order. Ambedkar rightly pointed out that 'from the point of view of the annihilation of caste, the struggle of the saints did not have any effect on society'. The traditional caste system was more directly challenged during the British Raj.

CASTE ASSOCIATIONS AND THE RESILIENCE OF SANSKRITISATION

The development of the means of communications in the XIXth century led to the opening up of the jati which, till then, was confined to a reduced territory, delimited by matrimonial relations (in North India caste endogamy and village exogamy are compelling rules). Hence the emergence of horizontal solidarities and the territorial extension of the frontiers of caste. The members of a same jati were enabled to migrate to find jobs or even obliged to do so, if they were transferred within the British administration for instance. The State building process played an important role since it led to the establishment of an all India bureaucracy. Transfers of bureaucrats out of their native place often generated feelings of anomie and made the finding of the suitable match for endogamous marriages more complicated; hence the idea to create associations which could link members of a same caste. These institutions were also stirred up by the census, which was a key element in the formation of the colonial state. From 1871 onwards the British enumerated the castes (like the religious groups) and therefore these 'human groups (castes) [we]re treated to a considerable extent as abstractable from the regional and territorial contexts in which they function[ed]'. This effect reinforced those of the state construction process but the census also raised among several castes the sentiment of having common interests since the British did not content themselves with enumerating them; they also classified them. In 1901, the Census Commissioner, Risley, decided to give the ranking of the jatis in their local context and their varna, which was a much more delicate enterprise. Castes immediately organised themselves and, as Ghurye points out, even formed councils to take steps to see that their status was recorded in the way they thought was honourable to them. Caste associations were therefore created also as pressure groups whose aim was to improve their rank in the census. This process was especially prominent among the low castes and therefore gives 'An indication of the widespread desire for mobility among the backward castes...'. Each census provided castes with an opportunity to petition the government for getting a higher place in the order of precedence and for being recorded under new, sanskritised, names. In 1911, 16 did so and in 1921, 20 in northern India, including Kurmis, Gadariyas, Kacchi, Ladhs and Ahirswho wanted all to be recognised as Kshatriyas. Indeed, this move was in keeping with the logic of sanskritisation since the objective was not to opt out from the system but to rise within it according to its own rules and values.

However, castes associations secularised and became gradually mutual aid structures, in charge of founding schools for the caste's children, creating co-operative movements and claiming new advantages from the state. The caste associations, from then on, tended to become interest groups. The Rudolph therefore underline their modern character-in a western sense. They behaved like a collective enterprise with economic and political objectives, in a way, which brings to mind the image of "lobbies". They had their head office, their publications, their list of members, and their organisation chart. Generally, their leaders did not come from the most prestigious clans or families but from those of the castemen who were the most educated, able to negotiate with the state and often as ambitious as the political entrepreneurs of Joseph Schumpeter. In many cases, they came from the younger generation. However, the transformational potentialities of caste associations must not be exaggerated since they were not conducive to social change per se.

The associations representing upper castes were often very conservative, as evident from the case of the Kanya-Kubja

Brahmins, a jati widely dispersed across Uttar Pradesh, Madhya Pradesh and Rajasthan. In 1884, a Kanya-Kubja caste association was created in Lucknow. An all India association grew out from it in 1901 and established local branches all over the Hindi belt. It was founded for helping the Kanya-Kubja Brahmins to compete with Kayasths, Banyas and other Brahmins of North India in terms of education and administrative jobs. It supported the development of educational institutions, boarding schools, sponsored grants and newspapers which were intended to foster solidarity within the caste. The number of local branches increased until the mid-1930s when then it declined, partly because of the Congress' opposition to caste movements. However, it started to rise again in the 1950s in order to protect the Kanya_Kubja Brahmins against the "threat" that represented affirmative action measures in favour of thelower castes.

Among the non-dvijas, caste associations often merely served as vehicles for sanskritisation in North India. The Kayasths of North India were probably the first to show the way in that direction. In late XIXth century, Munshi Kali Prasad, a Lucknow-based rich lawyer from this caste, wrote Kayasthas Ethnology, a book where he showed 'to which of the four great divisions of the Aryans in India [,the Kshatriyas,] the Kayasthas belonged'. Subsequently, the Kayasths claimed that they were the descendants of the Emperor Chandragupta. In 1873 Kali Prasad set up in Lucknow a fortnightly magazine Kayastha Samachar and a Kayasth Dharma Sabha whose main task was to educate the caste's children. A primary school-Kayastha Pathshala-was opened in Allahabad for poor and orphan children of the caste. In 1877, it became an Anglo-Vernacular middle school, then a high school and in 1895, an intermediate college. The Kayastha Conference was founded in 1886 on the basis of the Kayasth Dharma Sabha. The first resolution it passed at its first annual meeting in 1887 stressed the need 'to improve the educational and moral status of the Community' by opening new schools for which money was raised by the association. It also tried 'to encourage the community to undertake commercial and other respectable pursuits and not to rely solely on clerical or literary avocations'. The Conference aimed at uniting the Kayasths and therefore decided 'to prepare a National Directory of the Chandraguptavanshi Kayastha community', which was intended 'to promote union and co-operation by a knowledge of their distant and scattered brethren'. It established mutual aid programmes for the neediest Kayasth families to enable them to finance the study of their sons or the marriage of their daughters, etc. Parallel to this strong emphasis on socio-economic developments, the conference did not neglect the initial sanskritisation objectives of Kali Prasad. It had a Temperance section and repeatedly-and allegedly successfully-requested the Kayasths to give up drinking.

The Kayastha Conference is revealing for the ambivalence of caste associations: on the one hand, it endeavoured to promote the status of the Kayasths in the sanskritisation logic; on the other, it was created to fight against the restrictions of job opportunities in the administration of British India. However, the Kayastha Conference still endeavoured in the 1920s-1930s to sanskritise caste rituals and invited its members to emulate the 'dvijas'. Certainly, this attitude stemmed from modern motives since the main reason for sanskritisation was to standardise the Kayasth culture and to create a homogenous social group, however, sanskritisation remained the key idiom, with its emphasis on positional mobility instead of structural changes, to use Srinivas' words..

The most important social change that caste associations have achieved probably concerns the unity of the caste groups. They have successfully incited the sub-castes to adopt the same name in the Census and to break the barriers of endogamy, even if, within a caste, the members of the upper class still tend to inter-marry-but then it is more economic endogamy than purely caste-based endogamy.

Once again, the Kayasths are a case in point, not only because their association established a network covering several provinces, including the hindi belt and Hyderabad, but also because, in Hyderabad at least, 'the ease with which marriages across former boundaries are accommodated is striking'. For Leonard, this change 'might confirm an ideological shift from caste to ethnicity and class'. The question I would like to investigate in this chapter is whether the ethnicisation of caste-or at least the discourse of ethnicity-developed as early among the lower castes of South India (where Leonard's Kayasths have emigrated, by the way), and in the North. The ethnicisation of caste seems to have begun first in South India. This process has been observed by Robert Hardgrave in the case of the Nadars of Tamil Nadu whose caste association, the Nadar Mahajana Sangam was founded in 1910 and promoted what he calls 'caste fusion', as 'the unit of endogamy expanded'. S. Barnett maintains that this kind of fusion tended to transform castes into ethnic groups.

His demonstration is based on another Tamil case study, the Kontaikkatti Vellalars who do not represent a large number of people but are influential since many of them are landlords. From 1920 onwards, the caste association has encouraged them to expand endogamy in new territories and to other Vellallars in order to make up for their numerical weakness. It may then be one of the first examples of caste federations _ a notion to which we shall return in the next section. For Barnett these innovations confront the entire ideological field of caste hierarchy, since 'blood purity', on which _ according to him _ relies ritual purity has lost its importance. The relevant unit is not the original jati any more, but groups of castes, which represents the transition from caste to ethniclike regional caste blocs.

"Ethniclike" because each such unit is potentially independent of other such units, defined and characterised by a heritable substance internal to the unit itself and not affected, in terms of membership in the unit, by transactions with others outside the unit. Rather than the conceptual holism of caste, we begin to see the antecedent autonomy of its component parts. In an ethniclike situation transactional ranking no longer orders the parts of the whole, and caste interdependence is replaced by regional-caste bloc independence.

However, intermarriages are only one aspect of the ethnicisation of caste which also implies a collective history-at least a golden Age-and a separate, cultural identity. The subjective representation of the collective self is most important for the issue we are dealing with. Caste is partly a mindset. It is based on beliefs in hierarchies relying on purity and impurity-what Ambedhar called 'graded inequality'. Alternative social imaginaries might be conducive to the emancipation of the lower castes. As M.S.A. Rao argues: "The problem of identity is crucial in the formation of protest groups and for collective mobilisation':

Deprived sections of society in different parts of the world have organises themselves into protest movements to fight against discriminations of various kinds based on colour, religion, caste and tribe. Their problem, however, has been one of establishing a new identity-the kind of image that they want to protect in order to gain self-respect, honour and status.

Such a change in collective identity is precisely at stake in the process of ethnic identity building by lower castes. This kind of ethnicisation of castes or caste federations are much more conducive to social change than caste associations or caste fusion pure and simple. As we shall see such developments were much more prominent in western and southern India than in the North.

ETHNICISATION OF CASTE IN WESTERN AND SOUTHERN INDIA

Phule's bahujansamaj: the lower castes as an aboriginal people. The ethnicisation process which took place in western and southern India was partly due to the impact of the European ideas, as propagated by the missionaries and the schools. (utiliser S. Bayly)

The ethnicisation process is well illustrated by the Satyashodak Movement developed by Phule in the Bombay Presidency in the late XIXth century, which was not a caste movement since it intended to represent the 'bahujan samaj', the majority of the people, the masses. Jotirao Phule (1827-1890) was a Mali (market gardener), a cultivating caste in close contact with towns where its members sold their products. In one of these towns, Poona, Phule could attend a school of the Scottish Mission. What he learnt about the Blacks in the United States suggested to him a comparison with the lower castes-hence his book, Slavery (1873) that he dedicated 'to the good people of the United States as a taken of admiration for their sublime disinterested and self sacrificing devotion in the cause of Negro Slavery; and with an earnest desire, that my country men may take their noble example as their guide in the emancipation of their sudra Brethren from the trammels of Brahmin thraldom'.

The writings of Thomas Paine exerted a special influence on Phule who discovered the individualist values of liberty and equality in The Age of Reason and Human Rights. This source of inspiration developed in conjunction with that of Christianity. For Phule, Jesus-Christ epitomises equality and fraternity. He also regards him as the spokesman for the poor people. However, Phule did not convert to Christianity and even translated the Christian idiom into a new discourse focused on King Bali, the subterranean god who reigns in the underground world according to Hindu mythology.

Through the vernacularisation of Christian values and symbols, Phule endowed them with a new, positive identity to his people. He even gave them a new history on the basis of some of the findings of Orientalism. In 1792, William Jones had deduced from the discovery of the Indo-european linguistic family the notion of a common, original race whose branches had migrated towards Europe and India. This theory was developed during the nineteenth century by many German philologists such as Albrecht Weber, R. Roth, A. Kuhn and J. Möhl (whose books were published in the 1840s-1850s). In their writings appear the notions of 'Sanskritic race' or 'Vedic people'. These speculations reached India from the late 1850s onwards through Max Müller, who tended to be somewhat more cautious, and Muir who published in 1860 a study on 'The Trans-Himalayan Origin of the Hindus, and their affinity with the western branches of the Aryan race'.

The first Hindu nationalist ideologues of the late 19th century and early 20th century _ from Dayananda to Tilak _ borrowed heavily from the European orientalists. Among other themes, the one they used assiduously related to the common racial origin of the European and Indian people and its corollary, the southward migration which they interpreted to prove that the Hindus were the first race and that they once dominated the whole world. This myth helped the first Hindu revivalists to regain certain self-esteem by claiming that their ancestors were the first inhabitants of the world. Phule used the Aryan theory to his own advantage: the fact that upper castes leaders traced their origin from Aryan conquerors could be used to argue that they descended from foreigners and that their culture, including the caste system was alien to India's original people.

Phule, therefore, portrayed the Aryans as invaders who had settled in India at a rather late period to subjugate the first inhabitants of India and destroyed their civilisation. For him, the low castes were the descendents of these people. In this reinterpretation of the past, the invaders are identified as Brahmins whereas the indigenous groups are described as descending from the original ruling class, the Kshatriyas. In Phule's ideology, this category does not refer to the second varna but includes all original Indians, from peasant castes to Untouchables. For him, they formed a people, united by the bond of a common origin and of a warrior ethos:

"The Kshatriyas in India (the land of Baliraja) that is the original masters of the land here where known as Astiks, Pishachas, Rakshasas, Ahirs, Kakatas, Bhut, Kolis, Mangs, Mahars etc. They were extremely adept in fighting without the aid of arms (weapons) and were famed as brave and valiant warriors. They were of an epicurean (joyful) temperament and were given to the enjoyment of the goods things of life. The kingdoms of most of these rulers (chiefs) were in a prosperous condition, and it would be no exaggeration to say that the land of King Bali was literally flowing with milk and honey".

This description does not only present the original rulers of India as brave warriors but also emphasises their sense of manliness and honour while fighting (they did not use weapons) and their good nature. Such a narrative prepared the ground for the stereotype of the 'good salvage' that will be applied to the Indian aborigines. The king of these original Kshatriyas, Bali, is described by Phule as reigning over a rich country and this prosperity was the very reason for the Aryan invasions:

The extreme fertility of the soil of India, its rich productions, the proverbial wealth of the people, and the other innumerable gifts which this favourable land enjoys, and which have more recently tempted the cupidity of the Western nations, attracted the Aryans [...] The original inhabitants with whom these earth-born gods, the Brahmans, fought, were not inappropriately termed Rakshasas, that is the protectors of the land [...] The cruelties which the European settlers practised on the American Indians on their first settlement in the new world had certainly their parallel in India in the advent of the Aryans and their subjugation of the aborigines [...] They originally settled on the banks of the Ganges whence they spread gradually over the whole of India. In order, however, to keep a better hold on the people they devised that weird system of mythology, the ordination of caste, and the code of crude and inhuman laws to which we can find no parallel among the other nations.

Phule's endeavour had a pioneering dimension since he was probably the first low caste leader who avoided the traps of sanskritisation by endowing the low caste with an alternative value system. For the first time, the low castes were presented as ethnic groups which had inherited the legacy of an antiquarian golden age and whose culture was therefore distinct from that of the wider Hindu society; secondly, his efforts in favour of the low castes were not confined to his castemen only: he wanted to unite the Shudras and the Atishudras (dalits). As early as 1853 he opened schools for Untouchables. He projected himself as the spokesman of the non-Brahmins at large and, indeed, kept targeting the Brahmins in vehement pamphlets where he presented them as rapacious moneylenders corrupts priests eager to extort as much as they could from poor and ignorant villagers.

Phule was also the first low caste organiser. In 1875 he was attracted by the Arya Samaj, but he kept his distance from this movement because he did not trust the upper caste reformers who pretended to fight against the social system even though they observed its rules. Phule also remained aloof from the Congress, which he regarded as a Brahmin movement. Nationalism, according to him, was an illusion created by upper caste manipulation to conceal the inner divisions of Indian society. He founded the Satyashodak Samaj in 1873 in order to strengthen the sentiment of unity among the low castes. He narrated pseudo-historical episodes bearing testimony of the traditional solidarity between the Mahars and Shudras and protested against the Brahmins' stratagems for dividing the low castes. At least in the late 19th century and early 20th century, the Satyashodak idiom embraced rich peasants as well as agricultural tenants who belonged to very different castes and in some places 'the Sathya Shodhak message seemed to have reached even the untouchable'. A major spokesman of the non-Brahmin movement in Maharashtra in the 1910-1930, Mukundrao Patil, the son of Phule's colleague, Krishnarao

Bhalekar, was for instance a radical defender of the Untouchables even though he was a rich peasant. He advocated 'the general Satyashodak ideology, of opposition to Sanskritisation and assertion of the " non-Aryan " unity of Maharashtrian natives'. By that time, Phule's view of the non-brahmins as non-Aryas had made an impact on the small dalit intelligentsia. In 1909, Kisan Faguji Bansode (1870-1946), a Mahar from Nagpur, warned the upper castes in the following terms:

The Aryans-your ancestors-conquered us and gave us unbearable harassment. At that time we were your conquest, you treated us even worse than slaves and subjected us to any torture you wanted. But now we are no longer your subjects, we have no service relationship with you, we are not your slaves or serfs...

The Satyashodak Samaj eventually attracted even Marathas such as the Jedhe family who from Poona realised 'the futility of a purely Maratha politics'. Keshavrao Jedhe adopted 'the long-held Satyashodak view of history: Brahmans were outsiders to the country and to the ethnic community of true " Hindus "; they desired only their own caste superiority and consolidated their power through treachery, through falsification of historical records, and by weaving a web of religious slavery which set up a social hierarchy of superiority and inferiority and divided the masses'. Maratha princes such as the Maharajah of Baroda strongly approved of Phule's ideological commitments and donated large amounts of money to his movement. A direct descendant of Shivaji, the Maharajah of Kolhapur, Shahu, who reigned between 1894 and 1922 and who was 'intensely proud of his Maratha lineage', was even more supportive. He recruited Maratha Satyas Satyashodaks in his administration. In 1902 he even reserved 50% of the vacancies in the state administration for 'the members of the backward communities'.

Shahu patronised the establishment of the Satyashodak Samaj in Kolhapur in 1911. He promoted inter-caste dining and introduced the Inter-caste Marriage Act in 1918at Kolhapur. In 1920 he appointed Maratha priests to circumvent the Brahmins and soon after established the Kshatriya Vedic School to train Maratha priests. The very name of this school suggests that Shahu was still acting in the framework of sanskritisation.

Indeed, he tried to secure for the Marathas the status of Kshatriyas and in fact he broke with the local Brahmins in 1900 when they refused to recognise his family's claim to this status and accordingly refused to perform certain rituals. He wanted to 'kshatriyase' the Untouchables too. He used to give them symbolically swords and Maratha names. He called them 'Suryavaunshi', pretending that they could trace their lineage to the sun God, Surya. Shahu cannot be described as a Maratha leader also because of its efforts to federate the low castes. In the communal representation scheme that he introduced in 1920 in the Kolhapur municipality 85 castes were grouped into 20 'unions of castes'. The Marathas, the Rajputs and the Kunbis formed a constituency in themselves. Yet, the main reason why the Sathyashodak Samaj could not become a common platform for all the non-Brahmins on the basis of a non-Aryan identity had much to do with the attitude Marathas. Most of them refused to mix with lower castes and stuck to the sanskritisation process of other with which Shahu has still affinities. For instance, Bhaskarrao Jadhav, in Marathe ani Tyanci Bhasha, displayed much ambivalence: on the one hand he admits 'the prevalence of Dravidian customs and racial intermixture among Marathas, and on the other asserts, without any qualification, (that) the Marathas are definitely " Aryan Kshatriyas "'. Therefore, even those who had followed Phule's message for some time, eventually joined hands with the Brahmins-dominated Congress, or were co-opted by it. Congress leaders such as N.V. Gadgil, who was very much aware that the nationalist movement could only acquire a mass-basis if it attracted low caste people, contacted K. Jedhe and made an alliance with him in the early 1930s. A Maratha-dominated Satyashodak Samaj, which had remained aloof from the Congress, till then, decided to join the movement. Gradually, the Maratha rose to power within the party.

In spite of this ultimate failure, from Phule to Shahu, the low castes movement of Maharashtra was characterised by very distinctive features with long terms implications. For the first time, all non-Brahmin castes were invited to unite on the basis of a common ethnic background-as the original inhabitants of India-endowed with a Kshatriya ethos and to fight the Brahmin domination. Even though the Satyashodak idiom was imbued with the symbols of kshatriyahood, this movement escaped the sanskritisation process since the upper castes were not seen as role models but as invaders whose culture could be despised. A similar pattern developed in the South with the Dravidian movement.

FROM NON-BRAHMINISM TO DRAVIDIANISM

In Madras Presidency, the Non_Brahmin movement was instrumental in engineering forms of caste fusion and succeeded in endowing the lower castes with an ethnic identity relied on two grounds: they were not only presented as the original inhabitants of India, as Phule had already argued, but also as former Buddhists. This twofold argument was first articulated in the first decade of the XXth century by Iyothee Thass, a Pariah converted to Buddhism.

He pointed out that ancient India had been prosperous and most humanly governed under Buddhist kings but that they were dislodged from power by Brahmin invaders who imposed the caste system. The Buddhists were then marginalised and considered as unclean and low. Their religion had endowed them with a specific culture that eschewed violence, forbade the taking of alcohol etc. Thass even maintained that in the past India was called Indirar Desam, the land of Indirar, Indirar being the Buddha after he succeeded in controlling his five senses (indiriyams). This original civilisation was none other than the Dravidian civilisation and Thass therefore chose to call its castemates, the Pariahs, 'Dravidas'. Therefore early as the late nineteenth century, the Non-Brahmin movement claimed that the lower castes were the original inhabitants of India. Again, British Orientalism had prepared the ground for this development. The Reverend Caldwell (1819-1891) had already suggested that Sanskrit had been brought to South India by Aryan, Brahmin, colonists and that the original inhabitants were Dravidians speaking Tamil, Telugu etc. Gradually, the non-Brahmin South Indian associations adopted the suffix 'Adi'-initial, primordial-in their titles. The Pariah Mahajan Sabha, which had been founded in 1890, became the Adi-Dravida Mahajan Sabha, which, in 1918 appealed to the government to replace the pejorative word Pariah by Adi-Dravida, denoting the original inhabitants of Dravida land. In

1917 an Adi-Andhra Mahajan Sabha had come into existence the same way. In fact, this association was initially called Andhra Panchama Conference but the chairman of its 1917 session, M.V. Bhagya Reddy (1888-1939), in his presidential address, declared that the so-called Panchamas were the original sons of the soil and they were the rulers of the country'. Hence the change of name of the Sabha. Varma was a Mala and in the 1931 census about one Ahird of the Malas and Madhigas gave their identity as Adi-Andhras. One of the most influential proponents of the Dravidian ideology was M.C. Rajah (1883-1947), a Pariah who became secretary of the Adi-Dravida Mahajan Sabha in 1916 and who presided over the All India Depressed Classes Association since in 1928. As a nominated member of the Madras Legislative Council since 1920, Rajah moved in 1922 a resolution recommending that the terms 'Panchama' and 'Parya' are deleted from the Government records and the terms Adi-Dravida and Adi-Andhra substituted instead.

This identity-building process was led one step further by Ramaswami Naicker, alias Periyar, a religious mendicant who had been completely disillusioned by the Congress and Gandhi while he was taking part in the Vaikom satyagraha. If Phule had drawn some of his egalitarian inspiration from Thomas Paine, Periyar was much impressed by Robert Ingersoll. Like Phule and Ambedkar, he was egalitarian in a western, individualist vein.

The notion of human dignity was so central to his thinking that after quitting Congress in the mid-1920s, he launched the Self-Respect Movement, which immediately endeavoured to pressurise the Justice Party in order to make it the true advocate of the lower castes. Another of his key words was Samadharma that referred to the general principle of equality. But Periyar regarded it as a Buddhist notion. Like Thass, he presented the lower castes as descending from the first Buddhists and endowed them with a Dravidian identity, especially after his mobilisation of the late 1930s against the attempt of the Congress government of Madras at promoting Hindi in the schools of the Presidency. The Dravidar Kazhagam (DK) that he founded in 1944, though its mouthpiece, Viduthalai, considered that the Congress was behind 'the exploitation of the northern bania and his Aryan [brahmin] mentor'.

Thus, 'samardharma came to stand in for a civilizational and cultural alternative: a social order based on radically different principles from the present, which needed to rest on premises derived from a non-Aryan, non-Sanskritic ethos'. Periyar had an explicitly ethnic conception of the low castes' identity. He compared their situation to that of the blacks in South Africa. The Non-Brahmins who all shared a Dravidian identity had therefore to get united. As a result, Periyar advocated the coming together of the Christians, Muslims and low castes Hindus, and, within the latter; of the Untouchables and the Shudras. Such a rapprochement took place indeed since Nadars and Adi Dravidas (Untouchables) were the mainstays of the Self-Respect movement and then of the DK. But there were also Vellalas, Mukkulathavar and even Chettis among the lieutenants of Periyar. The scope and strength of this social coalition must not be exaggerated since old lines of cleavages persisted. As in Maharashtra, the 'non-Aryans' did not form a solid block at all. M.C. Rajah criticised the 'natural animosity' of the Justice Party towards the Untouchables and in 1922-23 his South India Adi-Dravida Congress broke ranks with the party. However, the ethnic ground of the Non-Brahmin discourse which, from Thass to Periyar combined Buddhist and Dravidian references had enabled its leaders to unify low caste people and mobilise them against the 'twice borns'. As early as 1920, 'a non-brahmin constituency with its own distinctive political claims had emerged in Madras' and enabled the Justice Party to win the elections. This ethnicisation process was fostered by the political reforms since the British were much willing to recognise ethnic and/or caste groups as legitimate units for representation in the political arena.

The impact of compensatory discrimination The formation of caste federations and the ethnicisation of caste, two inter related processes, were fostered by the British policy of compensatory discrimination based on the reservation of seats in the bureaucracy and in the assemblies. The very decision to grant such or such statutory representation to such and such group in these assemblies contributed to the crystallisation of new groups which resented their non-(or their under-) representation. The State was therefore indirectly reshaping society. Caste groups, often with low status, were prominent among those, which mobilised against the state's decisions. The Non-Brahmin movement of Madras Presidency was especially active. In April 1920, Lord Chelmsford received a Memorandum protesting against the reservation of only 28 seats out of 65 for the Non-Brahmins in the Legislative Council of Madras. Interestingly, the signatories emphasised their caste and ethnic differences for justifying their claim: The Brahmins differ from the non-Brahmins in caste, manners, customs and interests and even in personal law in some respects. The former is Aryans and the latter are Dravidians and thus they differ in race. In the past the Brahmins have practically monopolised all or almost all the seats in the Local and Imperial Legislative Councils. The disabilities under which the Non-Brahmins have been suffering were fully set out in the Memorandum which Rai Bahadur K.V. Reddi prepared and submitted to the joint Select Committee on Government of India Bill.

The Non-Brahmins asked for more seats in Madras assembly because they were 'different'. During the 1920 election campaign, their leaders requested 'all non-Brahmins in this presidency to immediately organise, combine and carry on an active propaganda so as to ensure the return to the reformed Council of as many non-Brahmin as possible'. This tactic yielded dividends since the Justice Party came first in the elections. In their plea to the British, the Non-Brahmins also emphasised their marginality in the state services and the 'disabilities' from which they were suffering. This discourse fitted well too in the British approach since the Government regarded also political representation as a means for compensatory discrimination.

This policy made a similar impact on the low caste movement in Western India. In Bombay Legislative Council the Marathas showed the way in the 1920s. Their principal patron, the Maharajah of Kolhapur, Shahu Maharaj, had circulated a memorandum 'on the necessity of separate Communal electorates for the Marathas, etc., for electing members to the new Councils under the Reforms scheme', where he wrote: The Marathas have distinguished themselves in the [first world] war certainly not less, if not more, than the Sikhs or the Mohammedans who have been given separate electorates. They are almost given to agriculture, military service or employment as mill-hands. Being thus not a commercial or educated community, they are poor, and without resources, influence and organisation. In this respect they are even worse of than Telis, Tilaris, Goldsmiths, Sutas, Lohars and even Mahars, Mangs and other Untouchables, to whom many a business line and handicraft are open [...] Five great monsters do a lot of mischief to the village agricultural community which mostly consists of the Marathas. The Kulkarni [Brahmin] is the biggest of them all [...] Next to the Kulkarni is the Brahmin Sawkar [money-lender] who has appropriated to himself a very large portion of the village lands. The Ahird in this order is the school-master and his brother the college-professor in big cities [...] [The fourth] is the Brahmin bureaucracy watered and nourished by Government themselves [...] The village priest, securely and permanently installed by Hindu religious puranas invented and developed to maintain the Brahmanic supremacy is the fifth monster.

Shahu demanded separate electorates instead of reserved seats on which, he said, he was 'sure that weak, unprincipled undesirable Marathas will be elected who would be used by Brahmins as cat's paw for them to draw the apples out of the fire', the same kind of argument used by Ambedkar before the Poona pact. However, the British were not prepared to grant a separate electorate to the Marathas. Some of them preferred to focus their demand on larger quotas and they had understood that to pressurise the British more efficiently they had to appear as representing more than one caste. They held, under the auspices of the People's Union, whose patron was the Maharajah of Kolhapur, a Conference of the Hindu Backward Classes in June 1920. The British, so far, designated the Marathas by their caste name but the conference considered that 'the term "Maratha and allied classes" should include all the Backward communities'. Maratha leaders obviously aspired to play a pivotal role in the shaping of a caste federation which would adopt the official designation 'Backward classes'. Therefore, the conference made 'an emphatic protest against the misleading statement made in public to the effect that the Marathas, Malis etc. do not belong to the Backward Classes when their percentage of education is very low'. The main demand of the conference was that the 8 seats reserved to the

Marathas and allied castes in the Montagu-Chelmsford report should be extended to 15. Simultaneously, the Secretary of the Poona-based All India Maratha Mali Union made a similar representation to the British:

The word 'Maratta' [sic] means all the backward classes. As a matter of fact not only the Marattas but all other allied communities have fought in the last world war for the Empire and all such communities are anxious to get the privilege of reserved seats in the council to be hereafter elected. Among the allied communities of Marathas, Yadav Gavlis then opportunely discovered that they had strong affinities with the Marathas. The President of the Yadav Gavli Association, Raghunath Vithal Khedekar, was an exceptional personality whom we shall meet again while dealing with North India in the following section. Born in Bombay in 1873, his father had been Private secretary of the Maharajah of Bhavnagar, one of the most progressive states so far as the upliftment of the lower castes were concerned. After studying medicine in the United Kingdom, he started practising in 1902 in Bhavnagar and Kolhapur, where he met Shahu Maharaj. The first Yadav association had been founded in 1903 by a relative of his father. In the early 1920s, Khedekar protested that the Southborough Committee should consider the Yadav Gavlis as Marathas :

The Yadav Gavli community claims descent from the Great Yadav families to one which Shri Krishna the 8th incarnation of Vishnu belonged. The whole of the North India, Gujarat and Deccan were only ruled by the Kings of the Yadav families [...] They have kept up their Kshatriya caste traditions, customs and occupations [...] They have given considerable recruits to the government and have been regarded as Marathas and included in the Maratha regiments.

In the end, the Yadav-Gavli association demanded the 'inclusion [of this caste] in the list of the Marathas and allied communities of the Deccan for franchise purpose'. Access to political power was of course the main reason for this social rapprochement. Eventually, Khedekar was deputed by the People's Union, the Deccan Ryots Association and the Yadav Gavli Association for making a representation to the Joint Select Committee. He explained: If the term 'Maratha' be defined as meaning 'anti-Brahmin' in the regulation to be framed under the Indian Act, it will remove all misunderstandings and ill feelings in the Maratha castes and it will allow Jains and Lingayat castes to share the benefit of the reserved seats.

Marathas, who had already forged a 'backward' front with the Malis and the Yadavs were striving for shaping an even larger coalition including the Lingayats and the Jains under the all-encompassing label of 'anti-Brahmins'. Certainly, the loose structure of the Marathas lent itself to this kind of aggregative strategy. They have no clear-cut sub-castes, they are so 'amorphous' that 'it is hard to tell in some cases, whether a group is Maratha or of another affiliation called Kunbi'. This arrangement naturally 'facilitates incorporation into Maratha caste' of other peasant castes. But in spite of the Marathas' specificity, there is much to learn from this case study on the way state policies can indirectly refashion social groupings. The British approach of compensatory discrimination through quotas in the assemblies have accelerated the transformation of castes into interest groups and have fostered a process of amalgamation among the low castes. Leading castes such as the Marathas initiated federations whose aim was purely political. They had understood that the rules were those of the game of numbers which, alone could enhance institutional representation in the State. In Maharashtra this strategy was rather successful. Its architects could rely on the legacy of Jyotirao Phule's Satyashodak Samaj, which had established an idiom-the Bahujan idiom-encompassing all the Non-Brahmins. Another important factor laid in the pivotal situation of the Marathas who represented 20% of the population. They were certainly not able to federate all the Non-Brahmins but the mere fact that the British designed a category called 'Marathas and allied' showed that they had been successful to a certain extent. Among these allies were the Kunbis, who have always been regarded as more backward than the Marathas but who appeared in the same category. Now, the Kunbis accounted for 10% of the population of Maharashtra and contributed, therefore, to the irresistible rise to power of the Marathas from the late colonial period onwards.

In Maharashtra and Tamil Nadu, the ethnicisation of caste and the formation of caste federations, helped the non-Brahmins to get organised and to gradually assert themselves in the political arena. However, the most significant caste federations took shape in the South and in Gujarat. Caste federations and the rise to power of the low castes Kothari and Maru have defined caste federations in terms which would have suited well the Maharashtrian situation since they emphasise the role of individual caste associations in the shaping of such coalitions and put a stress on the political motivations: The concept of caste federation refers to a grouping together of a number of distinct endogamous groups into a single organisation for common objectives, the realisation of which calls for a pooling together of resources or numbers or both. By and large, the objectives pursued are secular and associational, although the employment of traditional symbols for evoking a sense of solidarity and loyalty towards the new form is not uncommon. The traditional distinctions between the federating groups are on the whole retained, but the search for a new organisational identity and the pursuit of political objectives gradually lead to a shift in group orientations.

This definition was evolved in the course of a study of the caste federation phenomenon in Gujarat where the 'Kshatriyas' indeed exemplified this phenomenon. Right from the 1910s the state Rajput leaders had constituted caste associations for promoting education. In the late 1930s, the descendent of one of its leaders, Natvarsingh Solanki, wanted to extend these associations to other castes which he considered as Kshatriyas. He tried to refashion the social identity of those groups in order to allow others to join hands with the Rajputs and in this way, to acquire more weight.

Gujarat's largest caste was the Kolis. They had been classified by the British as a 'criminal caste' but claimed that they were Kshatriyas and resorted to genealogists for being recognised aristocratic ancestors. In this, they purely imitated the Rajputs. Some Koli clans had been able to establish matrimonial alliances with Rajputs, as those castes practised hypergamy and/or had established small principalities before the British took over. Yet, they had retained some control over land under the Raj as landowners or rather big tenants. Many of them met the necessary conditions for being enfranchised when the British established provincial legislative councils. The right to vote therefore enabled the Kolis to use their main asset, their number" : in 1931 they represented about 20% of the population, almost the double of the Patidars (12.16%), the dominant caste, the main rival of the Rajputs, who represented only 4.85% of the population. Solanki opened his caste association to the Kolis for this very reason: for transforming it into a mass organisation. In 1947, the Kutch, Kathiawar, Gujarat Kshatriya Sabha was created after years of preparatory work.

The word 'Kshatriya' was a useful umbrella label to bracket the Rajputs and the Kolis together. The Kshatriya Sabha is a good example of the way castes, with very different ritual status for defending common interests. In this case, the Kolis and the Rajputs had the same enemies, viz., the Patidars. Certainly, this alliance has been legitimised in the idiom of 'tradition', by pretending that its components belonged to the same varna, but the use of the word Kshatriya was largely tactical and the original caste identity was seriously diluted.

The Rajput leaders of the Kshatriya Sabha emphasised that a Kshatriya is not to be defined by descent but by military values. Political calculations had therefore social implications. Several taboos were abolished. Rajputs and Kolis of the Kshatriya Sabha shared meals and the Kolis elite married their daughters to lower Rajputs-who practised hypergamy anyway-and this process fostered the rajputisation of the upper Kolis. Kshatriyas tended to form a new caste. The use of terms like Koli Kshatriyas and Rajput Kshatriyas certainly show that the merger was far from complete. But important dimensions of the caste system were eroded by the after-effects of basically socio-economic and political strategies.

In fact, the main demands of the Kshatriya Sabha after independence reflected a relative indifference to ritual issues in comparison to material objectives. For instance, the association claimed that the Kshatriyas were part of the "Backward Classes" and therefore should benefit from reservations in the educational system and in the administration. This claim was the exact opposite of sanskritisation. The Kolis benefited more than the Rajputs from the Sabha, which created boarding schools, grants, loan systems etc. in favour of the poorest of their community. This development contributed to the emergence of a Koli intelligentsia of Kolis which, even though it remained small gave the Koli masses a new confidence and self-esteem as a caste. The members of this elite 'interact[ed] frequently and chart[ed] out common political strategies'. Right from the 1950s, the Kshatriya Sabha tended to capitalise its electoral support to the Congress in exchange of tickets for a number of its members as party candidates. The party was not fully responsive, especially because of the Patidars who were very influential in the Congress. The Patidars disapproved of the Kshatriyas demand regarding land reform. The Kshatriya Sabha therefore kept its distance with the Congress before the 1962 elections and the party underwent a setback. Instead, the association gave its support, against large concessions, to the Swatantra Party, which became the leading opposition party in the state. This situation persuaded the Congress to change its strategy and to give tickets to Kshatriya candidates before the 1967 elections. The Kshatriya Sabha then supported the Congress, which regained a more comfortable majority than in 1962.

Caste federations turned out to be political interest groups with more leverage than caste associations, simply because they represented more people. In Gujarat, after the Congress split of 1969, a majority of the party conservative notables remained with the Congress (O) while a larger number of Kshatriyas joined the Congress (R). They gradually gained control over the state Congress. Madhavsingh Solanki, a Kshatriya of low birth, became Chief minister in 1976 and appointed a majority of ministers with the same background. During the electoral campaign of 1977 he initiated a new caste alliance regrouping the Kshatriyas, the Harijans (Untouchables), the Adivasis (tribals) and the Muslims (hence the acronym "KHAM"). This KHAM alliance was largely responsible for the Congress success during the 1980 elections. Between 1957 and 1990 the number of upper caste Congress MLAs decreased from 33 to 6%, those with a Patidar background remained stable at about one fourth of the total, whereas the Kshatriyas increased from 12 to 25% and the KHAM MLAs at large from 39 to 55%. While the 'Kshatriyas' of Gujarat represent the best example of caste federation, other instances occurred in South India. In the early 1960s, the Kallan, the Maravar and the Agamudiar, three lower castes who had already close ties with each other (especially ritual ones since they clamed that they descended from the same ancestors), decided to adopt the same name, Mukkulator (lit. three castes), in order to merge and to influence local politics.

The search for new forms of caste activity did not contribute to social change and to the rise of the low castes in the same way in Maharashtra, Tamil Nadu and Gujarat but the above case studies suggest a western and southern pattern. In these areas, the development of communications, the impact of western ideas-ranging from missionaries' propaganda and school teaching, the establishment of a pan-Indian administration and census operations, fostered the formation of caste associations. These institutions had sometimes a very conservative overtone and confined their discourse into the sanskritisation framework. However, they prepared the ground for two major developments, namely the ethnicisation of castes, of which the ideology of the 'bahujan samaj' evolved by Phule and the Dravidian movement were the best examples, and the federation of castes which was epitomised by the 'Kshatriyas' of Gujarat. Both phenomena were influenced by the orientalist discourse and responses to the British policy of compensatory discrimination. They were intended to help the low castes to reach power and they were successful to a large extent.

In North India, none of these processes reached their logical conclusion even through the British Raj had generated the same context as in the South and in the West. Caste associations often followed the sanskritisation path and neither prepared the group for an ethnic discourse nor developed into caste federations.

What low caste movement in the Hindi belt ?

In North India also British policies had changed the social and political context in such a way as castes could have felt the same strong incentive to get organised. Efforts were made in this direction but they did not bear the same fruits as in the South and in the West. While caste associations took shape at an early date, they did not join hands into federations and they operated within the logic sanskritisation. For instance, in 1928, the Indian Statutory Commission received an avalanche of petitions and memoranda from caste associations, which demanded larger quotas in the assembly. The Government was petitioned by the All India Kushwaha Kshatriya Mahasabha, 'on behalf of the kori, kachchi and murao castes'. The fact that the Kushwaha label stood for three sub_castes of castes of market gardeners shows that this caste association promoted the fusion process, but not to a very large extent : this process cannot be compared with caste federations in Gujarat. Secondly, the Kushwahas claimed the rank of Kshatriya, and another association of middle caste of peasants, which sent also a petition, the Kurmi Kshatriya Parishad Sabha, did the same. Sanskritisation continued to play a major role among the low caste associations. In the following pages we shall examine this issue through the case of the Yadavs and the Kurmis on the one hand and through that of the Untouchables on the other hand.

Sankritisation and lack of unity among the Yadavs and the Kurmis The 'Yadav' label covers a great number of castes, which had different names, initially: Ahir in the Hindi belt, Punjab and Gujarat, Gavli in Maharashtra, Gola in Andhra Pradesh and Karnataka etc. However, traditionally their common function, all over India, was to take care of bovines cattle as herdsmen, cowherds and milksellers. In their 'Tribes and Castes of the Central Provinces of India', Russell and Hira Lal note that 'In former times the Ahirs had the exclusive right of milking the cow, so that on all occasions on their must be hired for this purpose even by the lowest castes' In practice, the Yadavs today spend most their time tilling the land. In the Central Provinces, in the first decade of the last century, already two kinds of the Ahirs were cultivators and labourers and less than one Ahird were still occupied in breeding cattle and in dealing with milk and milk products.

While the Yadavs are speared our several regions, as noticed above, they are more specially concentrated in the Ganges plain where they represent about 10% of the population. They form one of the largest castes in Bihar and Uttar Pradesh with respectively 11 and 8.7% of the population. The 'casteregious' maped by J. Schwartzberg show that the Yadavs were the largest caste in almost all the districts of northern Bihar and in much of eastern UP in 1931 But the Yadavs are not a dominant caste, as pastoral activity did not go usually hand in hand with land possession and from the ritual point of view, the Yadavs are traditionally regarded as low caste peasants: The very mention of the community invokes, in Bihar, the image of dull, miserly and loud-mouthed people lacking in grace and culture. Besides, the Yadavs are considered as to be unusually prone to casteism and violence.

In the central Provinces, a proverb says ' A Gaoli's quarrel: drunk a t night and friends in the morning'. Russell and Hira Lal note that in this region too, 'The Ahirs are also hot-tempered, and their propensity for drinking often results in affrays, when they break each other's head with their cattle-staffs'. However, their association with another image, that of placidity and peace. One of the proverbs cited by Schwartzberg says: 'The cow is in league with the milkman and lets him milk water into the pail'. Hence an ambivalent stereotype-if this phrase is not a contradiction in terms. The Yadavs reportedly descend from immigrants from Central Asia, the Abhiras, who established kingdoms in North India, the most recent of which was built in Rewari, in Haryana in the XVIIth century. The scion of the dynasty, Rao Bahadur Balbir Singh, established the Ahir Yadav Kshatriya Mahasabha in 1910. This association claimed that the Ahirs descended from the Yadu dynasty (hence the term Yadav) to which Krishna-the cowherd god-belonged, and that, therefore, they were Kshatriyas. To promote a warrior ethos and the caste unity, the association leaders could easily rely on the caste history since Ahirs were easily presented as coming from the same ethnic stock and were known for their martial valour-the prince of Rewari took part in the 1857 Mutiny for instance. This is probably why M.S.A. Rao considers that the 'term Yadava refers to both an ethnic category and an ideology'. Certainly, the Yadav leaders succeeded in their fusion project since they persuaded their caste fellows to downplay the endogamous units into which they were divided. There have even been some inter-regional marriages. Fusion was made easier from the 1930s onwards when North Indian Yadavs started to migrate from their villages to towns and especially to Delhi. But this project did not incorporate a more ambitious ethnicisation process through which other Kshatriya castes would have been merged. So far as ideology is concerned, it was dominated by sanskritisation.

The Yadavs lent themselves for such sanskritisation because they had 'a special relation to the Hindu religion, owing to their association with the sacred cow' (and with Krishna, the cowherd God). And the Arya Samaj also exerted a strong influence over the Yadav movement. As early as 1895, the ruler of Rewari, Rao Yudhishter Singh (the father of Rao Bahadur Balbir Singh) invited Swami Dayananda in his State. Branches of the Arya Samaj flourished soon after and Rewari provided a base from which Arya Samaj updeshaks (itinerant preachers) operated in neighbouring areas. The Arya Samaj was a reform movement, which has been too often regarded as purely Punjabi and confined to the urban middle class. In fact, it made inroads in the adjacent states at a quite early date and attracted then large numbers of low caste people. Dayananda even started his 'campaign against heresy and orthodoxy'-to use the words of an Arya Samajist-in the Kumbha Mela held in Haridwar. Subsequently, he toured in the United Provinces, in particular in the western part of the province.

He stayed eight times in Meerut, for instance, between 1866 and 1880-the Meerut City Arya Samaj was established as early as 1877 and others followed in Farrukabad (1879), Kanpur (1879), Benares (1880), Lucknow (1880). Eventually, the Srimati Arya Pratinidhi Sabha for the United Provinces of Agra and Awadh was founded in 1886. These local branches gradually extended their influence in the countryside. The anti-Brahmin stance of the Arya Samaj was especially appreciated by the low castes of the United Provinces. In Sathyarth Prakash (The Light of Truth), Dayananda has very strong words against 'the sectarian and selfish Brahmins', 'these ignorant, sensual, hypocritical, irresponsible and vicious people' who 'often dissuade persons from learning and ensnare them into their evil ways with the result that they lose health, peace of mind and wealth. Dayananda reproached the Brahmans with exploiting the superstition of the Hindus by projecting themselves as the only intermediary between man and god, a monopoly he compares to that of the Catholic Pope and which according to him was evident from the brahminical invention of idol worship: "These Popes fill their pockets by playing fraud upon you. In the Vedas there is not even a word to sanction idol-worship or invoking invitation and dismissals'.

Dayananda eulogised the Jats for forcefully resisting the Brahmins' 'popish' attitudes. He narrates the story of a Jat whose father was dying and who was asked to give his only cow to the priest as a 'dying gift', allegedly for helping the dying man to cross the river. The Jat had to agree since the priest had already talked to his relatives who put pressure on him. But he went to the priest's house soon after and boldly accused him of being 'a great liar' since he had not taken the cow to the river bank but was milking i t. He then contested the authority of the Garuda Purana, the book the priest mentioned as dictating his conduct: 'This book has been written by your forefathers to secure livelihood for you...'. The Jat took the cow back to his home and Dayananda concludes, 'If other persons also behave like the Jat, then alone can the popish fraud be stopped'.

Jats were very pleased by the way Dayananda praised one of them and they naturally shared his indictment of the Brahmins. However, Dayananda's indictment of the Brahmins did not amount to a complete rejection of the caste system. What he condemned was the hereditary caste. He contended that in the initial varna vyavastha children were placed in each varna according to their individual 'merits, actions and temperaments'. He specifically recommended that the 'fixture of the varnas according to merits and actions should take place at the sixteenth year of girls and twenty-fifth year of boys'. Like Gandhi later on, Dayananda was not against caste as such since, according to him, provided it was not a hereditary system, the castes endowed society with a virtually harmonious structure. Moreover, he considered that marriages should 'take place in the same varnas (classes) and the varna should be based on merits, profession and temperament'. It means that not only Dayananda adds one more criterion to the definition of castes-the profession-but also that endogamy, which is a pillar of the caste system, needed to be enforced.

Dayananda did not fight caste taboos either. For instance, he considered that a Brahmin needed only to eat food prepared by caste fellows because 'The nature of genital fluids made in a Brahman's body due to special kind of fooding is different from that made in chandalas body on account of bad diet. The body of the candalas is full of rotten particles due to rotten diet'.

Dayananda, therefore, maintained also the hierarchy in diets which is part of the caste system. He was obviously a clear proponent of sanskritisation and the Arya Samaj exerted a strong influence in this direction over the lower castes of North India. The first anti-Brahmin movement of North India was probably the Arya Samaj. But in contrast to what happened in Western and Southern India, this movement made a very ambivalent impact since it promoted sanskritisation. The activities of the arya samajists among the Yadavs of the Gangetic plains are a case in point.

Logically enough, the most obvious implication of the Arya Samaj in the North Indian countryside lay in the sanskritisation of the Jats, as evident from the ideology of the All India Jat Mahasabha which was founded in 1905 as 'an offshoot of the Arya Samaj'. On the one hand this caste association, as so many others, asked for a special treatment from the Government; on the other hand it claimed that Jats were Kshatriyas.

Arya Samajists exhorted the Jats to give up the consumption of alcohol and meat and recommended that severe restriction should be 'imposed on the movement of women'. The schools established with the association's support had often telling names-such as the Jat Vedic School founded in Rohtak in 1913- and generally taught Sanskrit in order to enable the Jats to teach Sanskrit and therefore occupy ' a profession which for centuries was the exclusive monopoly of the Brahmin'. The Arya Samajists propagated the same kind of ideology among the Yadavs.

The Arya Samaj updeshaks continuously canvassed for the adoption of the sacred thread by the Yadavs. Their campaigns were especially successful in Uttar Pradesh and Bihar. The Yadav rulers of Rewari, Rao Yudhishter Singh, true to his role as protector of the cows founded a Goraksha Sabha (association for cow protection) in conjunction with the Arya Samaj-which had started to create such sabhas all over North India. The arya samajists also enrolled the Yadavs in the cow protection movement. This movement, initiated in 1893 and relaunched at different points of time in the first two decades of the century, attracted many Yadavs who were anxious to emulate the upper castes. In the Bhojpuri region, Gyan Pandey, who emphasised 'the special role of the Ahirs' in this movement points out that 'we have evidence here of a relatively independent force that added a good deal of power to cow-protection activities [...]-marginally " clean " castes who aspired to full " cleanliness " by emphasising the purity of their faith and the strictness of ritual adherence to it on the issue of cow-slaughter'. Such a process can hardly be presented as 'a relatively independent force'. Obsessed with an imitation of the upper castes, the Ahirs could not develop an alternative value system. Both phenomena may not be mutually exclusive, however. The same Ahirs who took part in the cow-protection movement and could also petition the Bihar Census Commissioner for being recognised a Kshatriya origin also refused to do begari (forced labour) for the upper castes. Revisiting the notion of sanskritisation, Srinivas himself points out that it 'embodies a strong element of protest against the high castes: "We dare you to stop us emulating you" seems to be the spirit underlying emulation'. A specialist of the Yadavs, M.S.A. Rao also questions the opposition between sanskritised movements and egalitarian movements: "... the backward classes attempt to acquire, simultaneously goods and services belonging to religious, educational ", economic and political fields. That is, they claim higher ritual status, right of entry into caste Hindu temples, or establish a set of institutions parallel to the Brahmanical ones. They claim higher educational benefits, employment opportunities and political representation. From the point of view of the social movement approach all these demands belong to the same structural (conceptual) plane as expressions of egalitarianism. While the difference between sanskritisation and other low castes' movements needs not to be exaggerated, there are still differences and it is very difficult to follow Rao when he pretends that 'the Yadavs were not imitating the "twice-born castes" when they were donning the sacred thread, but were challenging their monopoly over this privilege'.

They tried to upgrade themselves while recognising the symbols of the Brahmins as superior-thesis the sanskritisation perspective. This approach does not necessarily imply a sense of equality since the caste in question may try to be recognised as higher in order to look down at the others which were on the same level. (The propensity of the Yadavs towards sanskritisation in evident from their attempt at "aryanising" their history. The first "history" of the Yadavs was written by R.V. Khedekar's father, Kithal Krishna Khedekar in the late XIXth century. This work was taken up by his son and published in 1959 under the title The Divine Heritage of the Yadavs. The book situates the origins of the Yadavs in the Abhiras and then the ruling dynasties mentioned as Yadavs in the Mahabharata and the Puranas. The descendants of Krishna naturally form the core group of this heritage. But dynasties regarded as Jats and Marathas, like those of Kolhapur, Barada and Bharatpur are also included in this historical reconstitution. This openness could have been part of an attempt a t federating different castes but in fact, the Yadav 'historians' admit t h a t these groups have succeeded and try to highlight the superiority of their caste. The ethnic dimension of their 'narrative' is therefore narrower than that of Phule or Dravidians. They try to demonstrate that Abhiras were Aryan origin. Lucio Michelutti shows that in the wake of Khedekar, K.C. Yadav and then J.N.S. Yadav-two of the most prolific Yadav intellectuals-base their claim on inscriptions which may suggest that the Ahiras were the main ruling dinasty of North India as early as the second century Before Christ. Rewari was generally presented as the last representative of the Ahira kingdoms.

This largely mythical history enabled Yadav intellectuals to invent a golden age. Khedekar pretends that 'Even in the vedic age the Yadavs were upholders of the Republican ideals of Government', under the aegis of Krishna himself. More importantly, he stresses the Aryan origins of his caste:

The Yadavs were those 'ancient Aryans who were the custodians of this Bharat Varsha and who possessed the highest virtues which attracted God to be incarnated amongst them, to play with them, to sing the sweet melody of the Bhagavad Gita in order to bring peace and prosperity in the world. Without the help of the Yadav, Shri-Krishna could not have done anything'.

This narrative certainly aims at giving the Yadavs an ethnic identity, but this ethnicisation process is embedded in the sanskritisation logic. In contrast to the lower castes leaders of Maharashtra and South India who tried to invent a Bahujan or a Dravidian identity which presented the Shudras and

Untouchables as the originals inhabitants of the country against the Aryans, the Yadavs claim that they are Aryans in order to exhauce their status within caste society. W.R. Pinch cites 'Yadav-Kshatriya historians who, in the 1930s, held that Yadavs were 'the ancient citizens of the land of the Aryans'-they did not pre-date the Aryan invasions. On the contrary, they were described as having 'their origins in the main Chandravamsh [lunar line] branch of kshatriyas'.

The All India Yadav Mahasabha, through which Khedekar federated regional associations based in Punjab, Uttar Pradesh and Bihar in followed the sanskritisation path under the guidance of Rao Balbir Singh, the ruler of Rewari who still played a prominent role in the Yadav movement. Interestingly, he was elected to the Punjab assembly in 1937 on a Hindu Mahasabha ticket. The programme of the AIYM is easy to summarise. It advocated vegetarianism and teetotalism. It militated in favour of the adoption of the name 'Yadav' all over India and so far as material interests were concerned, it incited the Yadavs to embrace new professional careers and put pressure on the British to make the army recruit Yadavs as officers.

While the AIYM helped the Yadavs to get united, in 1945 dissidents founded a rival caste association, the All India Yadav Sangh whose activities were even more sanskritised _ it took part in the 1966 anti-cow slaughter movement for instance. The main weakness of the Yadavs was their incapacity to make alliances with other castes of similar rank, like the Kurmis, who suffered from the same problem themselves!

The Kurmis are also concentrated in Bihar and UP where they represented respectively 3.6 and 3.5% of the population in 1931. The Kurmis generally work as cultivators and are looked at as middle caste peasants but they claim to be Kshatriyas. The ground for this 'kshatriyaisation' process was prepared by the Ramanandi sampraday which, as other sectarian movements, 'welcomed shudras as equal members of the monastic community'. The Ramanandis exerted a strong ideological influence over the Kurmis. Monks codified caste myths, established for them 'genealogical ties to either Ram or Krishna' and inculcate them 'a pure lifestyle' based on vegetarianism, teetotalism etc.. By the last decades of the

XIXth century, Kurmi leaders were the first among the low castes to fashion caste stories emphasising 'an ancient past of kshatriya distinction that had long since deteriorated into present-day shudra dishonour'. These stories, which were gradually propagated by printed bulletins, relied on the Vaishnava mythology as spelled out by the Ramanandi order. Kurmis were presented as descending from Ram's two sons, Kush and Lav-the Kushwahas (Koeris, Kachhis and Muraos) also claim that Kush was their ancestor but interestingly not attempt at merging these two groups ever took shape.

The first Kurmi caste association was founded in 1894 in Lucknow to protest against the British decision to reduce the recruitment of Kurmis in the police. The Kurmis of Awadh then created a Kurmi Sabha and declared that other castes like the Patidars (from Gujarat), the Kapus (from Andhra Pradesh), the Vokkaligas (from Karnataka), the Reddys, the Naidus (from Madras Presidency) and the Marathas (from Maharashtra), were also Kurmis. The association gained momentum in 1901, during the census operations when it claimed that Kurmis were Kshatriyas. The All India Kurmi Kshatriya Mahasabha, which was officially registered in Patna in 1910, combined the defence of the caste secular interests and sanskritisation. On the one hand it canvassed for the use of the sacred thread among Kurmis. On the other hand, it started to ask for quotas in the administration as 'backward classes' but its action met a faint response.

Kurmis and Yadavs, even though they occupied similar social positions failed to get united. The first attempt was made in Bihar in the 1930s. It involved the Yadavs, the Kurmis and the Koeris, a caste of agriculturists representing 4.1% of the state population. Members of those three castes joined hands in 1930 to contest the local district board elections. They lost badly but in 1934 formed the Triveni Sangh, a political party named after the confluence of three rivers, (the Ganges, the Yamuna and the Saraswati, now disappeared) in Allahabad. In 1936 about one million members had allegedly paid the four-anna (one-quarter of a rupee) fee. However, at the same time, in 1935, the Congress formed the Backward Class Federation 'to counter what they viewed as the dangerous class features of the Triveni Sangh and Kisan Sabha movements'.

Congressmen deprived the low caste movement from some of its leaders by co-opting Kurmi leaders (such as Birchand Patel) and Yadavs (such as Ram Lakhan Singh Yadav). And then they refused to give tickets to Triveni Sangh candidates. The party suffered from a serious setback during the 1937 elections but in the few places where i t won-like Arrah and Piro-Shahabad district _ upper caste landlords retaliated violently. The Triveni Sangh and the Kisan Sabha also failed to make an alliance because of the traditional antagonism between the low castes represented by the former and the Bhumihars who dominated the latter.

Many years later, the Kurmis tried to play a pivotal role in a similar arrangement. During the 30th session of the All India Kurmi Kshatriya Sabha, some of the delegates suggested that the word 'Kshatriya' should be removed from the name of the association and a resolution was passed to discourage the sanskritisation process. In the same way, it was decided to constitute a caste federation with the Koeris. The Kurmis leaders were not planning to create a new caste through intermarriages, but a union they called 'Raghav Samaj'-after one of the names of the Lord Ram-, a choice they justified by presenting the Kurmis and the Koeris as descending respectively from Lav and Kush, two sons of Ram. This attempt reflected the weight of the Biharis within the association. While the sessions of the Sabha were often presided over by Marathas, Patidars etc., in the 1970s about 30% of the executive bureau members were from Bihar (and 17-18% from Uttar Pradesh). The attempt to federate the Koeris and Kurmis was rather inconclusive, no doubt because of difference in their status and economic activities; the Kurmis were cultivators who produced staples like cereals whereas the Koeris were traditionally market gardeners.

The failure of the Yadavs, Kurmis and Koeris to form caste federations in North India can be explained from different points of view. One explanation lay in the fact that the Yadavas 'consider themselves to be natural leaders of backward classes'; their leaders even argued that their caste fought against injustice during the Dwapara Yug under the leadership of Krishna and that they should now show the way in the battle against the upper castes exploitation. This approach did not enable them to forge stable caste federations. According to me the division of the lower castes are more resulting from the influence of the Arya Samaj and its ideology of sanskritisation. This ethos prevented the low castes from developing a common, ethnic as well as 'federated' identity like in the West or in the South. The same kind of reasoning can be made about the untouchables' movement.

The North Indian Untouchables and the limited ethnicisation of caste The Untouchables of North India were also exposed to the influence of the Arya Samaj at the turn of the XXth century. Briggs emphasises that 'During 1911, preceding the Census enumeration, both the Arya Samaj and the Mohammedan communities made special efforts to enrol Chamars, especially those who were Christians'. This competition was part of the politics of numbers. It concerned a small minority since in 1911 there were only 1,551 Arya Samajist Chamars in the United Provinces, but most of the Jatav leaders were exposed to it. Their name, in itself is very revealing. Jatavs are Chamars, untouchable leather workers, who claim descent from the Yadu race, which, allegedly, entitled them to be known as Kshatriyas. The Arya Samaj missions were responsible for propagating these views. They were especially successful through their schools among the sons of Agra Chamars who had become rich thanks to leather trade. Manikchand Jatavaveer (1897-1956), one of the founders of the Jatav Mahasabha in 1917 was a teacher in a school of Agra run by the Arya Samaj.

Sunderlal Sagar (1886-1952), another co-founder of the Sabha in Agra was even versed in Sanskrit-so much so that he was called Pandit. A Ahir co-founder of the caste association, Swami Prabhutanand Vyas (1877-1950) was an Arya Samaj monk. They all preached moral reform, vegetarianism, teetotalism and temperance for achieving a cleaner status. That was also the first inclination of Swami Achhutanand (1879-1933) who was to become the most important Scheduled Caste leader of the United Provinces in the 1920s-1930s.

A Chamar, Swami Achutanand was born in a village of Farukkabad district in the United Provinces. His father was a foot soldier and his uncle a subedar in the army of British India-like Ambedkar's, his family benefited from the government's policy of recruiting untouchables in the military personnel. He was attracted by the itinerant life of Hindu ascetics while he was still very young. He followed his guru in Bengal and Gujarat till he was 24 and then joined the Arya Samaj. He worked as an updeshak of the movement, under the name of Hariharnanda, from 1905 till 1912, mainly in Shuddi Sabhas which were in charge of 'purifying' untouchables. But then he revolted against the Arya Samaj and spends five years working at exposing the organisation under his new name, Swami Achutanand (deriving from 'Achut', Untouchable). In a violent indictment of the Arya Samaj, he declared once : 'This sect has been constructed in order to save the Brahmin religion from the attacks of the Christians and Muslims. [...] Its profession of purification are a frand and a clever verbal gimmick of the varna system'. He ridiculed the Arya Samaj schemes of inter caste marriages, asking the leaders of the organisation why they do not arrange for such marriages also with twice-borns if they were true reformers. In a conference he organised in Allahabad in 1930 he attacked the Arya Samajist reinterpretation of the varna system in the following terms :

Earlier, caste and varna were based on birth. Now, they are being said to be derived from the talents and achievements of a person as preached by the Arya Samaj. If this is true then left the dwij [twice-born] marry their sons with our simple and homely daughters for the next generation as to vindicate this truth.

Swami Achutanand enunciated the outlines of his Adi-Hindu philosophy for the first time in 1917 twenty years after Thass in a collection of poems and couplets. According to him, the Untouchables were the first inhabitants of India and the rightful owners of this land. The Aryans came from outside, 'as refugees' who, by resorting to tactics and strategies, captured power and subordinated the autochthonous people : 'They did not win over our own ruler by their good and noble deeds but by clever manoeuvres and later called them demons and Asuru and Satan. They destroyed our culture and civilisation and made us untouchables and outcastes in the heart of our own society.

Swami Achutanand maintains that the Adi-Hindus had their roots in the Indus Valley civilisation in the region of

Harrapa and Mohendjo Daro. He explained the difference between Shudras and Untouchables by arguing that with the coming of the Aryans those sections of the defeated people who accepted the varna system became Shudras and those who did not became Untouchables. There were also those who ran away and began to live in the forest and in the mountains to become tribals or Advasis. The Adi-Hindu philosophy was well designed for promoting the unity of the Shudras, the Untouchables and the Tribals since it endowed those three groups with a common-cultural and ethnic background : once upon a time, they were parts and parcels of the same people. Swami Achutanand-like Ambedkar-did not pay any real attention to the Advasis but he did try to unite the two other groups in a political perspective: 'If these two categories were to come together and make an organisation then they would count for 20 crores [200 millions] and become the most important majority group-the Bahujan Samaj-in society and could make a government of their own...' Swami Achutanand adopted the same expression-Bahujan Samaj-as Phule. However, the organisation he launched in 1919 was called the All India Achut Caste Reform Sabha. According to his biographer, the first Adi-Hindu council was started in Andhra, then in Delhi in 1922, in Madras (the Adi-Dravid Sabha) and in Punjab (the Adi-Dharma Mandal). In Lucknow and in Poona, a journal named Adi-Hindu was started and, in Punjab, another newspaper Adidas was also launched for publicising the ideas of Swami Achutanand.

The Adi-Hindu movement gained momentum in 1922, when Swami Achutanand protested against Gandhi's Non Cooperation Movement and especially his boycott of the Prince of Wales' visit. Swami Achutanand emphasised that the Congress was an organisation of 'twice born Brahmans who are as foreign to India as are the British'. He argued that the Untouchables should not oppose the British, on the contrary, it was an opportune time for demanding them basic rights. He said he was favourable to the visit of the Prince of Wales and the British appreciated : when Lothian Committee organised its hearings in Lucknow, he was called upon to give a testimony about the Untouchables' conditions. Later on, in the early 1930s, he asked the British for the introduction of separate electorates.

The Congress leaders took exception of his pro-British stands. He was accused of being a Christian in disguise and an agent of the British paid for dividing the Hindu community. But in fact, the (upper caste) congressmen's hostility came from his emancipatory discourse and the way he was mobilising the Untouchables against the caste system. His strong criticism of the Manusmriti was especially resented. A poem called " Manuswriti is burning us " was read at the end of the UP Adi-Sabha Conference in 1927, the very same year when Ambedkar had the text actually burnt in Mahad. In reaction, the Arya Samaj started an All India Shraddhanand Dalitodwar Sabha whose objective was to break up the Adi-Hindu movement. With the help of G.D. Birla, M. M. Malaviya also started an All India Achutodwar Sabha, which organised meetings between 1924 and 1927. Later on it merged with the Congress-backed All India Dalit Varg Sabha.

There were direct confrontations between Swami Achutanand and Congress leaders in several occasions. Once, during the Mahakumbh Mela of Allahabad, the Arya Samaj organised an All India Dalit Liberation Conference under the auspices of Purushottamdas Tandon, a conservative Congressman, one of Malaviya's lieutenants in UP politics. In this forum, Tandon spoke about the Hindu mythology and how the Nishads found liberation by washing the feet of Ram and worshipped him. This discourse infuriated Swami Achutanand whose reaction radicalised the Conference, so much so that two resolutions were passed. One stated that all dalits can sell food items at the railways stations. The other one that the washing clothes and making shoes was the vocational task of the Adi-Hindus and that any twice-born Hindu engaging in this matter should marry his children amongst these castes and share their food. The later resolution amounted at consolidating the caste system.

Swami Achutanand's attitude towards the caste system remained ambivalent indeed. For instance, in the Adi-Hindu Sabhas the caste and sub-castes were all represented : instead of trying to eradicate them, Swami Achutanand recognised castes amongst the Untouchables. More importantly, his egalitarian discourse was largely framed in a religious mould drawing its inspiration from the bhakti tradition. Swami

Achutanand, even after leaving the Arya Samaj remained a sadhu. He was given his official name, 108th Swami Achutanand in revealing circumstances. In the late 1920s he organised in Delhi, outside the Red Fort, the foundation meeting of a Jati Sudhar Achut Sabha (Dalit Sabha for Caste Reform) when he challenged any Brahmin to shastrarth for the interpretation of the classical Hindu text and epics. He was opposed by a well-known Pandit, Akhilanand Kaviratan but declared the winner and conferred the title of 108th Swami Achutanand by an assembly of 'high class Brahmins and leading Arya Samaji leaders of Delhi and northern India'. It was certainly on their part a shrewd way to coopt him. He obviously resisted this attempt but did adopt the style of many Dalit saints before him. He draw his inspiration partly from the bhakti idiom. According to C.P. Jigyansu, 'His style of address was poetic and musical, similar to the Bhakti leaders of the 16th or 17th century, but his discourse was radical and biting'. This is a very apt way at describing the ambivalence of Swami Achutanand. His biographer pertinently emphasised that the 'Adi-Hindu agitation had started in a religious mould'. Indeed, after severing his links with the Arya Samaj, Swami Achutanand studied the writings of the Sikh Gurus, Kabir, Dadudayal, Namdev and Redam Sahib. He borrowed from them a very particular method of exposition since he 'relied a lot on the discourse of the Bhakti movement. Singing, chanting formed an essential part of his meetings. This old style of discourse is very particular to the cultures of the oral tradition where songs, poems and other narratives formed an essential ideological component of the preachings'. This modus operandi stood in stark contrast with Ambedkar's westernized style. While Swami Achutanand supported Ambedkar-for instance during his conflict with Gandhi over the separate electoral issue-he might have been uneased by his condemnation of the bhakti. Furthermore, Swami Achutanand organised some of his meetings during religious functions. In 1931, he held a conference on the preachings of Kabir in the heart of brahmanical orthodoxy, the Allahabad Maherkumbha Mela. Basically, Swami Achutanand discovered social equality in religion :

'Our religion is not Brahminism but Sant Dharma or Sufi way of life. Our religion does not believe in discrimination or differences between humans. For all humans are equal and have equal rights'. He also said :

We are outside the Brahmin religion. As we are not allowed to go to the temples, that proves the fact that we do not belong to Brahmin religion. Our religion is the way of the saints or the sufi way. This has been our religion since centuries or even longer. Our religion has produced hundreds of saints and their preachings constitute our religion. Our mothers and sisters since centuries have been praying to the mother earth because this land is the land of our forefathers and their forefathers. We do not need any other religion; our religion is already with us. We do not need any purification. Ours is the oldest religion, even older than the sufis of Palestine. Gautam Buddha propagated this religion. There is no discrimination or inequality or untouchability in it, as it is practised by the Brahmins.

There is no high caste or low caste persons there is only the human race and all are equal before God. This quotation is a good summary of the thought of Swami Achutanand. He emphasises that the Untouchables are the original inhabitants of India and that, correlatively, they are the torchbearers of the most ancient religion. This creed, however, recalls the bhakti cults since it emphasises the worship of saints and equality before God. Ambedkar always criticised the bhakti cults because they delinked equality before God from social equality-and he accused Gandhi to do the same.

Nandini Gooptu convincingly argues that the Adi Hindu movement arose in the wake of the resurgence of bhakti cults among the Untouchables in the late XIXth century _ early XXth century. Worshipping Kabir and Ravidas then became widespread among urban untouchables migrants in U.P, and ceased to be practised only by insular religious orders: new temples and statues were built, festivals and pilgrimages organised. However, such a promotion of what was after all a form of Hinduism was not likely to imbue the Untouchables with a separate identity like in Dravidian India. If 'bhakti was resurrected as a caste-based religious expression solely of the untouchables', it could not be practised 'as a form of denial of caste distinctions'.

Indeed, N. Gooptu admits that 'the criticism of the caste system by the Adi Hindu leaders was rather limited and had a narrow focus on the lack of rights or opportunities for the untouchables. The leaders did jettison the notions of "low" or "impure", but concentrated on proving that such stigma and disabilities should not be attached to them due to caste status. Nor did they attempt to question the concept that work was inherited. Instead they claimed that "low" work was not the true inheritance of the Untouchables. It was largely to buttress this claim that they asserted their pre_Aryan ancestry as the original rulers of India, for it enabled them to argue that they should re_inherit the ancient rights of which they had been deprived'.

Far from establishing a separate identity that would situate the Untouchables out of the caste system, the Adi Hindu movement used their so-called original identity as a means for promoting their status within the system. And correlatively, the bhakti resurgence did not imply a radical questioning of their belonging to Hinduism. They questioned Brahminism by adhering to a rather popular tradition but their practise of this religious cult recalls the modus operandi of the Hindu sects _ which precisely derived from bhakti _ whose egalitarian impact has always been otherworldly. While in Pundjab the Ad_Dharm movement was projected as a quaum, or independent community, rather than a panth, or religious path, in the Hindi belt _ the Adi Hindu movement could not achieve so much.

The movement also suffered from organisational weaknesses. While the 'informal nature of links between apex Adi Hindu organisations in the towns and local caste_groups in neighbourhoods contributed to the strength and breadth of the movement', by 1924 local Adi Hindu Sabhas had been set up in only four cities of U.P. (Kanpur, Lucknow, Benares and Allahabad). In fact the Adi-Hindu movement remained chiefly confined to Agra and Kanpur. Out of the 23 main Dalit leaders of the United Provinces in the first half of the century, almost 50% were from these two cities (eight from Agra and two from Kanpur).

In addition to these limitations, the movement also failed to unite the Untouchables, in terms of commensality or otherwise. Its leaders tried to organise inter_dining ceremonies but did not meet very enthusiastic responses. Untouchables leaders of North India could not agrec either about the strategy that was to be implemented vis-à-vis the British. The Yatavs are a case in point. In the late 1920s, the All India Shri Jatav Mahasabha submitted a very telling memorandum to the Simon Commission:

Our Mahasabha is fully alive to the fact that there can be no advancement so long as there is no real improvement in the political status of a community. It is idle to attribute the depression of the depressed classes to the religious and social system of the Hindus. If Government were to improve their political status by giving them honorary offices, adequate representation on local bodies and legislatures and in public services commensurate with their numerical strength, their social position would automatically improve and social injustice would become a thing of the past. For social position of the depressed classes would rise pari passu with the rise in their economic condition-a thing which is inconceivable in the case of any community without advancement of its political status.

Such a discourse foreshadows-or echoes-one of Ambedkar's main intuitions, namely that only power could enable his caste-mates to emancipate themselves. However, all the Jatavs did not share these views. For instance, a special meeting of the United Provinces Depressed Classes Conference was held on 14-15 April 1928 at Agra to protest against the participation of the Adi-Hindu movement to the work of the Simon Commission. In fact this movement was impeded by the activism of the Dalit leaders who stuck to the sanskritisation approach. It was especially affected by the competition of the Depressed Classes League that was founded at Lucknow in 1935 by R.L. Biswas with Jagjivan Ram as General Secretary and P.N. Rajbhoj as Secretary. The moving spirit behind this association-at least one of its chief architects-Dharam Prakash, was a staunch arya samajist who opposed Ambedkar's moves in favour of conversion and was elected to the Constituent Assembly, and then to the Rajya Sabha, on a Congress ticket.

In the 1930s, a similar division opposed the proponents of joint electorates with reserved seats, such as Bohre Khem Chand the president of the All India Shri Jatava Mahasabha (and the vice president of the All India Depressed Classes Association) and those who supported Ambedkar's demand regarding separate electorates, such as the United Provinces

Adi-Hindu (Depressed Classes) Association. This cleavage more or less coincided with the one opposing the proponents of sankritisation and those who were more favourably inclined towards an egalitarian, ambedkarite strategy, the important point being here that the former tended to dominate the Jatav movement till the 1930s. After the publication of the White Paper which was to be the basis (?) of the 1935 Government of India Act, the Agra based Jatav Conference sent a memorandum to the Deputy Secretary to the Government of India where it was said :

The Jatavs are the descendents of Yadu, the founder of Jadav [sic] tribe, from which the great Hero of Maha Bharat, Lord Krishna, came. But this position of superiority could not remain intact. Our community fell down from that great height to this degraded status in the Hindu fold [...] our present position is the outcome of the age-long inhumane oppressions of Brahminism or the Kshatriyas. We, Kshatriyas of the past, are labouring under various sorts of disabilities, restrictions and religious injunctions imposed on us by the Orthodox Hindus [...] But we are at loss to understand the exclusion of our (Yadav) Jatav community from the list of the Scheduled Castes given in the White Paper. The result of this horrible negligence would, no doubt, be the sacrifice of the interests of our community.

Such a discourse suggests that the Jatav movement was still under the influence of sanskritisation. Owen Lynch points out that 'The Jatavs were not attempting to destroy the caste system; rather they were attempting to rise within it in a valid, though not licit, way'.

The influence of Ambedkar made a strong impact on the Jatav movement in the 1940s so much so that the Maharashtrian scenario _ with Dalit acquiring a separate Buddhist identity could be used to avoid the trap of sanskritisation. Even those who did not convert themselves to Buddhism regarded the Untouchables as descending from the original Buddhists and, therefore, prided themselves of being the original Indians: 'Buddhist identity has replaced Sanskritic Kshatriya identity'. The Jatav movement could therefore rely on the same ethnic ground as the Bahujan movement in Maharashtra and the Dravidian movement in Tamil Nadu. Also, for the Jatavs, 'political participation' became a 'functional alternative' to sanskritisation, in the sense that they tried to achieve social mobility through access to power. This empowerment process was fostered by the British policies of positive discrimination and gradual democratisation since they both incited the caste to transform itself into a pressure group and to assert itself as a collective body. However, such a change was confined to the Jatavs of Agra. Except the president of the Scheduled Caste Federation of the United Provinces, Piarelall Kureel (1916-1984), who was a Kureel from Unnao district, most of the supporters of Ambedkar were Jatav's from Agra movement. A similar evolution only took place with the Noniya (salt makers) who abandoned the Arya Samaj for political action and the Mallahs (fishermen, boatmen) Babu Ramcharanji (1889-1935) who had founded the All India Nishad Maha Sabha in 1920 joined the Adi-Hindu movement in 1925 and became president of the Adi-Hindu Sabha in 1927. In 1933 the All India Nishada Sabha claimed that 'the Mallahs are the descendants of the ancient Nishadas and Chandalas of the Vedic age and they themselves and the Hindus in general regard them as such up to the present time'.

In many cases sanskritisation-on the basis of arya samajist influences or not-remained prevalent. In the 1911 and 1921 censuses, some 26 low castes claimed the status of the twice-born castes. Certainly, sanskritisation and social mobility were not mutually exclusive but the former reflected the pervasiveness of the value system of the caste hierarchy anyway. In 1935, after the publicisation of the government of India Act, the All India Dhobi [washermen, launder] Association protested against the exclusion of their caste from the Scheduled Castes which had been decided under pressures from other associations such as the Arya Samaj oriented United Provinces Razak (Dhobi) Association which pursued the sanskritisation path. The President of the latter organisation, for whom Dhobis were Kshatriyas, considered that giving his caste fellows the status of Untouchables would be 'a stigma on character and ability, an obstruction to self-advancement and improvement'. Similar conflicts happened in the case of the Khatiks, an Untouchable caste of meat cutters. The Dusadh Mahasabha also claimed that Dusadhs were Kshatriyas. The Bundelkhand Prantia Kori

Sabha, which claimed 20,000 members passed a resolution in 1936 to support the view that 'the Koris of India have always been classified amongst the touchable castes with the right to Samskaras' and that in the Manusmriti they are 'held to be born of a Kshatriya in a Vaishya mother'. Interestingly, the association referred to resolutions passed by caste panchayats in a dozen of districts distributed between Lahore and Jhansi, its headquarters.

Similarly, the salt manufacturers of North India, the Noniyas, who belong to the lower orders of the shudras, did not emancipate themselves from the sanskritisation pattern till the 1960s-70s. In 1898 rich notable of the caste established an association claiming for the Noniyas the status of Cauhan Rajputs. The 'New Cauhans' undertook to ritually don the sacred thread, something the upper castes strongly objected for sometimes. For William Rowe, the 'Cauhan Movement' provided the Noniyas 'a mechanism which allowed them to reduce the discrepancy between their contrasting positions in the ritual and economic hierarchies' but this movement 'does not challenge but rather upholds the traditional stratification system'. Interestingly, in the early 1960s, the 'new Cauhans' still considered the RPI 'as "the dirtiest party in India" (i.e., in its opposition to caste i t encourages interdining of castes and intercaste marriage...'. However, the youngest generation was dissociating itself from sanskritisation and get more politicises. Like in Madras and Bombay twenty years ago when the Montagu-Chennmsford reforms had fostered the organisation and politicisation of the lower castes, the Untouchables mobilised in the context of the 1935 Government of India Acts. However, too major differences remained. The above examples suggest that the proponents of sanskritisation remained strong and hindered the efforts made by others for uniting the caste against the brahminical order. Secondly, when castes reached this kind of unity they did not succeed in forging federations. The Jatavs organised a mere section of the Chamars for instance.

6

Social Background and Origins of Indian Dalit

The origin of the Dalit community, and of the caste system itself, is unclear. Adherents of the Aryan migration hypothesis theorize that the caste system was a product of the invasion, with the Aryans reserving the higher castes for themselves and relegating the darker-skinned, native inhabitants that they conquered to lower castes and untouchable status. An alternative theory accepts this general outline, but holds that Dalit existed before the Aryan migration as an oppressed class among the native Dravidian peoples of South Asia. In this latter theory, the Dalit status was simply preserved and expanded by the Aryans as part of the integration of Aryan and Dravidian societies.

In the context of traditional Hindu beliefs, Dalit status has often been historically associated with occupations regarded as ritually impure: any occupation involving killing or handling dead bodies, or anything involving disposing of refuse or human waste. Engaging in these activities was considered to be polluting to the individual who performed them, and this pollution was considered to be 'contagious'. As a result, Dalits were commonly banned from fully participating in Hindu religious life (they could not enter the premises of a temple), and elaborate precautions were sometimes observed to prevent incidental contact between Dalits and higher-caste Hindus. Historically, there may not have been clear demarcation between Dalit castes and the lowest Shudra castes. Before the freezing of lands and territories during the British colonial period, it may have been possible for Dalits to move up the ladder as Shudras or higher castes. In the same way, some people from the lowest Shudra communities may have been reduced in status to that of the Dalits. Culturally there appears to be continuity across the caste spectrum. In modern India the word 'Dalit' has been applied to all people who do not belong to any of the four castes of Hinduism. Defined in this way, 'Dalit' includes not only low-caste or outcaste Hindus, but also aboriginal followers of animist religions, and possibly may have included immigrant communities that subscribed to beliefs that were seen as incompatible with orthodox brahman 1st and Hindu traditions.

Dalits are not a single identifiable race or caste. Instead, they are divided into various subcastes known as or ' jatis', the lowest ranking of which is generally considered to be the Bhangis. Most genetic studies have found no significant evidence that members of 'untouchable' groups are substantially different from other groups in similar locations. Castes within a region are probably less genetically different than people of the same caste across different regions. While at least one studyfound a correlation between caste status and genetic markers seeming to indicate a more European lineage, no clear biological basis for caste distinctions has been conclusively revealed.

The absence of strong genetic differentiation between Dalits and non-Dalits is often regarded as evidence that the caste barrier was historically more permeable than commonly perceived. Intermarriage (which is again growing in popularity in Indian society), or sexual infidelity (the prevalence of which is difficult to assess) across caste lines may be more common than was previously thought. Additionally, Dalit diversity may be due to newly outcaste individuals or communities over the years. It is noteworthy that certain regional tribes that are considered Dalits are sometimes seen by Indians as racially distinct-they are often regarded as more closely related to Burmese, Thais, and other Southeast and East Asians. Many Dalits who have converted to other religions in the past few centuries continue to retain their Dalit identity. In the 1991 census, Dalits constituted more than 16% of India's population, with the greatest numbers living in Uttar Pradesh, West Bengal, and Bihar. They are also found in Nepal. In Pakistan, more than 60% of all Hindus are Dalits, keeping in mind that Pakistan is predominantly Muslim.

Dalits and Indian Politics

M.K. Gandhi made it part of the Indian National Congress's mission to eradicate untouchability. For this reason, untouchability has been officially abolished in India, although social practice has lagged behind, particularly in rural villages. In a few of these extremely traditional villages, Dalits are still not allowed to let their shadows fall upon Brahmins for fear of ritually contaminating them; and they are still required to sweep the ground where they walk to remove the 'contamination' of their footfalls. In some of these villages, rural Dalits are forbidden to worship in temples or draw water from the same wells as caste Hindus, and they usually live in segregated neighbourhoods outside the main village. In urban areas and most villages the old concepts of a rigid caste system and untouchability usually no longer exist, though most Indians still voluntarily hold on to their caste origins. Some seats in the National and State Parliments are reserved for Scheduled Caste and Tribe candidates, a measure sought by B.R. Ambedkar and other Dalit activists in order to ensure that Dalits would obtain a proportionate political voice.

Dalits and Religion

One of the tougher questions in modern Indian society is whether the Dalits are really Hindus. Traditionally, Dalits have been barred from many activities that were seen as central to Vedic religion and Hindu practices. The wide variety of practices and beliefs observed in Hinduism makes any clear assessment difficult. Defined narrowly as the practice of rituals associated with the Vedic teachings and Brahmin-centered orthodox religious complex, then many Dalits would be classified as non-Hindus. But if ' Hinduism ' is viewed in wider terms as simply a convenient label for the full range of Indian religious practices, then most Indians-including Dalits-would fit into that category. Many Dalits continue to debate whether they are 'Hindu' or 'non-Hindu'. Some have succesfully integrated into urban Indian society, where caste origins are less obvious and less important in public life. In rural India, caste origins are more readily apparent, and Dalits remain excluded from local religious life. Because many Dalits feel they must have a formal religion, they have been drawn to other religions to improve their social and economic standing by removing them from a religious environment where they are excluded and denigrated. Dalit politician and activist B.R. Ambedkar was influential in encouraging many Dalits to convert to Buddhism in order to escape the inequities of the caste system. Ambedkar himself converted to Buddhism shortly before his death. The interpretation of Buddhism popularized by Ambedkar and his followers borrowed heavily from the Theravada tradition and emphasized the Buddha's teachings on social equality, particularly his rejection of castes for Sangha members, and the Buddhist teaching that the 'true Brahman' is one who engages in ethical behaviour, regardless of birth. This movement is sometimes called Neo-Buddhism.

In recent years, the use of mass conversionas a Dalit political tactic (often to Christianity or Buddhism) has become controversial—some politicians called for bans on mass conversion ceremonies.

Dalits and Social Policy

The central government and many state governments reserve places for Dalits in all educational courses and government jobs, but many poor Dalits remain poorly educated. Most Dalits, like other poor Indians, cannot afford private schools and tutoring. The improvement of public education remains a priority for many Dalit activists, who believe that the poor quality of public primary schools prevents Dalits from taking advantage of the educational opportunities supposedly provided for them by quotas and preferred admission to institutions of higher learning. Education of rural Dalits remains particularly problematic. Additionally, a recent Supreme Court decision removed the quota system from private and unaided professional colleges, limiting preferred admissions criteria for Dalit students to government-run and funded educational institutions. Some Dalits believe that the jobs traditionally reserved for Dalits are no longer lucrative, and should be supplimented by reserved jobs in the private sector. Recently, some Dalit politicians attempted to secure action from international business groups and the World Bank that would provide reserved jobs for Dalits in foreign funded development projects, and foreign business investments.

Rural Dalits face many of the problems as other poor, rural Indians. Dalits in poor communities may be the target of the frustration and fear of non-Dalits. These individuals, often desperately poor themselves, may target Dalits who are seen as living 'above their station'-either through economic prosperity, or by acting without regard for traditional caste restrictions on behaviour and relationships.

CONCEPT OF DALIT : ORIGIN AND DEFINITION

The concept is believed to be originated in the 1930s in journalistic writings according to Michael, and as a Hindi and Marathi translation of 'Depressed Castes', the term the British used according to Webster. The term, however, was chosen, according to Zelliot, by the group itself and is used proudly. In her view, 'Dalits' implies those who have been broken, ground down by those above them in a deliberate and active way. There is in the word itself an inherent denial of pollution, karma and justified caste hierarchy. However, according to Massey, 'dalit' more as a concept and in its present use has its seed in the writings of two great Indian personalities, Phule and Ambedkar. He believes that Phule in his writings used the title Shudra-Ati-Shudra for Dalits and he knew it was a Brahmin conspiracy against Shudra-Ati-Shudra (both being Indigenous people) to divide them into two castes or classes in order to make them their slaves. Similarly, he says that for the 'Dalit', Ambedkar used the title 'untouchable' (achuta) in his writings. Guru also explains that the category dalit was first used by Ambedkar himself in his fortnightly Bahishkruit Bharat. He (Ambedkar) defined it comprehensively: Dalithood is a kind of life condition which characterises the exploitation, suppression and marginalisation of dalits by the social, economic, cultural and political domination of the upper caste brahminical order. But Massey makes one point clear that is many Dalits today prefer to be called Dalits (name self-given) as it is not merely a name or title but has become an expression of hope for them in recovering their past self-identity. Shah however argues that with the change in market structure in the post-independence and the rise in education among small sections of Harijans, small entrepreneurs and a white-collar middle class have emerged among the Scheduled Castes. These have become militant and call the Scheduled Castes the 'Dalits' that is a poor and exploited class.

Oommen, on the other hand, argues that the Dalits suffer from cumulative domination (socio-cultural, economic and political) and multiple deprivation. He has however excluded the section of the 'Harijan bourgeoisie' among the SCs from this category since they are economically well-off and politically privileged (even though not entirely emancipated from socio-cultural oppression). Thus, in his view, only those Scheduled Castes who have low ritual status, appalling poverty and powerlessness fit into the definition of Dalits.

Contradiction, Multiple Terms and Heterogeneity

According to Guru, the term 'dalit' is not accepted by all those who belong to this category. It has faced criticism, particularly by the urban, educated middle class dalits, as socially regressive, derogatory and hence undesirable. Thus, they look at the term with disdain. Guru also states that a small section of neo-Buddhists rejects the concept of dalit which includes all the oppressed classes and prefers to be called Buddhists and tries to restrict it to those who suffer from untouchability and other social handicaps. Some even prefer to confine the term Dalit only to Ambedkarite Buddhists, but for many others, Dalit is not necessarily only Buddhist but also all socially oppressed persons in general and untouchables in particular.

There is also a section of the community, according to Guru, who prefer bahujan over both the Buddhist as well as dalit categories. However, the problem with such a formulation is that it neglects the dialectical relationship between 'dalit' and 'bahujan' which has a bearing on the formation of the dalit category and its marriage with bahujan. Similarly, speaking on the notion of harijan vis-à-vis dalit, Guru argues that the category harijan is artificially imposed on the untouchables and is an ascribed one as it does not flow from the untouchables' own experiences. Given its divine association, it is inadequate for capturing the specific realities since it also replaces the need for internal critique. On the other hand, the category dalit derives its epistemic and political strength from the material social experience of the community which renders it authentic and dynamic rather than passive and rigid. Ambedkar also said that even though Gandhiji wanted assimilation of the untouchables with the mainstream, he made it impossible by his euphemism, Harijan. In his own words, '... such assimilation was not possible from the new name, Harijan given to the untouchables... his new name counteracted assimilation and made it impossible'. However, in Sharma's view, historically dalits imply not a structure, but a processual phenomenon emanating from a politico-legal entity known as 'Scheduled Castes' and the latter being an outcome of the preceding moral-political entity which Gandhiji referred as Harijan. What I believe is that the concept of 'Harijan' has to be seen in its proper historical context.

In the context of various dehumanizing terms such as Achhuta, Dhedh, Chandal being used for the Dalits, Gandhiji's euphemism did provide some respectability even though only in name. What is important to understand is the evolutionary framework and the specific context and time in which 'Harijan' appeared. Today almost all conscious and educated Dalits are scornful of this notion and reject it out rightly. So, now it is imperative to discard this notion in the context of contemporary discussion on dalit issues though it will be unavoidable in the context of a historical account of such issues. However, Dalits in general do not have any problem with the constitutional concept of SCs. They are relatively comfortable with it even though the notion, they believe, reminds themselves and others about who they really are and where their social space is.

However, it must be borne in mind that the category 'Dalit' is not a homogeneous category. It involves a number of castes. According to Shah, they have internal hierarchy. Neo-Buddhist Mahars look down upon with contempt on the other Scheduled Castes who have not converted to Buddhism. There is also conflict between the Mahars and the Mangs. In this connection, Michael Moffatt argues that the cultural system of Indian untouchables does not distinctively question or revalue the dominant social order. Rather it continuously recreates among untouchables a microcosm of the larger system. Even Ambedkar realized that 'graded inequality' within the untouchables was a hurdle in their emancipation from their controls of the caste Hindus. Similarly Shah argues that there are middle class Dalits and the poor Dalits whose problems and interests are of different kinds. While for the former, the problem of identity and reservation is important, the latter is grappled with the problem of poverty and exploitation.

Webster's Critical Analysis

Webster's critical analysis of two of the prevailing ways to define 'Dalits'-class analysis and communal analysis-holds much significance here to simplify the understanding of the concept. Those using a class analysis of Indian society subsume Dalits within such class or occupational categories as peasants, agricultural labour, factory workers, students and the like. This can be seen in most Marxist historical writings, the sub-altern studies volumes and to a lesser degree, in the Dalit Panther Manifesto. In fact, the concept was made popular by the Dalit Panthers in the 1970s. This class analysis is fraught with serious problems, according to Webster, since it not only fails to take account of the basic contradiction and oppression of the Dalits but also hides these by using categories which diverts attention away from them. By their own admission, Webster argues, Ambedkar as well as Jagjivan Ram indicated the existence of such contradictions.

Similarly, those using a communal analysis of caste tend to view only those untouchables as Dalits who remain Hindus by religion. If they convert to another religion, then they cease to be Dalits. Webster argues that this view is at serious odds with the realities uncovered by studies of castes among Christians and Muslims. Thus, he says that at least for Dalits, the stigma of untouchability and its accompanying disabilities based on caste are an Indian rather than Hindu phenomenon. And '... these were and still are the defining characteristics of a Dalit even if a Dalit moves up in a social class or changes religion.

CONCLUDING STATEMENT

It becomes clear that despite various interpretations, there is agreement that the 'Scheduled Castes' is an important component in the construction of the dalit category. And as is the common knowledge, other caste people or categories also face certain disabilities in the society but they have never experienced the totality of disabilities, more prominently caste disability like the Scheduled Castes. There is also dialectical relationship between the Dalits and other castes. All achievements: economic, political, educational howsoever gargantuan will stand dwarfed in the face of caste disabilities. A Dalit who is educationally qualified, economically well-off and politically privileged may get a better treatment than his caste brethren who have not got any secular achievements (Education, Wealth, Power etc.) like him but he is not completely free from socio-cultural indignities which Oommen has also admitted. So, though Oommen has excluded the 'Harijan bourgeoisie' among the Scheduled Castes from the dalit category, I am however inclined to view the category 'Dalits' as an inclusive one comprising all the caste people who suffer from caste ignominies irrespective of the fact that some of them are upward in secular fields. What I try to impress here is that caste disability is central to the construction of the notion of 'Dalits'; other factors do play a role but they are not central.

The communal view of defining 'Dalit' as a Hindu phenomenon has been critiqued by Webster. Though it is true that the Dalits even after conversion suffer from the same caste disabilities but theoretically religions like Islam or Christianity are egalitarian and there is no room for caste discrimination even though in practice, revealed from many studies, it is found to be there. Would the religions like Christianity or Islam admit to the existence and practice of caste-based disability in their religions? They could not as it would normatively negate the egalitarian character of these religions. So, on the one hand, there is absence of a formal acknowledgement of such an evil practice, on the other hand, there is indeed such a practice prevailing in reality. The contradiction notwithstanding, the Constitution also confines caste disability to being a Hindu phenomenon. Reservation is also given on this basis. So, for the purpose of the present discussion, we can restrict the notion of Dalit in its scope to include all those who are scheduled in the Constitution and are eligible for reservation even though Dalit Sociology is the perfect sub-field to generate a thorough discussion and debate on this issue. There is indeed a necessity for this as even though the caste system with institutionalized iniquitous social structure is a product of Hindu society (most sociologists believe so), over the years, it has been able to penetrate many other religions in India. Ambedkar had also admitted this. Recently, even the Supreme Court – the custodian and the interpreter of the Constitution – has admitted a petition relating to the issue of Dalit Christians being considered for reservation benefit. So this issue being a complex issue, I believe, it is in the fitness of things that a meaningful debate takes place.

EVOLVING NECESSITY OF INDIAN SOCIETY

Having made an effort (of course, not exhaustive) to demystify the notion of Dalit, it is, however, necessary to talk about Dalit Sociology now. We have already sub-fields like Political Sociology, Industrial Sociology, Rural Sociology, Urban Sociology, Sociology of Education, Sociology of Knowledge, Sociology of Agriculture, Sociology of Development, Sociology of Science, Sociology of Religion, Historical Sociology, Medical Sociology, Gender Sociology etc. to name a few. So another new accretion to the already existing sub-fields should not be a problem at all. In the course of evolution and growth of Sociology, many new sub-fields have come up keeping pace with the changing time and evolving necessity of a period and society. Dalit Sociology is the evolving necessity of today's Indian society. A distinct and wholly dedicated full-fledged sub-field can do justice to the myriad issues related to Dalits. It can also convey a substantive and symbolic meaning to the otherwise marginalized sections of the Indian society that Dalits and dalit issues are not only being tolerated but also being accepted. Substantive because issues of substance, concern, importance and meaning to the Dalits can be deliberated, debated, and disseminated. Symbolic because it will make Dalits aware of the fact (a sense of acceptance) that their issues are being represented as relevant issues.

Upper Caste Bias of (Higher) Education

Now the question that arises is why there is suddenly a necessity for Dalit Sociology. Interestingly, the necessity was always there, it is only being articulated in recent times. Sociology in Indian context has studied many issues including dalit issues, but, as many dalit intellectuals believe, the legitimate/due representation has always been lacking. It is because there were very less number of Dalits coming to higher education leave alone the issue of showing any interest in dalit issues. Except a few, non-dalit intellectuals did not have much fascination for such issues. So, besides a minor representation here or there, dalit issues have never been the dominant themes in sociological discourse. In fact, as Dalits complain, the values and ideals imparted in school, college and university curricula only represent upper caste values and have squarely ignored the dalit cultures and values. Thus, education in general and higher education in particular, instead of respecting the history and culture of different communities, has, in their considered opinion, become the promoter of higher caste values alone. As Ambrose Pinto argues, most stories, anecdotes and examples in our textbooks and syllabus are from the dominant culture... There is no place for dalit history, geography, medicine, anthropology and culture in the curriculum. Making similar observation Illaiah argues that the Dalit-bahujans find that their culture, life-style, production-based skill etc. are not part of the history. It is as if they never had a history. The literary texts are full of condemnation of their culture and are brazenly silent about caste inhumanity. They were never told that Phule, Ambedkar were as competent as Gandhi and Nehru were. They were always told only about Gandhi, Nehru, Subhash Bose and so on, people they could never relate to, people whose upbringing had nothing to do with their upbringing. Similarly, the nationalist movement was presented as a Brahmin-Bania fight against colonial power and the role played by the Dalit-bahujans was never mentioned, according to Illaiah.

A Historical Fact and Emerging Changes

It is, however, not surprising that dalit issues have not been given the due they deserve. It has always happened in history that who wields power dictates terms. Dalits were always made to live in a condition of subjugation, marginalization and dehumanization in the society. They were not allowed education, dignity and self-respect. So, powerless as they were, they could not possibly have strived for the propagation of dalit values and ideals. Even today, to a great extent, the condition of Dalits has not significantly changed. Many continue to experience ignominies, indignities and inhumanities, but things are not exactly the same today. Education has penetrated and awareness has built up. A few have come up economically, politically and educationally whom we can say middle-class Dalits. Dalit intellectuals are an important component of middle-class Dalits. It is these sections who are really spearheading the movement for a legitimate place for dalit issues in the academic discourse. The presence of Dalits both as students and teachers in the academic field has necessitated a re-look at the contents of knowledge being imparted. No wonder, there is, therefore, a clamour for correcting imbalances in the projection/non-projection of reality, especially with regard to dalit issues.

Dalit intellectuals themselves are engaged in extensive research into exploring their own past, unravelling their own history, genealogies etc. Since 'Dalits' is not a homogeneous category, different sections within it must have different genealogies and histories. They can contribute rich ethnographic data for sociological understanding.

Apart from the history of exploitation, discrimination and humiliation, they can also explore the saga of resistance, triumph, entrepreneurial trait and ability, other achievements and successes. There are quite a number of educated Dalits who are bringing out autobiographies and biographies which are also a source of rich sociological contents. Dalit Sahitya (literature) is another development which provides an opportunity for generating consciousness through writings, poems and poetries. Non-dalit scholars have also shown flexibility and shunned intellectual apartheid to take up dalit issue related researches. So, now nobody can say that there is dearth of literature on dalit issues to impact upon academic discourse, even though, there is still the need for a relentless effort to undertake more of such researches in an expeditious manner.

So, today, at the attitude level as well as at the literature level, the educational arenas/centres of learning are better suited to take up a study of dalit issues in its entirety along with the clamouring for the same by the dalit intellectuals. Dalits being an integral part of Indian society, their issues need to be an integral part of educational discourse. So, the need for Dalit Sociology can not be overemphasized.

Developing a Perspective from Below

Many dalit scholars have strived to make people look at the society and the world from an otherwise neglected/different/other/counter perspective, which has been variously called the perspective from below/the sub-altern perspective. Dalit Sociology can help shape and sharpen such a perspective by giving enough scope for it to find a place in academic discourse where dissemination can lead to debate and debate can lead to the development of sensitivity and refinement of attitude, outlook and perspective. It can prepare the ground for understanding the history of suffering of marginalized groups and from this standpoint, critique the dominant viewpoint. In fact, Ambedkarism is such a perspective, which inspires Dalits in their struggle for self-respect and assertion, and, at the same time, talks about a society where social justice is the main goal, and where everybody can live with his/her head held high. It can be a very important ideology in Dalit Sociology. Apart form this, there are other important ideologues like Phule, Periyar whose ideas inform a dalit's mind and inspire him/her in the struggle for emancipation.

Incorporation of 'Diversity' in Curriculum

Dalit Sociology can bring to the fore that Dalits are such individuals in society who always have to adjust. This is, in fact, not only true of Dalits, tribals etc. in India but also true of all underprivileged or disadvantaged anywhere in the world. They are the ones who have always to adjust/'fit-in', the institutions (educational) or others (people) do not adjust to them. The cultural difference: one at home/their own community, the other in society in general/educational centres in particular, very often results in the development of inferiority complex in them contributing sometimes to their underperformance, which is construed as student deficit.

This may not be true always because the potential is constrained at the outset by the prevailing social structure in society in general and educational centres in particular that do not leave any scope for it to unfold. Dalit students can recount many such experiences of subjugation or marginalization, which can help see things in perspective and this can enrich Dalit Sociology. It is important to mention that education and more particularly higher education must orientate towards the 'diversity project', which can include changes necessary to truly educate a diverse population of students for the society in which we live, and the changes may be incorporated in various aspects, most notably, in the curriculum and pedagogy, and teaching styles. The incorporation of diversity in the curriculum through Dalit Sociology can affect students' attitudes, knowledge and outlook and, at the same time, can demonstrate to students of so-called lower castes that the educational institution is working on change.

This, however, can help in unlearning and relearning much of what has been known. According to Morgan etal, a revealing work by Lopez using Michigan data in a longitudinal study of the impact of inter-group contact and coursework dealing with racial/ethnic changes in student attitudes, found that coursework had the most significant positive impact on attitudes toward educational equity. This finding is consistent with other evidence that coursework influences not only attitudes but knowledge, skills and cognitive development.

Astin, for example, in one of the studies found that 'students responded positively to diverse faculty, as well as to what they taught (multicultural courses or courses with multicultural issues imbedded in them). Students also noted positive cognitive and affective development if they participated in diversity activities: (1) taking a women's studies or ethnic studies course; (2) taking a world cultures course; (3) participating in racial and cultural awareness workshops; (4) discussing racial or ethnic issues; or (5) socializing with someone from another ethnic group'. In addition to the above, according to Astin, students also reported increased commitment to promoting racial understanding.

Astin sums it up this way: "[T]here are many developmental benefits that accrue to students when institutions support an emphasis on multiculturalism and cultural diversity". In fact, it is important that institutions committed to educating all students for a complex multicultural society should create curriculum that recognizes and engages diversity.

Through the contents of Dalit Sociology, the difference between 'the equality of opportunity of access' and 'the equality of opportunity of success' can also be highlighted as it is important that the two should not be confused. While the emphasis should be initially on the former, the latter should always be the final goal. So, the effort should be to create more equality in society. And Dalit Sociology has an important role to play in this.

Process of De-peripheralisation

We know that books by Dalits are rarely discussed. It is not that they are not discussed at all. But they are very rarely discussed. Dalit Sociology can provide a meaningful platform for surfacing of de-centered knowledges or to use Foucault's terminology, 'an insurrection of subjugated knowledges'. Through this, the process of de-peripheralisation can be said to, at least, begin. It is important that the excluded and silenced get an opportunity to make their points of view heard as, according to Anne Seller, the excluded and the silenced have a privileged vision, because they can tell that the silencing is working. This can help build an inclusive knowledge as the perspective from the below is incorporated in the knowledge pool. In fact, this is also compatible with the pluralistic stand of postmodernism. According to Seller, as Harvey expresses it: 'The idea that all groups have a right to speak for themselves and have that voice accepted as authentic and legitimate is essential to the pluralistic stand of postmodernism'. Postmodernism is, in fact, concerned with the validity and dignity of 'the other' and it has a commitment to the oppressed, says Seller. It must be mentioned here that Dalit Sociology is not an endeavour to produce value-free knowledge. In fact, as Seller argues, 'there is no such thing as a value-free education, we cannot produce and disseminate value-free knowledge'. As the knowledge of a particular group, it issues from a particular perspective, says Seller.

Women's Studies and Inclusive Education

According to Robert Engvall, questions have arisen more frequently in recent years over the treatment of diverse human experiences in the curricula of our institutions of higher education. He further says in the context of women's studies that cultural pluralism and increased awareness of the value of human diversity have heightened curricula response to the needs and wants of those seeking greater inclusion within the higher education sphere. The concept behind the invention of women's studies was the perceived need to overcome some of that bias and to bring to light previously omitted histories, literature, and ideas. He also holds that increased democratization has allowed former outsiders to openly question the role that bias has played in higher education and more fully explore the intersection of gender and race with other identities. What he says of women's studies and race holds true in case of Dalits in India. Indian society is characterized by cultural pluralism and there is also increased democratization in the society. This has resulted in the demand for inclusion of diverse human/cultural experiences in the curriculum. In fact, inclusive education (in the sense of including dalit issues) is integral to a democratic society. Explaining the meaning of inclusive education, Barton says: 'Inclusive education is not merely about providing access into mainstream school for pupils who have previously been excluded. It is not about closing down an unacceptable system of segregated provision and dumping those pupils in an unchanged mainstream system. Existing school systems in terms of physical factors, curriculum aspects, teaching expectations and styles, leadership roles, will have to change. This is because inclusive education is about the participation of all children and young people and the removal of all forms of exclusionary practice'.

Afro-American Studies: A Precedent

In the context of making a case for Dalit Sociology, it is worth mentioning Nellie Y. McKay here who says how Blacks struggled in the 1960s and 1970s to include their life/cultural experiences in the American educational system. According to McKay, 'In launching efforts to integrate the white mainstream academy in the 1960s and 1970s, black students and faculty, as "others," were violently opposed to the system that denied their human and intellectual worth. They determined to change the demography of the institution with their presence and to alter the premises of previously perceived knowledge to take cognizance of their racial and cultural experiences. Predictably, the system responded by resisting changes to its long-held authority. But the outsiders fought well, and when the dust settled, around the middle of the 1970s, Afro-American Studies, as a field of inquiry, had taken firm hold in white colleges and universities across the country.... They became the vanguard, and their successes paved the way for Women's Studies and other Ethnic Studies Programs that followed in the closing years of the 1970s. By then, too, the first group of black students and faculty on the front lines of the action, and the whites who had supported them in their struggle, had absorbed the worst of the system's resistance to change. It was time to look toward building a unified intellectual structure that was not a closed system of knowledge controlled by a privileged group of knowers'. From the above, it is clear how the Blacks had to struggle to include their cultural/racial experiences in the academic milieu, and how their struggle paved the way for other marginalized sections to press for the inclusion of their cultural/racial/gender experiences in the curricula. Similarly, the Dalits in India had to struggle hard to get self-respect, which was historically denied to them. And the struggle is still on. Society is yet to fully become sensitive to dalit rights, but it is, undoubtedly, in the process of purging itself of its traditional/discriminatory character. In such a context, I believe, unlike black issues, it may not be that difficult for dalit issues to be incorporated in the teaching-learning process in India. But, there is the necessity for continued pressure: intellectual, social and political. Dalit issues are indeed relevant social issues for sociological understanding. They can be legitimately seen as forms of knowledge because they have their own way of conceptualizing and making sense of reality, approaching a problem, and ascertaining truth. In fact, dalit issues can broaden epistemological base. And this fact cannot be lost sight of for a long period.

Moral and Sensitive Society

While 'knowledge is power', true knowledge is wisdom. And it should be everyone's effort to build a wise, moral and sensitive society. It may not be untenable to say that Dalit Sociology can help build a more wise, moral and sensitive society. While society will be immensely assisted in its effort to be able to groom sensitive, wise, responsible, moral individuals, Sociology is also likely to gain immensely because Dalit Sociology will be an important contribution to the pool of knowledge. It is important, however, that more and more non-dalit scholars should come forward to work on dalit issues. It is equally important that Dalits extend whole-hearted cooperation to such scholars without being obsessed with the idea of suspecting their intentions. True, it may sometimes happen that some non-dalit scholars may be selective in their portrayal of the dalit situation, but to criticize and discourage only on the basis of selectivity will be antithetical to the final goal of generating an attitudinal change and sustaining it over time. The debate regarding an insider's subjectivity and an outsider's selectivity is quite old. The change needs to be welcomed without, of course, sacrificing the motivation for constructive criticisms, since they are the necessary ingredients for the growth of knowledge. Another thing which needs to be emphasized is that Dalits themselves and scholars sensitive to dalit issues must find a place in different academic bodies which decide curricula and syllabi in order for dalit issues to find their due place. It is important to mention that Dalit Sociology becomes a compulsory rather than an optional subject in Sociology as a part of higher education programme. It is equally important that other social sciences also have dalit studies as part of their course structure.

IMPACT OF THE REFORMS ON DALITS

The social disadvantage suffered by dalits in India was taken note of in the Constitution of India which was drafted under the chairmanship of Dr. Ambedkar-a person who had spearheaded the most momentous anti-caste movement of the depressed classes. It provided dalits with many safeguards, viz., 1. social, educational, cultural and religious safeguards, 2. economic safeguards, 3. political safeguards and 4. safeguards for employment. The free market ethos of the Reforms, conceptually can neither confirm to the democratic spirit of the Indian Constitution of 'one vote, one value', nor can it coexist with the system of positive discrimination embodied in these safeguards. For, the market grants moneyed person more value, and overtly believes in the jungle law of 'might is right'. To a large extent, the primary motivation behind these Constitutional provisions was liberal democratic aspirations that characterised the freedom movement. However, these aspirations and the initial ideological zeal of the founding fathers withered away in no time and what survived was its utilitarian dimension for the electoral politics. The sorry state of the executive compliance with these Constitutional provisions amply bears out the fangs of the Indian society. The Reforms will bring a kind of legitimacy to this attitudinal resistance. These safeguards will stand eroded as the Reforms gain in momentum. Influence of the Reforms is bound to be all pervasive. However, only a few issues of importance to the dalit masses have been picked up for discussion here.

Financial Assistance in Education Institutions

Reservation in the educational institutions and the financial assistance in the form of scholarships and freeships constitutes perhaps the most important factor in the development scheme for dalits. For, it is primarily responsible to make the basic input of education available to them. Without education, all the constitutional safeguards including the reservation in services would be infructuous. Under this scheme the dalit students whose parental income is below a specified level, get freeship, reservation in admissions to all the colleges getting grants-in-aid from the government, and scholarships. Without this assistance, even today, it would be difficult for dalits to send their children to school. The Reforms have already resulted in freezing the grants to many institutions and in stagnating, if not lowering, the expenditure on education.

The free market ethos has entered the educational sphere in a big way. Commercialisation of education is no more a mere rhetoric, it is now the established fact. Commercial institutions offering specialised education signifying the essential input from utilitarian view point, have come up in a big way from cities to small towns. Their product-prices are not only based on the demand-supply consideration in their market segment but also are manipulated by their promotional strategies. In a true spirit of globalisation, many foreign universities, are invading the educational spheres through hitherto unfamiliar strategic alliances with non-descript commercial agencies, of course at a hefty dollar equivalent prices. Many elite institutions like IIMs, IITs, suddenly facing fund crunch had to raise their fee structure and other prices many fold. They were already beyond the reach of dalits. When they eventually turn self-financing, their prices would be benchmarked against their international counterparts, which any way would be affordable to the same top market segment that constitutes the focus of all the Reform-talk. As the job markets become acutely competitive, owing to a sharp decline in job opportunities, the polarisation between the elite and commoner would also sharpen. Various kinds of price barriers would be erected to thwart the entry of downtrodden. Even the sphere of primary education the coverage of which has been so miserably inadequate as to leave out multitude of children in villages as illiterate, could not remain unaffected, notwithstanding its already existing divide between the vernacular and English schools.

Corporatisation has entered this arena, transforming the education into an enterprise for profits. The quality of input these expensive schools will provide will benchmark the products in the contracting job markets. Even today, because of preponderance of the English language in business circles, the divide between village and towns is almost complete in the field of education. It is so difficult for a village student, educated in vernacular medium to compete with his convent educated (now an understatement!) counterpart in cities and towns. If this is the situation of general village population, the plight of dalits who besides being the poorest of the village population carry additional Bretton Wood of social discrimination, is indeed a worrisome matter. Despite several kinds of State assistance, dalits are plagued with alarming rate of school drop-outs. This may be explained out as much by the need for dalit children to supplement their meagre family incomes for meeting the two ends as also the erosion of their faith that education could be the instrument to change the pathetic course of their lives. This sense of alienation is going to grow with the progress of the Reforms.

Reservations in Services

Whatever may be the other costs, the government policy of reservations in employment sphere has undoubtedly played an important role for dalits. The policy broadly envisages representation of dalits in proportion to their population in all the public services which includes the government, public sector, autonomous bodies and institutions receiving grant-in-aid from the government. A cursory glance at the figures of this representation is enough to get a pathetic state of implementation. Howsoever, unsatisfactory the results of the implementation may be, the importance of reservations from the dalit viewpoint cannot be overemphasised.

As could be evidenced by the organised private sector, where it would be difficult to find a dalit employee (save of course in scavenging and lowliest jobs), without reservations dalits would have been totally doomed. The importance of reservations thus could only be assessed in relation to situations where they do not exist. Whatever be their defects and deficiencies, they have given certain economic means of livelihood and some social prestige to the sons and daughters of over 1.5 million landless labourers. Whether they get real power or not, over 50,000 dalits could enter the sphere of bureaucratic authority with the help of reservations. Besides these tangible benefits promised by the policy, it has instilled a hope in dalit community. This hope predominantly manifests in the form of spread of education among them. Their emotional bond with the nation and its Constitution despite heaps of injustice and ignominy they bear every moment of their life may also be significantly attributable to the Reservation Policy. The winds of privatisation under the Economic Reforms have already shaken the very foundations of the Reservations.

The Reforms clearly envisage the minimalist government. Wherever the Reforms patterned on the Structural Adjustment Programme of the World Bank were carried out, denationalisation of the public sector and privatisation have come in a big way. Being the late starter, India has not reached the scales achieved by others, say, the Latin American countries. However, the start has not been any unimpressive. Almost all sectors of economy stand opened up for private investment. The disinvestment in existing public sector companies has already been allowed upto 49 per cent by the policy. The public stake being more than 50 per cent, the public sector as such is not yet dismantled in policy. It continues to be the State, as before, and hence attracts application of the reservation policy. However, the Reform package has already endangered, if not abolished, the reservations through back doors. In the name of preparing the PSUs for global free market regime, the PSUs are being allowed/encouraged to have strategic alliances with private companies from India and abroad.

As such, over the last five years, many profit making PSUs have formed the joint venture companies (JVC). These JVCs are strategically structured as not to fall in the ambit of the PSU-framework. The typical equity stake for the PSU and private could be 49:51. There appears to be a great deal of receptivity for this scheme in the government circles. There are no policy barriers on the business to be pursued by these JVCs. Theoretically, an existing PSU can hive off its business divisions into private JVCs and transform itself into a financial holding company with a skeleton staff. Even if technically it remains a PSU, and assuming that it followed the reservation policy sincerely, it would have little scope to absorb dalits in its staff. Whatever may be the strategic considerations, the fall out of this process practically amounted to shutting the doors of these new age companies to dalits and to potential neutralisation of the reservation policy. The policy of limited disinvestment of PSUs not being in conformity with the spirit of the Reforms, is bound to be relaxed in favour of privatisation any time.

But still, all the PSUs may not get privatised at once. The better ones would be gobbled up by the bigger sharks. The worst ones may be closed down or distress-sold. And the middle ones may for quite some time, continue to be the relic of their past. Whatever the scenario, the residual structures of the 'reformed' PSUs are never going to be the same, as far as dalits are concerned. The ethos of privatisation and the excuse of competition, superimposed on the traditional caste prejudice, will never allow reservations to happen, any more. Other public services are also bound to slip out of the reservation policy. Most of the sectors, which were the traditional domain of the government investment, have already been released for the private investment.

Atrocities and Socio-Cultural Suppression

The caste atrocities are an integral feature of dalit life. The government machinery keeps on collecting their statistics year after year and issues it in a report of its Commissioner for SCs and STs (now the National Commission for SCs and STs). There are at least three Articles (15,17 and 23) in the

Constitution of India which seek to mitigate the evil. To give effect to these Constitutional provisions the following acts also have been in operation:

1. The Untouchability (Offences) Act, 1955, later amended and re-titled as the Protection of Civil Rights Act, 1955
2. The Scheduled Castes and Scheduled Tribes (Prevention of Atrocities Act) 1989 and The Bonded Labour System (Abolition) Act, 1976

Despite this, the statistics of the registered atrocities read like a balance sheet of a blue chip company with consistent rise every successive year. It is pertinent to remember that owing to the dependency relationship of dalits with the perpetrators of atrocities, not every occurrence of the atrocity gets registered. Rather, it can be safely assumed that behind each registered atrocity over ten atrocity cases go unreported. As per the latest statistics, every day nearly 50 cases of atrocities are registered all over the country. Over three dalit women are raped and six are disabled on each day round the year. The National Commission analysed the causes of each of the atrocities in a sample of 45 cases. The analysis shows that out of 45 cases 13 are clearly attributable to the economic reasons. The balance can also be explained out by some kind of weakness of dalits. Coupled with the weakness of dalits, their growing assertiveness and refusal to submit to the casteist dictates of the village lords, rebellion ethos assimilated through the Ambedkarian struggle and process of general awareness, also cause atrocities to increase.

The atrocities occur where the dependency relationships are more pronounced and bear economic implications. Villages, where dalits as landless labourers depend upon landlords or rich farmers for their livelihood and where the traditional caste equations have a potential to yield economic surplus to the latter, provide ideal setting for atrocities. What impact would the new regime have on the socio-economic setting of Indian villages? In face of it, the unbridled capitalism inherent in the Reforms is not compatible with any feudal structure. But this thumb rule does not seem to be entirely validated by the developmental experience in India. The capitalism in India did not have to sprout through the bedrock of contradictions of feudalism as in Europe. It was planted in the fertile soil of

Indian feudalism. It has grown here on its nutrients. Thus it would be too mechanical to have a theoremic expectation about the demise of feudalism and thence the end of the caste through the growth of capitalism. The caste institution moreover, has defied the classical mould of feudalism by possessing many unique features. The most important being its resilience and adaptability. What we experience in the mysterious growth of casteist politics today in India is precisely this ability of caste to adapt to changing times. The annihilation of caste is only possible through economic empowerment of dalit masses and waging an uncompromising and concerted struggle against its non--economic manifestations.

Can the new regime afford these economic empowerment of dalits? Can it, for instance, grant them land? Does it have the wherewithal or motivation to catalyse their struggles against the caste system? The answer to all these questions will be in negative. Instead of talking of land reforms, the new regime will promote depeasantisation of Indian agriculture and consolidation of their holdings to start corporate farming. Barring perhaps the example of East Asian countries, the Bretton Wood institutions sponsored reforms have always aggravated the economic inequality everywhere. The experience of other countries where similar Reforms were brought in, bears testimony to the fact that with increasing inequality the social tensions also increased as a result of the Reforms.

The capital influx in the rural areas will have natural ally in the rich farmers who have hegemonic hold over their areas. These sections, will be the main beneficiaries of the improved terms of trade and capitalist development in the rural areas. All the dalits would be thrown into the job market along with many non-dalit marginal to middle farmers. The vast army of unemployed thus created by this developmental dynamics will need appropriate instruments for being controlled. The history bears ample testimony to the fact that whenever the people tended to come together with a common identity, the ruling classes have deftly used the time-tested weapon of castes to divide them. Unlike elsewhere, the Reforms thus are likely to enliven and rejuvenate the archaic value system.

The economic reforms in the mould of macro-economic stabilisation and structural adjustment programme of IMF and World Bank have essentially a pro-rich bias. Wherever they were implemented, they have worsened the situation of the masses of poor people in absolute as well as relative terms. Some contrary data to this general observation (say, of the east Asian countries) are rather attributed to the departures from the standard blueprint given by the Bretton Wood institutions. The dalits in India, being the poorest of the poor have been hit the hardest. Their social disabilities, largely reinforced by and sustained on the economic deprivations, are bound to get accentuated with these policies. The Indian reforms were essentially 'crisis driven' and not 'strategy driven' when they were adopted. There have since been changes in the formation and key persona. The new government for instance has imparted them a form of 'strategy' through their Common Minimum Programme. However, there has not yet been any evidence of this strategy being any different from the course followed by the previous government. The complete discourse of Reforms appears to be either grossly off the mark of Indian reality or to assume out its momentous features. The broad Indian reality is that India has too many poor. As per the Human Development Report, 1996, there are 229 million income poor but more than twice as many, 554 million are capability poor. In terms of capability poverty, its 61.5 % population is poor. Its rank according to descending poverty among the 174 countries of the world, is 135. Even today India is predominantly an agrarian economy, with over 70 per cent of its population living in villages. No statistics moreover can adequately capture the heinous socio-cultural inequality that is an abiding part of Indian reality. It has acute inequalities not only in economic terms but in the socio-cultural terms.

The free market oriented reforms ought to take this grave Indian reality into consideration. Unless there is a wide spread purchasing power in the economy the market can never be free and sustainable. The reform strategy thus should embody sustainable economic empowerment of rural masses; investments to enhance their capability and effective measures for accelerated development of the disadvantaged sections like dalits. The pre-requisite to reforms therefore could be the radical land reforms, massive investments in rural areas into agriculture-related infrastructural projects, universalisation of primary education, primary health care system and reinforcement of positive discrimination in favour of dalits. The devil of casteism could be tamed only by freeing general masses of people from the anxieties and uncertainties about basic survival. The general condition of deprivation has rendered them vulnerable to be the preys to the frequent machinations of the vested interests that make them see the enemy within their own class. The relative equality thus can be the bedrock for launching the socio-cultural offensive in the form of mass-education programmes. But this all may still not be enough. The policy of positive discrimination in favour of dalits will have to be reinforced much more vigorously in all the sectors of economy, than ever before. They need to be reframed and simplified for effective implementation. Unlike the current provisions, this may be stopped once their representation comes on par with the general population. The specific reform package can be formulated in terms of the conditions existing then.

There arises a question of capital. Where will the capital for the investment in basic reforms come from? Not an easy question to answer, indeed. But some pointers may not be impertinent. It is acknowledged since number of years that India has a parallel economy in black money. The recent spate of scams is a mere corroboration of this hypothesis. The Reforms appear to have given them a boost. Whatever little that has surfaced can be likened to a tip of iceberg. Some five years ago, an unofficial estimate by the World Bank had put the unaccounted money of Indians kept in various tax havens at $ 100 billion. As per *Finance India*, (an article in the September 1995 issue) the range of capital outflows was from $ 1065 million to $ 370 million just in one single year-1993. Much of the $ 10 billion money in the non-resident account is said to be belonging to the resident Indians. The evidence of this kind abounds. As against this vast sum of our own money, what the government aims at out of the Reforms is the paltry sum of some four to five billion dollars of foreign direct investment a year to come in the country! The size of the money indicated above, that rightfully belongs to the people of the country, may be good enough for the task. But to unearth this treasure certainly requires a political will. India does not need capital as much as it does the political will to better its destiny.

THE SITUATION OF DALITS IN INDIA

Historically, the caste system classified people by their occupation and status. 'Each caste had a specific place in the hierarchy of social status'. Although in 'scriptural terms' social and economic status were supposed to be separate, the economic and social status of the various castes tended to coincide (Shah, 2006). However, since the 19th century, the link between caste and occupation has become less rigid as it became easier for people to change occupations. This change has accelerated with the economic boom which has taken place in India since the early 1990s. There has not, however, been a corresponding fluidity in caste, as intermarriage is very rare. Privileged sections of society tend to be from 'upper castes' while the disadvantaged sections come from the so-called 'lower castes'. Caste 'can be seen as the institution that has been structuring and maintaining for centuries relations of power among different communities, and seeks to legitimize these power relations through systematically dispensing mixes of economic and cultural assets/opportunities and deprivations to different communities.'

Many have commented on the robustness of the caste system, 'which has survived in the South Asian societies in one form or the other, despite the fundamental ideological and structural changes that have occurred through the spread of religions like Islam and Christianity as well as of model secular and egalitarian ideologues, all opposed to the very idea of hierarchy based on inherited statuses.'

For Dalits (the term meaning down-trodden or oppressed), at the bottom of this hierarchical system, it is their status as 'untouchables' which puts them at the heart of an insidious form of discrimination. This particular phenomenon results in the social unacceptability amongst people of other castes to touch the same food and utensils, draw water from the same source, or enter the same temples.

The specific structure and hierarchy related to castes is specific to various states and regions in India, with only the highest caste, the Brahmins, consistently faring better throughout the country. Not only are there differences in the names of the various castes, but the hierarchy between them may also be different between regions. However, castes who traditionally suffered discrimination based on untouchability, which was an element of the caste system throughout India, have been identified, enumerated and incorporated in the 'schedule' of the Constitution. 'The implicit criterion for inclusion in the Schedule Caste list is the social and religious disability suffered by a caste on account of untouchability, i.e. being at the pollution end of the social hierarchy.' In defining who would be included in the Schedules, the government originally used the 1931 census report, and to a large extent duplicated a list created in 1936.

Currently, the National Commissions for Scheduled Caste (SC) and Scheduled Tribe (ST) are vested with the responsibility of considering castes for inclusion or exclusion from the Schedule, which then needs to be ratified in Parliament. The discriminated communities are then officially designated as Scheduled Castes (SCs). Included in the SC category are communities from three different religions, Hinduism, Sikhism and Buddhism, all having within them communities traditionally suffering from untouchability. The term Dalit is the generally accepted term for the 'ex-untouchables', which corresponds to Scheduled Castes, which as mentioned above denotes the legal status as coined in the Constitution.

Mehrotra (2006) recognized that there has been political and social mobilization of SCs in India, particularly in certain poor states such as Uttar Pradesh (UP), which is one of the poorest states in India. However, this mobilization has failed to translate into positive change in the social sector for this excluded population. As Mehrotra wrote, 'while UP's mobilizers of the Dalits (SCs) have focused exclusively on capturing power, the gains to the lowest castes have been entirely of a symbolic nature.'

The Situation of Dalits in Nepal

As in India, the term Dalit is a politically coined word meaning 'the poor and the oppressed' and is less sensitive than the meaning of 'Harijan' or 'Acchhoot' or so-called 'untouchable'. The Nepal Legal Code of 1854, the Muluki Ain, formulated on the basis on Hindu Orthodoxy included five hierarchical categories. They are: i) Tagadhari (wearers of holy thread); ii) Non-enslavable alcohol drinkers (Namsinya matyali), iii)

Enslavable alcohol drinkers; iv) Impure but touchable (Pane nachalnya, chhoi chittto hlnu naparani); and v) Untouchable castes (pani nachalnya, choi chhito halnu parniya – caste from whom water is not acceptable and whose touch requires sprinkling of holy water).

It is believed that this caste hierarchy was influenced by political considerations and it was endorsed by state counsellors who were mostly from high castes. It is also accepted that the political ideology of Nepal as a Hindu state (which changed as of 2007 – Nepal has now been designated as a secular state) has remained highly exclusionary. Despite the legal provisions, caste-based discrimination continues to be practised.

Indeed, the Dalits themselves practise discrimination among their own group. Thus there are two kinds of 'untouchabilities': i) between upper caste and Dalits; and ii) within the Dalits. Dalit women and men suffer equally from the practice, but terai Dalits face more discrimination than those living in the hills. Unlike in India, Nepal has no single defined schedule of castes. Different Dalit organizations such as the Dalit Vikas Sammtte formed in 1997 and the National Dalit Commission have identified different groups as belonging to the Dalit caste. As the list fluctuates, the numbers of the Dalit population also vary according to different sources. Estimates range from 12% to over 20%.

Lack of national consensus on the Dalit population is one of the factors hindering a better understanding of the magnitude of disparity and discrimination faced by the Dalit community. The Dalit community in Nepal is also not homogenous. Dalits can be examined in three broad regional groups: i) dalits in the hill areas; ii) Dalits in the Newari community; and iii) Dalits in the terai areas. The practice of untouchability is more severe among the Madeshi community in the terai and in the hills of the Mid Western Region and Far Western Development regions of Nepal. Some Dalit groups fare better than others. For example, the literacy rate among the gaine (singers) is 49% and is higher than the national average. The lowest literacy rate is found among the Mushar community, who live in the terai. On most socio-economic indicators, Terai Dalits fare worse than hill Dalits.

The Phenomenon of Untouchability

In order to address the situation of Dalits, it is important to understand the phenomenon of 'untouchability'. The Hindu version of untouchability also has a racial basis as the impure status is based on birth and religion. Bhattachan *et al.* (2002) listed a total of 205 existing practices of caste based discrimination which can be grouped into nine categories. They are: i) denial of entry into houses, restaurants, temples; ii) inability to perform important religious service because wearing a sacred thread is not permitted, etc.; iii) access to common resources such as using water from tap or pond used by upper caste is denied; iv) denial of participation in public activities or entry into public places such as religious functions, government functions; v) forced labour or discriminatory practice of labour; vi) dominant behaviour towards Dalits such as Jadau system (practice of obeisance); vii) atrocities such as more rape cases among Dalit women than others; viii) social boycott – if a 'high caste hindu' member marries with a Dalit of either sex, he or she is banned from the society; ix) Attitudinal untouchability such as if one sees a kami (blacksmith) early in the morning it is considered inauspicious, or if there is a Dalit teacher then children of high caste groups will not attend the school.

Multiple, Overlapping Disparities and Discrimination

These affect Dalits in various spheres of life, including in education. Poverty In *Nepal*, Dalits are poorer than most other social groups. While the proportion of the population below the national poverty line is 31% nationally, 47% of Dalits live below the national poverty line. Eighty-six per cent of Dalit households have an income lower than the national average. Multiple regression analysis of Nepal Living Standards Survey (NLSS) II data also found: a) per capita consumption of Dalit households is about 46% lower than that of the Brahmin and Chettri (the highest Hindu caste groups); and b) the 'social penalty' for being a Dalit translates to Rs. 4,853 (or US$ 67) less per capita consumption.

Poorer families have less to spend on their children's education. Families in the poorest quintile spend NRs 416 per family on education compared with NRs 8,691 for the richest quintile. Most schools in Nepal rely on families to provide stationery, uniforms and many schools charge exam or registration fees. Child labour is prevalent among poor families, although employment of children under 14 years as labourers is prohibited by the Child Act 1991. NLSS II found that the proportion of children aged 5–14 who are working and not attending school is highest among the poor (21% in the poorest quintile) and decreases for the richer quintiles. The opportunity costs of schooling for poor families is significant. Many Dalit families also make a precarious livelihood, earning their income in the informal sector, through daily wage labour, often involving seasonal migration. This insecurity deters families from making longer term investments by educating their children. In *India*, scheduled caste (SC) children remain disadvantaged across many social indicators. Estimates from the 2000 National Sample Survey suggest that SC 'constituted 20 per cent of the rural population, but 38 per cent of the poor.'

Conflict

The internal conflict in *Nepal*, which expanded in scope and intensity from 1996, affected education and children in many ways, including accelerating the trend of migration (due either to security concerns or difficulties in maintaining livelihood). Family migration to urban centres may disrupt or end children's schooling for financial reasons, because of difficulties in finding places in crowded urban schools, particularly in the middle of a school year, or children not being able to keep up with the classes as the quality of teaching is poorer in rural areas. Lack of official documents, such as transfer or birth registration documents, can also present an obstacle when transferring to a new school. Migration of male family members may increase the work burden of the remaining members, particularly women, resulting in children being pulled out of school to take on their share of the burden. Children may also be sent away for fear of being arrested, tortured, abducted or recruited by the army, police or Maoist forces. The precise impact of the conflict on Dalit children and their schooling is unknown, but it would be safe to assume that they are more affected due to their lower socio-economic position in society. For example, a study by the Central Child Welfare Board and Save the Children Alliance found that one third of the 17,583 children found to be leaving Nepal for India during a three month period (July–October 2004) were Dalits. They were the largest group, followed by Chhetris and Brahmins, who together only constitute 33 per cent of the total population. Despite the progress towards peace in Nepal, issues still exist. Demonstrations by new groups continue to result in closure of schools, and previous dynamics at district level have not yet ceased entirely.

Gender

Since the Dalit society is also systematically integrated in the patriarchal mode of the Hindu caste system, in *Nepal*, the social and economic status of women is much lower than that of men. This is manifested in the lower health and nutritional status of Dalit women, as well as in the political representation of Dalit women, which is negligible. However, as compared with the high caste women, Dalit women have greater mobility. This is due to the economic need to go out and seek for employment and income for their families. Data on literacy rates show the gender disparity among Dalits. Whereas 44% of Dalit men are literate, only 24% of Dalit women reported they could read and write a simple sentence.

Terai Dalits have lower literacy rates than hill Dalits. Poverty affects schooling for girls more than for boys. The gender gap in enrolment is bigger in poorer households than in richer households.

In *India*, the literacy rates of women, SC and ST continue to be below average. The percentage of the ever-married women by caste who are illiterate in India, and in two selected states: Uttar Pradesh, which is one of the most disadvantaged; and Tamil Nadu, which is among the most advantaged states in India. One can see that there is a significant difference in the level of illiteracy in the two states among all the castes, therefore confirming the significance of disparities between regions in India. However, SC ever-married women were disadvantaged in both states, with 85% of SC women illiterate compared with 57.2% of other higher castes in Uttar Pradesh, and 64.1% of SC women in Tamil Nadu compared with 5.0% of higher castes. Dalit women have to face three pronged discrimination – they are women, they are Dalits and then they are Dalit women.

7

Structuring of Social Inequalities in Rural India

The Notion of Social Inequality

Social inequality is a perennial problem, and therefore, it is found universally in one form or the other. Its prevalence is a part of human existence. On the origin of inequality among men the following questions posed by Dahrendorf remain pertinent: (1) Why is there inequality among men? (2) Where do its causes lie? (3) Can it be reduced, or even abolished altogether? (4) Or do we have to accept it as a necessary element in the structure of human society? These questions are no doubt ubiquitous, yet specific societies have shown differential patterns and expressions of social inequality. However, before we take up the case of social inequality in rural India in particular, it would be proper to analyse in brief the concept and perspective on social inequality.

Dahrendorf distinguishes between inequalities of natural capabilities and those of social position; and between inequalities that do not involve evaluative rank order and those that do. Of these two pairs of distinction Dahrendorf works out four types of inequality: (a) natural differences of kind, (b) natural differences of rank, (c) social differentiation of positions, and (d) social stratification based on reputation and wealth. In all the four types "individual" is evidently the focal point of status-evaluation. Such a conception of social inequality based on distribution of property, wealth, honour and power among individual members would imply a certain ideological basis and a structural arrangement of people based upon those inegalitarian institutionalised norms. In the final analysis such a conception of inequality provides a logical legitimacy to social inequality, its functionality and inevitability. Based on such a plea social in-equality is visibly found in the division of labour, differentiation of roles and, in fact, in differential evaluation of different tasks and roles assigned to or taken up by different members.

We start with a simple conception that social inequality is found in one form or other, but it is not necessarily functional and inevitable. Division of labour of differential expertise is functional, and it is this which is required too. One may reject this view by dubbing it "idealistic" and "imaginary", but all human societies have been striving for such a formation of social relations all through their existence. Another view point is that social inequality is a multidimensional and dynamic aspect in the sense that its one pattern changes in part or full and another pattern emerges modifying or altering the previous one. There are two implicit points in this statement: (i) social inequality is not monolithic as wrongly conceived by some students particularly in the context of caste; and (ii) there has been a continuous (with variations in the magnitude) structuring and restructuring of social inequality.

In fact, it is erroneous to perceive inequality opposite of equality— both in theoretical terms and empirical contexts. Inequality is a "relational" phenomenon, that is, to be seen in terms of one-another rather in an absolute sense. In a family its members are unequal in regard to their kinship based statuses, but they are "equal" as members of an intimate primary primordial unit. Family members are different from members of a formal organisation. Even when there is "unequal" distribution of work or assignment of duties and responsibilities members of a family are treated as "equal". To evaluate social inequality in India from the point of "organisation" of an industrial western society would certainly undermine the role of India's social structure, culture, history and dialectics. Of these concepts, the first two refer to structural and normative aspects, and the latter two refer to change and contradictions. We may also state that there is no opposition between a structural analysis and a processual approach for studying

Indian society. These two together could explain the pattern of structuring of social inequality in a wholesome way. Also, we would explain the futility of the dichotomy between the western industrial society and the traditional/backward society, and the irrelevance of accepting the former as a refer-ence model for studying the latter.

We have no hesitation in accepting Beteille's view that a placement of people in layers (higher and lower) is inadequate for analysing social inequality. There is a need for understanding of ongoing, relations between individuals occupying different positions. But I notice some serious implications in what Beteille writes: "The problem of social inequality is above all the problem of how people interact with each other, how they compete and contend, how some succeed in moving up while others are pushed down despite their resistance." We are aware that this formulation about social inequality is not specifically meant as such for studying-Indian society, but formulations like this have quite often been used for analysing Indian social situation without realising the fact that it has emanated from the experience of modern, western Society. For example, if interaction among people is preordained by structural social ties to a large extent then competition would not become a pivotal aspect of social relation. There is nothing like a "success theme" in the Indian society the way it is reflected in the above quotation. There is an implicit theoretical viewpoint which can be accepted with some precautions only. "Rational" aspect assumes the element of volition which again is not quite a fact in India's context.

Statements about acceptance of western industrial society as a model for analysing Indian society abound in the contemporary literature. Competition for status and power is more in modern industrial societies than in traditional agrarian societies. Individuals are units of social ranking in the western societies whereas groups and collectivities are the main basis of states and power in Indian society. Likewise these contrasts, continuity, ascription and cultural norms are said to be predominant in the Indian society, and change, achievement and material values overwhelm the western world. It has very often been stated that social classes are a feature of modern industrial societies. Even Aron's dichotomy between the *nominalist* and the *realist* conceptions of class in terms of "individual" and "collectivity", respectively, as the basis of class identifications seems to be inadequate. The nominalist (psychological) basis is not independent of the realist (collective consciousness) in the Indian context as the two have been inseparable parts of India's social formation.

The question is: Is the notion of Homo Hierarchicus synonym of India caste system? Another question is: Are there no elements of Homo Equalis in India's system of social stratification? We do agree with Beteille that "the idea of hierarday entails that of inequality...", but inequality does not necessarily mean "hierarchy"; that is, rigidity of high and low statuses. Rigidity of caste-based statuses is not more than those based on apartheid, estatehood and feudalism. Students of Indian Social History have amply shown discontinuities, breakdowns, changes and contradictions in India's caste system in particular and in Indian society in general. Multi-dimensionality not only of India's social fabric but also of the caste system has already broken the determined monolithic of Homo Hierarchicus. To accept Homo Equalis as ideological basis and also a fact of life of modern western industrial society is simply a myth, and to take it as a reference model for Homo Hierarchicus in Indian society is perhaps a very serious ignorance (conscious or inadvertant) on the part of students of Indian society.

Notions of both inequality and equality are built into the ideology and practice of the caste system. The position of priesthood speaks of superiority of ritual status, but the notion and practice of "contra-priest" indicate the role of secular duties and if obligations certainly with ritual coverage. Relations between *jajman* (patron) and *kamin* (client) are not simply of higher and lower, superordinate and subordinate positions, but they also define rights and obligations of the lower sections along with the dominant ones. Therefore, we propose to cast a fresh look at the explanations of social inequality in rural India.

Approach to the Study of Social Inequality

There are a number of approaches to the study of hierarchy and inequality. Following the Hegelian view we would say that the "world of things" is dominated by the "world of thoughts".

"Hierarchy is the domination of thought, the domination of the spirit." Marx also considers hierarchy more in terms of an ideal form. Inequalitarian relations are determined by the existential conditions that exist in a given society. The existential conditions as depicted by Marx are reflected in the following statement:" As individuals express their life, so they are. What they are, therefore, coincides with their production, both with what they produce and with how they produce. The nature of individuals thus depends on the material conditions determining the production." Marx simply does not speak of "structure" of existential conditions, but also analyses the process of change in these conditions.

Tribal ownership, ancient and state ownership, feudal or estate property ownership and capitalism are not only evolutionary stages but also, when put together, form the core of "Marx's method for studying society and history. In each stage, Marx makes a mention about division of labour and distinctions between town and country, and, in fact, about nature of a socio-economic differentiation. Antagonism and contradictions are the causes of differentiation and change. The notion of basic structural change is an inseparable part of Marx's understanding of society and history as it is evident in his analysis of stages and groups of people in these stages.

Structuring of social inequality is a continuous process. Marx's view in this regard is: "The social structure and the state are continually evolving out of the life-process of definite individuals, but of individuals, not as they may appear in their own or other people's imagination, but as they really are; i.e., as they operate, produce materially, and hence as they work under definite material limits, presuppositions and conditions independent of their will.". Further, he writes: "Consciousness can never be anything else than conscious existence, and the existence of men is their actual life-process." "Life is not determined by consciousness, but consciousness by life."

We consider these eclectically taken statements from the German ideology in the form of a method for studying social inequality. Men are seen by Marx in their actual life-process. The practical process of development of men is taken into consideration for understanding of social reality. How social life is produced? What is its mode of production? What units are produced as a result of certain social conditions? What is the nature of social interaction between the groups produced through such an evolutionary process? We find a sort of answer to these questions in the following: "History is nothing but the succession of the separate generations, each of which exploits the materials, the capital funds, the productive forces handed down to it by preceding generations, and thus, on the one hand, continues the traditional activity in completely changed circumstances and, on the other, modifies the old circumstances with a completely changed activity." Thus, in fact, Marx visualises continuity of tradition and emergence of modernity side by side. Structure of social relations is determined by the direction of change. Structure and process are, in fact, co-existent.

Another methodological perspective is given by Max Weber. Gerth and Mills write: "Much of Weber's own work is of course informed by a skillful application of Marx's historical method." Weber criticizes Marx for an untenable monocausal theory, a segmental perspective and reducing the multiplicity of causal factor to a single factor theorem. However, Gerth and Mills comment that Weber's work may be seen as an atternpt to "round out" Marx's economic materialism by political and military materialism. Despite ideological and methodological differences between Marx and Weber, the two are interested in grasping the interrelations, in other words, the social structure itself. The principles of rationalisation, depersonalisation and routinisation are key to Weber's thinking and understanding of society. The individual and his action as the basic unit are core of Weber's *interpretative sociology.* All forms of associations and institutions should be reduced to "understandable" action. Thus, methodologically Weber's theory of stratification is subjective. Gerth and Mills observe: "The nominalism of Weber's method may be understood in terms of his attempt to avoid a philosophical emphasis upon either material or ideal factors, or upon either structural or individual principles of explanation."

Nadel works out a definition of "structure" and based on that examines the relevance of the "structural analysis". "Structure indicates an ordered arrangement of parts, which can be treated as transposable, being relatively invariant, while the parts are themselves variable." Nadel speaks implicitly of "dynamic equilibrium." The structure of a society in terms of "network" or "system" of relationships could be only a starting point for analysing the process of change in the social relationships. Nadel writes: "It (structural analysis) enables us to present our data neatly, synoptically, and with some elegance." "Time", "reality" and "function" are three cornerstones of the structural analysis. Therefore, the structural analysis is not just confined to "the continuity" of a social life, its persistence and invariance", it accommodates the elements of "time", "variance" and "changes" and even "volition", hence a "dynamic analysis". Nadel agrees with Forte's view about social structure as "a sum of processes in time". All societies, therefore, combine necessarily structure and process (change). Ordering and reordering, and distribution and redistribution, imply both structuring and restructuring of social relations. In fact, there is no contradiction between structure and process, and the two are built into each other, and hence put limits upon each other.

Bailey, no doubt, unlike other researchers, discusses "problems and methods" of his study of Baderi village in Orissa. In his analysis of "structure and system", Bailey seems to have made a claim for making a structural analysis of political change. Bailey writes: "A structural analysis emphasizes the regularity, the continuity, the permanence of certain forms of social interaction, and of groups of persons. It also emphasizes system..." For Bailey the word "structure" refers to a higher level of analysis of interconnections between various sub-structures. Bailey compared to Nadel puts more emphasis on coherence and continuity. For "rationalising" this view Bailey states that at empirical level there is no antipathy between conflict and a structural analysis. But he also reiterates his "structural-functionalist" stance by saying that the structure itself contains rules for the resolution of conflict, and conflict even plays a crucial part in maintaining the structure. Obviously, implication of such a view is that nothing transforms, replaces and displaces particularly in the Indian context. Caste, village community, its power structure and its linkages with higher levels are visualised as "static". Formulation of the structural analysis is guided more by the coloured colonial misconceptions rather than by the rigour and logic of the approach itself. If a society has not been "static" or "unchanging" or it has not been changing as per the perception of change of colonial rulers and some scholars (particularly the western ones), it is erroneous to start with a "static analysis" of Indian society. Besides this, "a dynamic analysis" is understood, again erroneously, as a result of some external factors which implies that all changes are from without and not from within. History of India's social formation is full of contradictions and changes emanating from within its structure and normative pattern. Therefore, Bailey's notion of structure as a higher level of analysis, in effect," a low level of generalisation".

Social Inequality in Rural India

Along with the developmental of the order of the four ranks, namely, Brahmins, Kshatriyas, Vaisyas and Shudras, the development of state, law, religion, science and philosophy also took place in ancient India. Walter Ruben holds the view that the structure of ancient India society can be described in terms of agrarian production and the relations of the different social strata to property, especially the soil. Thus, the rank-orders in the village community depended upon the quality of agricultural land and infrastructure for cultivating it. However, Ruben does not seem to be right in assuming that the village community was stationary and inflexible. Guild (*sremi*), caste (*jati*) and devotion (*bhakti*) were later developments. Ruben also along with some historians prefers to characterize the Indian society by the Asiatic mode of production. Ruben writes: "Thus, we may like to characterize Indian history as that of a society based on the Indian variant of the Asiatic mode of production with strong elements of slavery in antiquity and of feudalism in the middle ages, succeeded by capitalism which mainly came to India in the form of British colonialism till capitalist India became" independent in 1947." Such a unilinear mode of change undermines variations within each of the elements of one stage into the next one. The hypothesis referring to replacement/displacement of social structure underlies such a process of evolutionary scheme.

Romila Thapar emphasizes two major aspects of the functioning of social groups and their mobility in the study of a society. She refers to pastoralism, settled agrarian economy and an emergent commercial-urban economy as features of Vedic, Mauryan and Gupta periods, respectively. She also observes that change at the level of elite groups were most obviously brought about by foreign invasions and migrations. The migrations affected status relationships and the rules of marriage. Thapars view that ancient Indian society was not a rigidly structured society is based on the fact that a hierarchy of statuses was absent. The Verma concept did not refer to an actual description of the social functioning, and therefore, Indian society was not a frozen one. There were periods of change which influenced social institution as and other domains of social life.

Thapar brings out a distinction between ritual status and actual status in terms of economic and political power. Despite a hazy line of demarcation between the two and the ideology of *varna ashram dharma,* there were secular bases of social stratification. Rigidity of *varna* was weakened by the emergence of "mixed castes". Tribal identity and occupational identity paved a way for "mixed castes". No doubt ritual status was fixed, but change in its rigidity was brought about by improving it or by denying its importance. This was more of an ideological sort of change. There was mobility also in terms of actual status as it was not necessarily defined by and dependent upon the ritual status. Emulation of actual status required a change in the re-distribution of society's resources. Also the examples of tension between the ritual (Brahmanic) and the actual (the Kshatriya) statuses have been brought to our notice by several scholars. However, it would not be correct to say that the two statuses were completely independent of one-another. For example, caste system has performed innumerable functions including economic and political, and this is one strong reason for its continuity and change.

A study of social stratification based on evidence from Buddhist sources reveals two schemes of categorisation of people: (i) *varna, jati and kula;* and (ii) a Brahmanical division of society, namely, Brahmanas, Kshatriyas, Vaisyas and Sudras on the one hand, and another based on non-Brahmanical sources categorising people into Kshatriyas, Brahmanas and Grahapatis on the other. The Brahmanical scheme uses *varna* and *jati, and* the non-Brahmanical categorisation is based on the term *kula.*

The latter represents "a division of society into the domains of power, ritual and the economy." In the Buddhist literature, the Kshatriyas are invariably enumerated above the Brahmanas. Also tension is noticed between the Kshatriyas and the Brahmanas. The Buddha refuted the claim of Brahmanical superiority. One finds a two-tier system of social ranking in the Buddhist literature. The system of social stratification is not as normative as portrayed in the Brahmanical texts. Occupational divisions among people were the basis of their identification. Thus, a system of stratification existed independent of the Brahmanical scheme

According to Kosambi the essential relationship in India is not based on kinship. Production and mutual exchange of commodities and bonds of production hold society together. Caste was related to economic hierarchy and the two together paved way for feudalism. Feudalism was a form of social order. In the medieval period of Indian history, namely, from twelfth century till the advent of the British Rule basic structural changes occurred in the traditional Indian society. These changes comprised the land tenure systems such as Iqta, Mansabdari and Jagirdari etc., which in turn, brought about changes in the ruling class and the rural landed aristocracy. Below the rural aristocracy were big peasants. There was considerable stratification within the peasantry.

S.Nurul Hasan writes: "The zamindar class played a vital role in the political, economic, and cultural life of medieval India." However, Hasan makes this reference in the context of their role in extracting the agricultural surplus, appropriation and control of rural economy. "At the same time, the separatist, localist, and parochial trends received powerful patronage from the Zamindari class." The class of zamindars was highly differentiated. Hasan classifies them into: (1) the autonomous chieftains; (2) the intermediary zamindars, and (3) the primary zamindars. The second and the third categories were found at the village level. Chaudhuris, Khots and Muqaddams were intermediaries, and the primary zamindars included the holders of proprietory rights.

Inequalities in the pre-British period existed in myriad ways. There were people who did not pay land-revenue, and some paid only a nominal amount. There were others who paid the maximum. Such economic disparities were associated with caste hierarchy as well. The system of land-grants (Jagirs) promoted creation of landed enclaves from among the ruler's caste and his kin groups. Some favourites, professionals, dancers and singers and servants were also given Jagirs in lieu of their services. The entire system became quite complex and inequalitarian. There were as many as forty-five *jagirs* and one hundred seventy-five taxes in the erstwhile state of Jaipur. The *jagirs* were arranged in a rank-order based on their size and revenue, and the Jagirdars enjoyed power and privilege in accordance with the ranks of their *jagirs.* Taxes were also socially patterned as they were imposed differentially in terms of caste ranks and other positions.

There were socially structured land control relationships in terms of the landlord and the tenant. But they were not monolithic as they were divided into innumerable strata. A social formation viewpoint explains that various landed strata were linked to definite socio-cultural and economic and political roles. Besides this, each caste group, for example, was differentially associated with other caste groups. A potter used to supply earthen pots to various families in the village community. He was treated as a *kamin* or servant by the Rajput landlords, but the "untouchable" castes or even castes of "equal status" could never treated him as a *kamin,* though like the Rajput landlords they were also his "patrons". Further, it would be wrong to assume that a potter was a *kamin* in all situations. He used to behave as a "contra-priest" on the occasions of marriage etc., in the families of castes higher than his own. A contra-priest is a person who is required to perform certain ritual functions on auspicious occasions at the families of castes higher than his own caste. Thus, inequality and equality co-existed, and no caste, class and power groups enjoyed absolute power. The very nature of inter-dependence upon each other provided certain rights and privileges to all social groups. But these were certainly of an uneven nature.

Frykenberg's suggestion for formulating new theoretical models seems worth mentioning here. His two ideas are: (i) "ideas of movement, namely, about process and causation; and (ii) ideas of "structural relativity", that is, of dynamic relationships of social entities moving within a defined structural whole." Frykenberg considers ideas of structural relativity as intrinsic to the study of process and structure: "The dynamic relationships of all social entities moving within a defined structural whole can hardly be analysed without me invention of working models, some simple and some extremely complex." Land, labour and lord are appropriate elements according to Frykenberg. The British Rule brought about drastic changes in the institutions of property, government and law, and these three significantly affected land, labour and lord socially as well as economically.

Private ownership of land, land settlements, Zamindari and ryotwari systems, centralisation of governmental authority throughout the length and breadth of the country, bureaucracy, judiciary and new legislations changed the structural and normative patterns during the British period. Due to these changes despite unwillingness of the British raj the caste system became weak as a social hierarchy, and became stronger as a source of mobilisation for social, economic and political gains. This process of caste mobilisation for extra-ritual ends received further boost in the post-independence period due to adult franchise, elections, migration and education.

Both Cohn and Metcalf arrive at a similar conclusion in their studies of the eastern districts of Uttar Pradesh. Cohn writes: "Most of the Rajputs whose Zamindari rights were sold continued to live as they lived before in their villages and talukas, dominating lower-caste cultivators and offering sustained and at times effective opposition to auction purchases." Thus, change in status from Zamindari to ex-Zamindari or what Metcalf calls "from *raja* to landlord" could not substantially affect adversely their dominant position in Indian rural society. Change in legal status does not necessarily change the "actual status" of the people.

This sort of hiatus between the ideal or expected change and the actual change and situation would not permit analysis of social change and mobility in terms of closed systems. Therefore, there is a need to go beyond the study of caste system and social mobility because social reality was much broader than what caste could encompass. Changes emanating from external sources, for example, during the British period, in terms of legislations, land tenure systems, technology, education and administration cannot be studied simply from a caste point of view. Unexpected or latent structural and cultural changes emerged during this period resulting into restructuring of hierarchical relations.

My own study of Rajasthan shows that the Jagirdars and Bhomias were allowed to retain best lands at the time of the resumption of jagirs. Some lands were not resumed at all. Jagirdars mobilised their caste association, namely, the Rajasthan Kshatriya Mahasabha, for allotment of *khudkasht* land, compensation and assessment of *jagirs* for land revenue. The government bowed to the pressure of the jagirdars. The substantial tenants were able to manage transfer of large landholdings in their names depriving the smaller tenants of their due share. This was a significant step in structuring social and economic inequalities. The legal status was withdrawn but there was no corresponding effect on the actual status. Downward mobility was not a significant result of this legislation in several cases. Upward mobility was, however, quite a noticeable phenomenon in the case of tenants.

An Analysis of a Few Selected Studies

We do not intend discuss the patterns of social stratification in terms of caste class and power as such in this essay. But a reference to Louis Dumont's structuralist stance in regard to intercaste, intracaste and intra-familial racking is not completely out of context. The principle of hierarchy do not only applies to caste, but also to principles of values, occupations, food and clothes and "bride-givers" and "bride-takers". Dumont looks for cultural meaning of affinity and consanguinity.

In Dunmont's Homo Hierarchicus Y. Singh discerns four notions of structuralism: (i) ideology, (ii) idealistics, (iii) transformational relationship, and (iv) comparison. Hierarchy is an ideational notion; it pervades all aspects of Hindu society. Everything is seen in terms of "pure" and "impure", its binary tension and dialectics. Since pure and impure are parts of the same principle, they are complementary. But hierarchy is seen through the super priority of the pure over the impure. Dumont observes that there has been change in the society and not of the society, hence rules out a structural change in India's caste system.

Since we are interested in discerning change in the existing patterns of social inequality, we do not wish to go into the genesis of various approaches and methods of the study of social stratification. It would be appropriate to lay lands on a few selected studies. Anand Chakravarti discusses inequalities in rural India based on status, economic differences and power. The analysis of social inequalities in terms of these three spheres is based on the assumption that a lower status in one sphere is not necessarily accompanied by the same in the other two spheres. Of these three domains caste status is fixed by birth. But it is to be seen how ritual basis of caste continues to play a decisive role in determining social, economic and political status.

Structural incongruities have certainly emerged in the post-independence period. Caste has become segmental entity as it has lost its "organic" character. The pure does not encompass today the less pure or impure. In fact, if the "less has acquired strength in economic and political spheres, it encompasses to a large extent "the pure". The nature of inter-caste relations is not so much valued today in terms of commensality as it done in terms of wealth and power. Pollution-purity and untouchability have become more of casual rituals than a day-to-day reality. This is due to structural changes introduced in the countryside over a period of last four decades. Motivational factors or rational outlook have not brought structuring of social inequalities as much as the latter has changed values and aspirations of the rural people. Two studies, one by F.G. Bailey and second by T.S. Epstein focus on structural change in the countryside. Bailey examines relationship between caste and new economy. As a result of the abolition of the traditional land tenure systems new frontiers, namely, economic, political and administrative have taken land to market. Bailey analyses new economy, land transactions, services and trade. The landlords have become ex-landlords, and the functionary and service castes have become landowners. The latter have taken their traditional produces to market and have earned profits which were not available to them in the traditional system.

Epstein's study shows that structural innovation, namely, irrigation has brought about significant change in the village economy, but restricted social change by discouraging migration, education and employment outside the village. Lack of such an innovation resulted into migration, education and employment. Epstein analyses structural change in two villages of Karnataka in terms of crops, houses, landholdings, livestock, family incomes and expenditures and market networks.

Social inequality is a structural and historical reality observable in diverse forms and in different contexts. Social inequality is, therefore, related to structure, ideology and behaviour of the people. Its consequences could be seen in terms of arrangement of the people and expressions of their life-styles and careers they pursue. Structure of inequality in a given society is generally found having dissonance between different dimensions. For example, the three dimensions of social inequality, namely, social, political and economic are not of the same magnitude in terms of producting inequalitarian relations, and therefore, they do not necessarily correspond with each other having one-to-one relationship. Thus, social inequality may be pronounced in one specific domain, whereas in others it may not be of the same magnitude. Such a state of inequality is normally a result of specific structural conditions and processes of change. Men are, therefore, not equally unequal. Impact of inequality is also uneven. Even ascriptive bases of inequality such as age, sex and kinship positions do not have a uniform pattern of social effects.

Social inequality is a very sensitive aspect of our social life. The notion that a person is higher than someone else or that one has a realisation that his position is superior to some other member of his village community makes it sensitive and evaluative. It is not psychological evaluation that matters so much. Such evaluations are based on differential possession of resources including house, household goods, property, education, lucrative job and political power. Since role of these factors in determining social inequality has increased, the role of descriptive factors such as birth, sex, age and fictive status has declined considerably.

Fallers states that social inequality has both normative and structural phenomena. The normative aspect refers to evaluation, and the structural aspect refers to distribution of material resources and power. Berreman makes a study of four dimensions of social inequality, namely, behavioural, interactional, material and existential. Social inequality is a lived-in-experience and a stark reality. It is a relative phenomenon.

Let us illustrate the structural basis of social inequality from our field studies in Rajasthan. The Brahmins are regarded high in ritual rank-order by other castes, but their influence and power in other domains depend mainly upon their economic and educational achievements. In one of the six villages, we have studied, Brahmins are dominant not because of their high ritual status, but because they enjoy dominant positions in economic and educational spheres. This is so to a large extent because being Brahmin they have more access to higher education and white-collar jobs than other caste groups. But it is not that all the families from among the Brahmins or even all the individual members from Brahmin families have such a privilege and opportunity. In another village Brahmins have incongruity between their ritual status and economic and cultural (educational) achievements, and therefore, they do not enjoy power and dominant position in the village community. Out of the remaining four villages, in one only Brahmins have consider able influence in the affairs of the village because of their better economic and educational status. Thus, social inequality is a very complex phenomenon. It is not that high ritual status of Brahmins has become altogether redundant and insignificant. It is accorded importance on certain religious, ritual and ceremonial occasions, but it is ephemeral. A Brahmin priest becomes a commoner as soon as the particular episode is over. However, there are still some noticeable cultural and social distinctions between different caste groups particularly in regard to life styles, performance of rituals and observance of some practices.

In regard to Rajputs, hierarchy based on the size of the *jagirs* and the zamindars is not closely associated with commensal and ritual bases of caste-based inequality. Norms in relation to pollution-purity and "untouchability" were never a significant element of the syndrome of life-styles of Rajputs. They were always non-vegetarian and drinkers of alcohol, and their food habits made them to think that Brahmins and Banias particularly would observe norms related to pollution-purity and untouchability as they were vegetarian, teetotaller and performed rituals and worshipped gods and goddesses. Thus, theoretically, the Rajputs were number-two in the caste hierarchy, but in practice they were number-one in political sphere, and did not bother about their ritual rank as such. Generally, they were not engaged in gainful educational achievements. Because ofthe abolition of the jagirdari and zamindari systems, they have been affected severely. Now a good number of Rajputs are self-cultivators like their ex-tenants, and, some of them today own much smaller landholdings than their own ex-tenants. A substantial number of Rajputs work as police constables and soldiers in the army. Rajputs are one community which has witnessed a radical downgrading of their social status in the village community.

Conversely, the Jats who were tenants of the Rajput landlords, have improved their status considerably in economic and political spheres. In the economic sphere the loss of Rajput landlords has been their gain as they have acquired substantial landholdings. In the sphere of political power, they have taken maximum advantage of adult franchise and their preponderant numerical strength by arousing caste consciousness and mobilising their members on the caste basis.

Thus, two obverse structural processes created new cleavages within different caste groups and also brought about some "levelling" effect on the structure of social inequality. Some of the Rajput families, though could not retain their traditional glory and power, have tried to retain best lands, and diverted their savings and assets in economically gainful activities and enterprises. Similarly, the Jat cultivators who were substantially benefited by the land reforms further consolidated their economic position by extracting maximum advantage of developmental schemes and facilities and by adopting new devices in the field of agriculture. Those groups and families which received a jolt could not recoup from that crisis, and have ended up with not only downward social mobility but also in some cases reached the level of pauperisation. There are families from amongst almost all caste groups in this category.

Form of Social Inequality

Louis Dumont's structuralism and its application by several

others to the study of India's taste systems have led us to think that there exists the dichotomy of hierarchy and equality, and holism and individualism. Srinivas seems to the Dumont's approach to the study of social inequality. He writes: "In short, there is, on the one hand, the syndrome of tradition, hierarchy and holism while on the other hand, that of modernity, equality and individualism. There is no liberty in traditional societies for liberty can only be predicted of individuals and not of groups." The obvious confession is that Hindu society is hierarchical and the modern western society is egalitarian.

If we look at the Indian scene today, it is quite evident that individuals migrate to towns and cities for higher education and better employment. Srinivas writes: "Caste society is holistic and hierarchical and is inimical to individualism but in spite of this individualism surfaces in the *sanyasi* or renouncer, who transcends society." Srinivas and Dumont see individualism only in renouncing of the world and not in migration of a Marwari Bania from western Rajasthan to Assam, Bengal, Bihar, Tamil Nadu and Karnataka. A Rajasthani "untouchable" labourer has been migrating to Delhi and Punjab for seeking employment particularly in the years of drought and famine. Always a selected few have gone out of their native places for higher education and white-collar jobs. These are vital sociological facts of India's rural life in the context of inequality.

According to Dumont the basis of the caste system is the opposition between the pure and the impure, but with increased recession of pollution-purity syndrome, hierarchy does not continue to be an ideology. There is also no combination of "two forces", that is, Brahmins and Kshatriyas (status and power). The intermediate castes have extracted maximum economic benefits from "green revolution", and political gains from adult franchise and elections because of their numerical superiority and improved economic standing. Dumont and Srinivas both do not see any exploitation in the jajmani system, because it is not recognised as such as per the norms of the system. Exploitation of the *kamin* (functionary) castes and "untouchables" was not only obviously perceptible, but was highly institutionalised. Today, we have new forms of "exploitation" which are not clearly visible under the new system of relations of production in agriculture and politics and elections. I have discussed elsewhere that occupation, education, power and styles of life are the main aspects of change in social stratification. Distinctions based on these aspects are evaluated as the yardsticks of higher and lower status. There is no denying of the association of caste ranks with these aspects, but incongruities in them are indicative of weakening of the traditional social inequalities, and congruities speak of the continuity of caste groups or some families with fairly good economic position.

New forms of inequalities along with continuity of traditional inequalities in some measure in regard to various caste and class groups and families have emerged due to historical and cultural legacies and present-day distributive disparities. Class distinctions have even accentuated within the caste groups. Caste groups or some families have hindered not only emergence of class consciousness but also created new enclaves of power and privilege. There is an undeniable element of casteness when only Harijan labourers are burnt alive, but at the same time this is also a case of class atrocity as the Harijans are generally poor and who indulge in such inhuman acts are rich and resourceful.

The ownership, control and use of land in relation to caste partly become the basis of relations in rural India. Beteille identifies three forms of inequality: (i) between landlord and tenant; (ii) between landowner and wage labourer; and (iii) between large, medium and small proprietors. Issues related to agrarian structure and change are sharply focused in a study of the district Basti in Uttar Pradesh.

The two main issues are: (i) the "land grab" movement in 1970 by the poor and ancless peasants; and (ii) the structural and emergent factors resulting in the termination and failure of this movement. The questions raised by Rajendra Singh in this study are quite relevant for analysing agrarian and social inequalities in the village community. The questions are: (1) How have various agrarian reforms affected caste, class and land relations? (2) Who have been the gainers and who the losers of land as a result of these reforms? (3) What is their caste and class position today? (4) What is the impact of these reforms upon the emerging pattern of power structure in the district?

Explorations, to find answers of these questions, show that there was an increase in the number of zamindars and the growth of class solidarity among them. There was pauperisation both of zamindar and *mahants.* And finally, a strong lower middle caste, rich "peasantry, emerged. We have discussed this process of change in terms of "proletarianisation" of the Jagirs and Bhomas and "bourgeoisiefication" of the tenants in my study of six villages in Rajasthan. "Downward" social mobility was quite pespective in the case of a large number of landlord families.

Today social inequalities in rural India cannot be diagnosed in terms of caste or class categories because of the very nature of social formation that has emerged in the post-independence period. Singh observes:" After examining the Basti situation find the inadequacy of class as well as caste. The agrarian society in Basti conforms neither to a class nor to a caste model. Class dichotomies and conflicts can be seen in the context of caste which mould the subjective perceptions of the people in the countryside. Since mobility has been both upward and downward simultaneously, it is evident that various caste and class groups are highly differentiated. The hypothesis that the rich are getting richer and the poor poorer is not correct in all cases. Gail Omvedt endorses Singh's view that "caste" is not necessarily equivalent to class, but it very clearly puts some limits.

The idea of "continuous hierarchies and discrete castes given by Dipankar Gupta refers to a commentary on Louis Dumont's notion of caste as Homo Hierarchicus. Gupta writes:" Any notion of hierarchy is arbitrary and is valid from the perspective of certain individual castes. To state that the pure hierarchy is one that is universally believed-in, or one which legitimises the position of those who participate in the caste system, is misleading." Besides pollution-purity, distinctions and "diacritical notches" are observed strictly in the caste system. Castes equally pure refrain from merging their identities. Distinctions related to pollution and purity do not systematically affect caste status. In view of these formulations Gupta examines the *jajmani* system, sanskritisation, caste and politics and caste-class and social class. Inconsistencies and incongruities in behaviour of members of different caste groups in these spheres can be understood in terms of their discreteness. The mode of production is a social formation in which we find interconnections of caste, kinship, family, marriage and even rituals with the forces of production and production relations. Social inequalities are seen by Gough in terms of the emergence of a new bourgeoisie, the polarisation of the peasantry, and the pauperisation of the working class. Namboodiripad and Ranadive analyse class relationships as a domain assumption in the treatment of caste and kinship in India. Even *varna* and *the jajmani* systems are explained in terms of class relations and embedded in the mode of production. Caste is analysed also in terms of physical force and economic power. Castes operate as enclaves functioning parallel to eco-systems. Marriages take place within these eco-systems, hence these become operative caste-boundaries.

We have analysed nature and patterning of social inequality from the point of both structure and process. Structuring of social inequality refers to "structure in time". Our analysis shows that there are both internal or historical contradictions and external influences along with structural and normative sources of inequality. Placement of groups, families and individuals in high and low positions based on wealth, property, occupation and education refers to structural sources. Normative sources refer to evaluative standards. These are applied differentially to various spheres such as social and cultural (caste)· power and economy. We have analysed the question: Whether these spheres of social inequality are indepenent of each other or they are inseparable aspects of the same social formation.

Neither caste nor class alone can be a sufficient approach for studying social inequality. In fact we have examined that social and economic dimensions of inequality co-exist and are automatically affected by each other. Upper castes have slided down in their status, and some of them have improved their position. Such a pattern is found almost among all caste groups. Thus, apparently equal groups are inequal in myriad ways and in their resourcefulness. Besides this, the social groups which occupied lower positions also enjoyed some rights and privileges.

Social inequality is structurally relational and relative phenomenon. Structural factors have brought about marked and manifest changes in the structure of social inequality. Ancient, medieval, British and contemporary periods in Indian history have shown role of these factors in terms of migration, invasions, warfare, land reforms, administration and education etc.

The caste system, which has been a pivotal infrastructure in shaping social relations, has not been "static" and "unchanging" as it is depicted in various writings. In fact, it has pervaded almost all aspects of social relations, and therefore, to see it as confined to ritual or religious phenomena would amount to undermining of its pervasiveness. Both the contexts of caste, namely, historical and contextual, would permit us to know that the structural and the normative dimensions are inseparable and therefore a dichotomy of caste and class or a trichotomy of "caste, class and power" as forms of social inequality or as systems of social stratification bring out only a fragmented picture of India's rural social formation. A social formation point of view for studying social in-equality is based on the understanding specifically of the structure, culture, history and dialectics of India's social fabric.

8

Scheduled Castes and the Struggle Against Inequality

TOWARDS A PARTICIPATORY FORM OF RESEARCH

One basic issue which needs close attention in any serious discussion, not only of the problems of the Scheduled Castes but of all social problems, is the place of theory in social analysis. Increasingly, social activists have begun to lose confidence in theoreticians. This is especially the case of those engaged in the problems of the marginalised groups such as the Scheduled Castes. Theories, these social activists seem to say, are abstract entities produced in glass houses built by the theoreticians. They are, the activists feel, far removed from the reality they are trying to cope with, often viewpoints of specific groups developed in their peculiar cultural milieues to serve their own interests.

Moreover, 'prefabricated' theories, social activists feel, can only hamper social praxis. Theory building, if necessary at all, must come, according to them, as an end product of social praxis, not precede it and control it. This disenchantment of social activists with theoreticians 'has come from a number of sources. First, hard pressed as they are with many urgent and practical problems, social practitioners have little time to conceptualise their problems. Such exercise, they feel, is a luxury which they cannot afford. Second, most activists seem temperamentally disinclined to engage in analytical thinking. Third, the theoreticians, on their part, seem to be equally incapable of entering into a dialogue with the men in the field and join them in their struggle to articulate and conceptualise their experience.

While the disenchantment of social activists with theoreticians is understandable, it must also be admitted that every social praxis implies a theory. Attempts to articulate the theory implied in praxis, would be a profitable exercise especially when such theoretical formulations seem to come in conflict with existing theories. They can be genuine discoveries which challenge accepted theories and implied assumptions, and can open up new vistas for our understanding of social reality. Discussion on the relevance of theory brings us to the question of ideology. It is generally accepted that there is no such a thing as a totally detached and objective research. Every individual and every theory is to some extent a product of a particular historical epoch, often the product of a particular cultural group and hence will be influenced by its nuances and concrete concerns. The subjectivity involved in social research is sometimes interpreted to mean that all research is 'committed.' 'Committed' here means not merely that social researchers should be aware of their subjective limitations and therefore should question, at every stage, their findings and their motives. It is taken to mean that all social research comes from specific 'interest groups' and serve their needs. According to this interpretation, social research in the West is framed to serve the Western societies, particularly the capitalists. Social research in India too, according to this view, is planned and executed either as an appendage to the Western exercise, or as a service to the well to do upper classes and castes.

Others, especially those who are engaged in the problems of the Third World countries and more specifically, working with marginalised groups in these countries, would argue that social research, in order to be relevant, *must* be 'committed'—committed, to be specific, to the problems of the marginalised groups and to an ideology that is beneficial to their cause. This is more so, according to this view, since social science research so far, seems to have been planned and manipulated by interest groups in order to exploit the economically disadvantaged and other marginalised groups such as the Scheduled Castes and Scheduled Tribes. At this point, we may refer to what is known as participatory research, and which seems to take a middle path between research as detached analysis of social reality and research as ideologically committed action-programme. Although the concept and method of participatory research is still evolving, the general trend seems to be to make research an instrument to assist actors in the field to come to an enlightened understanding about the nature of the situation in which they are, and what to do about it. In the words of Paulo Friere, the aim of participatory research is 'to provide the people with their own voice' rather than to estimate and report the success of experimental manipulation in a field setting.

Participatory research generally includes three stages: (1) information gathering on the context of action, (2) discussion between actors and researchers on the information in order to clarify problems and work out guidelines for action, and (3) concrete action programme. Step three leads to step one and the process is repeated. What role does the researcher take in a participatory form of research? What level of emotional or ideological identification with the actors is possible or advisable? One may point out here the distinction made by Ralph Turner between taking the role of another and taking the stand-point of another. According to Turner, the researcher in participatory research should place himself in the role of the actor, but refuse to take the standpoint of the actor. This would require a great deal of personal discipline, and understanding between the researcher and the actors. The task of the researcher can be particularly difficult when there are antagonistic interests or political rivalries among actors within the same project. The success of the dialogue between the researcher and the actors in the field will, to a large extent, depend on the ability of each side to respect each other and their professions and to listen to each other in a spirit of openness.

Among those 'researchers' who work among the marginalised' groups such as the Scheduled Castes and Scheduled Tribes, it is possible to detect two broad theoretical orientations. The first, perhaps the more popular one, can be called the Marxist ideology in so far as it uses some form of 'Marxist analysis' to understand social reality. Although there are different schools of Marxist orientation, one version of it is presented here.

This version of Marxist analysis stresses the predominant role of the relations of production in determining societal formation and controlling societal functions. In this view, 'caste is class on primitive level of production.' Class functioning can be seen, it is argued in (1) the pattern of ownership. (2) the use of labour, (3) the nature of the market system and (4) the consumption pattern of different classes in society.

Marxist analysis generally stresses that, among different types of relations of production in a society, one or other form tends to dominate over the others. The dominant relations of production would impose their laws of functioning on the other relations of production which are subordinate to them, and would determine the general character of the super-structure of that particular society. The complexity of the economic structures, with the dominance of the relations of production found therein, explains, according to this view, the complex character of the juridico-political structure of their historically determined society. In India, it is argued, the capitalist form of relations of production has dominated over the others. The capitalist system is supposed to have provided India with legitimisation for the existing mode of production and distribution, motivation for linking personal identity with the prevailing mode of production and symbolic interpretation for their current boundaries of life.

Those who follow this theoretical orientation would argue that in the capitalist system, the dominant castes exploit the weaker sections through subtle ideological, cultural and cleverly construed symbolic representations. Thus in India the caste system is seen as being used by the emerging capitalist class as a vehicle of exploitation to maintain their economic, social, political and ideological domination over the rest of society. It is only in this context, they argue, that the marginalisation of some sections or the 'atrocities on Harijans' can be adequately understood.

Other researchers, who are also concerned with the problems of the marginalised groups, are not so happy with the Marxist ideology or the form of social analysis developed by the Marxists. They too feel that classical social theories, and forms of social research are inadequate to meet the needs of the time, and are eager to develop some form of participatory research. However, the Marxist attempt to reduce all social phenomena to economics and economic-based class formation, they feel, does not do justice to the complex social reality.

Ethnic, socio-cultural and religious dimensions of reality, these researchers feel, cannot be reduced to mere economic reality or interpreted as epiphenomena resulting from the material basis of production and the relations of production. While recognising the important contribution made by Karl Marx to the understanding of society, especially by explicating the conflictual nature of social process and the strong economic base in this conflict, they would go beyond Marx and try to integrate the different dimensions of social reality into social analysis.

Among these social analysts too, there is no single unified approach. One version among them would stress power relations in society as the basic element in the societal process. The process of power formation, it is admitted, is definitely influenced by economic forces, but it is seen as a universal social process in which ethnic, cultural, regional and political groups tend to become polarised into those who control power and those who are dependent on others for their existence. The phenomenon of the Scheduled Castes and their struggle for equality, according to this understanding, is a specific instance of the power-relations in society.

The Policy of Reservation

One specific issue concerning the Scheduled Castes, which has been exercising the minds of many people is the policy of reservation. Reservation for the Scheduled Castes includes three specific areas to be filled on the basis of their proportion in the population: reservation of electoral seats in the parliament and in the state legislatures, reservation in government jobs, and reservation of seats in educational institutions.

There are two important questions to be asked about the practice of reservation. The first question is whether reservation is a legitimate way of doing things in a secular society where equality and equal rights of all are to be respected. On this question, there is no agreement. On the one side, there are people who bold that reservation in general cannot be reconciled with the principle of equality and the principle of merit, namely, that reservation by its very nature, excludes meritorious and perhaps more qualified individuals from competing for the reserved job. Professor Andre Beteille, who led one of the discussions on reservation pleaded for eliminating reservation at least from important areas.

On the other side, there are those who argue that reservation does not violate the principle of equality. According to them, it is not even an exception to the principle of equality. They would see reservation as a specific instance of application of the principle of equality and equal opportunity. An abstract rule of formal equality which prescribes uniform treatment for all individuals on the basis of merit, they argue, cannot do justice to those who have been marginalised and incapacitated from competing in the social arena. In order to make equality and equal opportunity available to all, they further argue, it is necessary to use the concept of proportional equality which takes into account social and other disabilities which hinder equality of opportunity. Although, historically, reservation was introduced in the Constitution primarily to offset the effects of inherited inequalities and to remedy the effects of historic injustice on certain communities, they are convinced, it is possible to go beyond this interpretation and conceive reservation as a specific form of proportional representation, on which secular democracy is based. Such proportional representation in modern pluralistic societies, they argue, cannot be conceived merely on individualistic terms. It should be conceived primarily in terms of group representation. On the second question, whether reservation policy has actually achieved what it set out to do for the Scheduled Castes, also there is no agreement. The type of questions one must ask oneself in this connection are whether it has been given a chance to succeed at all, whether opposition to the policy from some powerful groups, who stand to lose by the policy, can be taken as a criterion for its non-acceptance by the nation at large, and whether initial difficulties in its implementation or the side effects can be taken to mean that the policy itself is counterproductive.

Dealing with Untouchability

Another issue concerning the Scheduled Castes which

demands serious attention, is the problem of untouchability. Although untouchability was abolished in the Constitution of India, all available data indicate that the practice of untouchability continues unabated, especially in the rural areas. What is the source of this persistence of the practice of untouchability in Indian society? Is it primarily a religious phenomenon? Or is it mainly based on economic factors? How does one explain the apparent ineffectiveness of law in this matter? What are the sources open to the marginalised groups to empower themselves in the fight against injustice and inequality in society? While the strong 'religious' connection in the practice of untouchability cannot be ignored, it would seem that the religious approach propagated by Mahatma Gandhi and his followers for the removal of untouchability does not seem to have produced any significant results. According to Gandhiji, the removal of untouchability must be achieved by the upper castes, who practice untouchability. The upper castes, in Gandhiji's opinion, should be made to realise that the practice of untouchability is not based on Hindu Dharma. It is only a change of heart on the part of upper caste Hindus, according to Gandhiji, that could bring about the removal of the practice of untouchability. He strongly advised the 'Untouchables' themselves not to revolt against the upper castes or demand changes in caste practices by themselves.

This was diametrically opposed to the views of Dr. Ambedkar. According to Ambedkar, the practice of untouchability was part and parcel of Hindu religion. However, he argued that the only way for the 'Untouchables' to liberate themselves was to increase their power to bargain rather than introduce religious reforms. This would require, as Ambedkar saw it, serious planning to improve the conditions of the 'Untouchables' in the fields of employment, education, and political organisation. In the social scene of India today, both these views co-exist without much dialogue. It would seem, however, that the number of those who opt for solid economic development and political organisation of the Scheduled Castes as the answer to the untouchability problem is increasing. Implied in this orientation is the conviction that, whatever one's religious beliefs, one will be able to impose a certain mode of behaviour on others only as long as he has power to make others follow his will. An important issue which has not received the attention it deserves is the problem of Scheduled Caste women. There seems to be a marked difference in the pattern of discrimination of Scheduled Caste men and women. In the work-place the Scheduled Caste women seem to be much less paid and much more exploited than their counter parts. Education is much less available to them than to men.

Those Scheduled Caste women who get some educational experience find much greater constraint in social adjustment and social acceptance than Scheduled Caste men. Programmes for the Scheduled Castes usually end up with men and very seldom reach the women. Whether it is the question of welfare programmes or the question of reservation of seats in educational institutions, the concern often seems to end up with men. All this indicates that serious attention has to be given at all levels concerning the problems of Scheduled Caste women in national planning.

The Problem of Conversion

Finally, there is the most vexing issue of religion. The problem of religion is today related to a number of sensitive areas. One of these areas is the phenomenon of conversion. Conversion movements among the Scheduled Castes are not new. Often these movements were an attempt to raise their social status in society. However, conversion is, at the same time, related to political sensibilities. The dominant Hindu Community in India has become exercised over the conversion of large number of Scheduled Castes to Islam and Christianity. This concern has been shown in different ways such as claiming the Scheduled Castes as part of the Hindu society, reconverting those who have joined other religions and restricting welfare programmes and other government benefits to those who profess Hinduism. Even the process of law has been influenced and sometimes manipulated by certain groups to discourage conversion. An example of this can be seen in the definition of the Scheduled Castes given in the Presidential order of 1950 which restricted the term, and hence, all the special benefits guaranteed for the Scheduled Castes, to only those who professed Hinduism or Sikhism. All this has seriously affected the functioning of secular democracy in India.

When at midnight of August 15, 1947, the bells of freedom rang throughout India, it had a double significance for the people of India. It meant the rejoicing of a nation which had achieved independence after nearly two centuries of colonial domination. At the same time, it was also a commitment, the acceptance of mutual responsibilities by the people of India to make this country a better place to live for all. On the one hand, it was a dream come true, a 'tryst with destiny' as Pundit Jawaharlal Nehru said on that day. On the other hand, it was a freedom which had yet to be achieved. India would not really be free, Nehru reminded the people, until every tear was wiped away from her face, the tears caused by poverty, discrimination and exploitation.

The experiment in democracy in India, for the last thirty five years, does not seem to have succeeded in making equal opportunities available to the marginalised groups such as the Scheduled Castes and Scheduled Tribes. In this connection the remarks of Shri Yogendra Makwana, then Minister of State in the Ministry of Home Affairs, led to a lively discussion at the Workshop. In recent years, the Scheduled Castes themselves have begun to be increasingly aware of this reality and have begun to question the wisdom of many things being done in their name. They are also becoming politically more conscious and horizontally mobilised. While the Scheduled Castes today do not have enough power to dictate national planning and policy decisions, those who are in responsible positions today can ill-afford to ignore the legitimate aspirations of nearly 100 million people in this country who could, till now, be taken for granted.

Perhaps the most important discovery was the realisation of the need for close collaboration between research scholars and social activists in the field. Most participants became aware that the problems of the marginalised people have no easy solution. They also became deeply conscious of the need for serious dialogue. Most theoreticians seem to build up models of social processes without sufficient rooting in the existing reality. Most activists, on the other band, seem to be so involved in the process that they can easily loose the proper perspective of the social programme in which they are deeply immersed. Serious and honest dialogue between the two can help both in their search for understanding and for discovering meaningful solutions to the problems they face. In all this, it is important that the dialogue takes place not merely between the research scholars and social activists in the field, who are often outsiders to the local people. The dialogue should involve the local people and their leaders. Both the research and the action programmes should become a search with the people who are actually involved in the process.

Such a process will not only result in a deeper understanding of local problems and the development of well-knit local units, but will also facilitate building up inter-linkages between action groups in the field and horizontal mobilisation, giving rise to concrete strategies to empower the marginalised people in India to secure equality, justice and freedom.

THE CONTINUITY OF DISABILITIES OF SCHEDULED CASTES IN INDIA

The post-Independent SCs were known by a variety of terms at different times. During the Vedic age the present-day Scheduled Castes people were included in the category of Shudra. It is clear from a mention what Atri declared a washerman, a leather-worker, a cane worker, a fisherman, and a Bhil as Antyajas or outcastes (Ghurye: 1969; 98). In traditional India the untouchables were known as the 'antyas' or 'bahyas' people living outside villages and towns (Sharma: 1958; 130) The British Government identified them as 'untouchables,' 'depressed classes' and Scheduled Castes' at different times. Since the Vedic age to the present-day post-Independent India, a Hindu Society has a history of SCs of their disabilities. Here the changing nature of their disabilities has been delineated.

DISABILITIES OF SHUDRAS IN AN ANCIENT INDIA

An account of religious, economic and civil disabilities, and also the severity of punishment to the Shudras has been sketched below:

Religious Disabilities

A number of religious disabilities were imposed on Shudras. They were allowed to use the current exclamation namah. They were not to be admitted to the Upanayana and the study of the Veda *(ibid.,* 119). Neither they were allowed to listen to or recite the Vedic hymns. Also, they were not allowed to follow the Ashram system. If a Shudra recited Vedas his tongue was cut off. It is because they were regarded unfit for twice born and so they had no right to wear the sacred thread and also they were made disqualified to receive religious blessings. Shudras were not admitted to the ceremony of sacrifice. Dutt elaborated that; 'though the Shudra was present at the Ashwamegha sacrifice in the capacity of a watchman, the privilege of abhishekh (ritual sprinkling) was not given to him and he was not to be admitted to the hail of sacrifice.

He was also deprived of the right of initiation and the right of drinking soma at sacrifices' (Dutt 1968; 87-88). They were not allowed to milk for fire-oblation). A marriage of Shudra was also not regarded as sacrament but was regarded only as a sexual union. Shudras were prohibited from practising austerities. In this regard, a story of the Ramayana is quoted that Rama had killed a Shudra for practising austerities. It is well-known fact that the temples built by the labour of Shudras were not open for them. Similarly, a Shudra could not attain individual salvation after death, which was a privilege to other three Varnas. Thus, a Shudra was unfit for initiating a ceremony of twice-born, for studying Vedas or reciting the Vedic hymns, for performing a sacrifice, for offering fire-oblations and for practising austirities.

Economic Deprivation

According to the Mahabharata the Shudras can have no right to own property. He was not permitted to acquire wealth. Kautilya mentioned regarding the means of livelihood of Shudras. They had two sources of livelihood, i.e., service of twice-born castes and their own professions *viz.,* artisans, dancers, actors etc..

Shudras were always associated with the removal, street sweeping and cremation of corpses. The duty was imposed on them to pick up and carry the dead bodies of animals and human beings. They were employed as agricultural labourers and slaves. Dun remarked that the professions of 'Shudras were regarded as impure and they were degraded to the level of the slave. Also, the outcastes persons were deprived of the occupations of the twice-born. The food and clothes remnants and castaways by the three Varnas were the sources of support for survival to the Shudras. Thus it is clear that the Shudras' economic life was degraded to the lowest position.

Disabilities in Civil Life

A Shudra had no right of sitting, conversing, or going along the road with twice-born men and if he does so he should receive corporal punishment. It is quoted that if a Shudra commits adultery with woman of the twice-born, he shall suffer capital punishment, Various prohibitions against a Shudra were to be observed by a twice-born person viz., not to go on journey in the company of a Shudra, not to eat food or accept water given by a Shudra, not to marry a Shudra female by a Brahmin, not to express sentiments of compassion about a Shudra and so on. The Chandals were treated as untouchables Manu declare them to be worthy of being settled outside the town-limits. Ghurye quoted that the objects like vehicles and seats defiled by the touch of a Shudra were to be rendered unfit for use unless water was sprinkled over them. That is to say that the position of Shudras in ancient India was degraded down to the animals.

Severe Punishments to The Shudras

In Manusmriti Shudras have been discriminated against for punishment. *A* severe punishment is laid down to the Shudras on the violation of the rules of the Shastra. For abusing a member of the Dwija caste the Shudra's tongue was to be mutilated. In case a Shudra abused a Brahmin by using his name he was punished by inserting in his mouth a red hot iron bar. For preaching a Brahmin a Shudra was punishable with pouring burning oil down his throat and ears. It is pointed out that the most severe punishment was to be awarded to a Shudra and the least to a Brahmin. In this way the Shudras were not only discriminated against in the matter of punishments but also they were severely punished.

SOCIAL DISABILITIES DURING THE MARATHA PERIOD

During the Maratha period (1600-1818 A.D.) in Maratha country, i.e., the present Western Maharashtra the traditional order of the Hindu society seems to be unchanged. A sovereign Maratha kingdom is identified from the emergence of Shivaji Chhatrapati. King Shivaji made clear his policy towards the various castes in his Royal Order issued on January 28, 1677 AD that: "The practices of each caste as handed down by tradition should be scrupulously observed". And King Shivaji preserved the system of Chaturvarnya without disturbing the framework of society during his rule. During the Peshwa period i.e., the 18th century a number of interdictions were imposed on the members of each caste regarding marriage, dining, drinking and social contact. In Maharashtra the Balutedarj system is known for its village economy. The essential feature of the system is that the artisan castes and the other untouchable castes had to provide services essentially or occasionally to village people. In the system, especially the position of the Mahar was as bad as a slave. It is because a Mahar had to perform a number of duties. It is mentioned that under the Peshwas the Mahars, the Mangs and the Chambhars were untouchables and also they were living outside the village. Regarding the interrelationship certain strict rules were imposed on the members of each caste. The Brahmin was not permitted to employ a woman as a maid-servant from the untouchable castes i.e., Mahar of Chambhar. Some mentions are on the historical documents that the upper caste-Hindu men were not permitted to have illicit intercourse with a Mahar or Mang woman and the identified upper caste-Hindu men were to be excommunicated, and when a lowest Mang had intercourse with a upper caste-Hindu woman he was to be murdered. In case of crimes such as theft, robbery and dacoity severe punishment was awarded to Mahar criminals. A practice of forced labour was prevalent and the Mahars, the Mangs and the Chambhars were employed towards it. The lower Castes were forbidden certain usages and customs e.g., doning the sacred thread etc., practised by the Brahmins. An untouchable girl, a student of Mahatma Phule's school of the 19h Century has stated in her essay, that 'it was not possible to the Mahars and Mangs to pass through the roads of Peshwa's palace in Pune city'. From the above account it is clear that the position of the members of the untouchable castes was degraded below the level of the animal.

DISABILITIES OF UNTOUCHABLES DURING THE BRITISH PERIOD

Till pre-British regime the supremacy of the Brahmins and their authority over the Shastras was neither disturbed nor challenged. The Hindu kings also restored the order of the Hindu social structure and system. But, with the advent of the British a number of new systems emerged and developed, viz., a Government of modern legislations, a modern bureaucracy and administration, new means of communication such as posts and mass media, a system of modern formal education based on scientific and rational temper, the growth of industries in cities and its large-scale organisations and a number of Christian missionaries to the educational and medical services of the poor.

In spite of these many new things, a Hindu society remained unchanged. The important thing which is to be noted here is that, at the initial stage the British Government had adopted the policy of non-interference in the internal affairs of the Hindus' religion and customs. Nevertheless, the new systems in the British rule affected the traditional institutions of the Hindu society with certain limitations. It was not possible to change the entire order of Hindu society at once. Therefore, we come across with a number of complaints regarding disabilities suffered by those untouchables of the British India.

In the Maratha country the various duties of the village which were imposed on the Mahars continued even during the British period. In the Bombay Presidency of the British India the Mahars had to perform a number of duties as inferior hereditary officers to the various Government departments *viz.,* irrigation, revenue, education, police and local self government.

The Mahars were to be called upon to render their services at any time of day and night. In return to their services they had two sources of livelihood i.e., a piece of main land and the baluta (grains from the peasants). That is why Dr. Babasaheb Ambedkar described the Watan system as an atrocious and barbarious system. An incident is mentioned that, one Mahar with socks and boots was not allowed to enter the main village and also the act of putting tiles by a Mahar on his house was not tolerated by the caste Hindus, and those who did so against the practice a social boycott against the community was declared. A case is reported that till 1926 a Bhangi (sweeper) was not allowed to board a tram in Bombay city.

The untouchables were not admitted to the public places such as watering places, wells and dharamshalas. It is evidenced from the resolution passed in the Bombay Legislative Council. A case is mentioned that in the year 1836 a Mahar boy was denied admission to the Dharwar Government School. In many schools the Mahar boys were not allowed to enter the classroom but they had to sit at Varandah. It is mentioned that in the year 1927 in the city of Bombay, the depressed class children were given separate pots for drinking water. The doors of the Hindu temples were closed to the untouchables is a widely known fact. The famous temple entry agitations which were led (consequently those went failure) under the leadership of untouchables at Nasik, Amravati and Poona in Maharashtra, and also under the leadership of Mahatma Gandhi at Guruvayur in Kerala are the sufficient examples to suggest that the untouchables had to suffer from such disability. In the year 1929 Dr. Ambedkar had given an account of the socio-economic disabilities of the untouchables of the times, that: Untouchables could not enter the Police, the Army and the Navy as their touch was causing pollution, the professions like trade and industry were closed to them, they were not free to dress and live as they liked, they might not wear better clothes than the high caste-Hindus, they had to live in hut, and could not take the bridegroom on a horse in procession through the main streets of the village, if an untouchable was a victim of the majority tyranny the Police hardly was to come to his rescue.

It is mentioned that in the year 1927 a medical practitioner not only refused to enter the untouchable's quarters but he refused to see the patient and to apply the thermometer also. The complaint was reported in the year 1928 that the High case-Hindus of some villages in Indore district had framed certain rules against the Balais. The rules imposed were:

1. Balais must not wear gold lace and bordered pugrees.
2. They must not wear dhoties with coloured or fancy borders.

3. They must convey intimation of the death of any Hindu to relatives of deceased—no matter how far away the relatives stayed.
4. In all Hindu marriages, the Balais must play, music before the processions, and during the marriages.
5. The Balai women must not wear gold or silver ornaments; they must not wear fancy gowns, or jackets.
6. Balai women must attend all cases of confinement of Hindu women.
7. The Balais must render services without demanding remuneration, and must accept whatever a Hindu is pleased to give.
8. If the Balais do not agree to abide by these terms, they must clear out of the villages. This example is sufficient to indicate the caste tyranny.

It is mentioned that it was not possible to invite a respectable untouchable to a house of caste Hindu, and in case it is done the caste council would not only condemn him but also would pass a judgement against the householder as unfit for social intercourse. An incident of some villages in Solapur district was reported that the effort of the Mahars of giving up of the carrying of the carcasses of dead animals at self-improvement was not tolerated by the caste-Hindus and in consequence the villagers had declared the economic boycott.

PRACTICE OF UNTOUCHABILITY, ATROCITIES

During the post-Independent period in spite of the Constitutional and Statutory measures and also making the practice of untouchability punishable under the Protection of Civil Rights Act the condition of SCs has not improved and the disabilities on the grounds of untouchability continued adding incidents of complaints regarding the practice of untouchability, harassments, torture, atrocities and tyranny. The account of their social, economic and educational sufferings is stated below.

Observance of Untouchability

A number of Reports of the Commissioner for SCs and STs inform us regarding the prevalence of the practice of untouchability. There are some common forms of untouchability which are being observed not only in villages but in towns and cities also. In many parts of the country untouchability has been rigidly observed against the Bhangis or the Mehtars in towns and cities as well. Generally the high caste persons neither receive nor eat cooked food given by the persons from the lowest caste groups. In many parts of village India, the village wells are not open to SCs. They are not allowed to use hand pumps constructed in many villages. It has been the common experience to the SC persons that they have been denied rented accommodation not only in villages but in cities also. The barbers and the washermen refuse services to the lowest castes on the grounds of untouchability. In Rajasthan the SC persons had no access to inns. The lowest ex-untouchables were not allowed to sit on the same cot with high caste persons or in presence of the high caste Hindus.

In some parts of India the lowest ex-untouchables could not ride a horse. As stated in the Fourteenth Report of the Commissioner for SCs/STs (1964-65) in some areas of Tamil Nadu the SCs were not allowed to carry dead bodies, to wear shoes, to ride on cycles through the localities of caste Hindus. In an area of Union Territory of Delhi the lowest castes were prevented from using public roads. In some villages the entry in hotel was barred. In some places tea was served outside the hotel or in separate tumblers or coconut shell kept outside the stalls and also water was poured from a distance. Whenever the lowest caste persons were invited to the house of higher caste on occasions they were made to sit separately. As stated in the Twelfth Report of the Commissioner for SCs/STs (1962-63), the survey observed discrimination against SCs in Gujarat State that, the SCs had to wash their clothes or take bath at separate ghats of the tanks and also they were compelled to use the river-water down stream only. Further it is reported that separate drinking water arrangements were made for SC employees in the Municipal and Grampanchayat offices. And separate burial or cremation grounds existed for the SCs. In some villages of Gujarat, the SCs were served clothes, flour, sweetmeat and grocery from a distance by the caste-Hindu shop owners.

According to the Eleventh Report of the Commissioner for SCs/STs (1961-62) in some of the villages of Madhya Pradesh the ex-untouchable persons were not allowed to put on a turban with turrha. In some villages marriage processions were not allowed to pass through the localities of high caste Hindus. In some parts of India a music-band was not allowed to play at the marriage. And the women were not permitted to wear ornaments made of silver.

The ex-untouchables were neither allowed to enter temples nor were allowed to offer sweets or flowers to the deity. In Mathura-Vrindavan if an ex-untouchable disclosed his identity he was not allowed to enter the temple. In some villages of Bihar the SCs were not allowed to attend the Kirtan. The same Report stated that in some interior villages the ex-untouchable pupils had to sit separately. Also, in some schools they were not allowed to touch the bucket, glass or Iota kept there. In some villages the high caste-Hindus did not allow the ex-untouchable children to join the schools. In the University of Allahabad the SC IAS trainees were refused tea by the manager of the canteen.

In the Fourteenth Report of the Commissioner SCs/STs (1964-65) it is stated that in a village of Gujarat a SC teacher was not allowed to enter the store-room of the school. In some hostels attached to Government schools and colleges of Jammu and Kashmir State the SC students were discriminated against in common rooms and kitchens.

In some cases the higher officers have used disrespectful and objectionable language against SCs and also insulted them. It has been reported that in some village Panchayats the SCs were not allowed to sit on chairs. In village of Gujarat in the year 1977, the caste Hindus did not allow to enrol the ex-untouchables of the village as members of the village Milk Cooperative Society.

According to the Twenty-sixth Report of the Commissioner for SCs/STs (1978-79) the ex-untouchables were assaulted and insulted while taking seat in a bus or by chance touching caste-Hindus or their vessels, and such cases were reported from the state of Gujarat, Haryana, Kerala. Pondicherry, Madhya Pradesh, and Uttar Pradesh. The extent of untouchability can easily be understood as the number of registered cases under the Protection of civil Rights Act, 1955 has increased in the country from 526 in 1971.

Cases of Atrocities, Harassments, Torture and Insults

Day by day incidents of atrocities on SCs are increasing. The figures show that the atrocity cases during the year 1979 were 13,975 in number which rose to *15,054* in 1982. A variety of forms of atrocities were committed such as murder, rape, molestation of women, illegal dispossession of land of SCs, burning alive (as occurred at Belchi, a village in Bihar and also at many other places), violence resulting in grievous hurt, arson, burning of houses, preventing from cultivation of land and harvesting of crops, unlawful eviction from the land in possession and the like. And the causes of atrocities have been reported that of social awakening and assertion by the SCs on account of problems relating to the practice of untouchability, harassment, land disputes, housing, non-payment of minimum wages, forced labour, refusal to carry out the traditional caste duties etc.

A number of complaints have been reported relating to the denial of justice to SC employees in service matters. The cases of harassments of SC persons were reported not only from the offices but also from the experiences of varied interactional levels with the caste Hindus. A variety of cases of complaints of harassments, tortures, insults were reported such as insulting by using caste name, commenting on the colour of the skin, depriving from opportunity to appear at the examination or depriving from confirmation and promotion chances in the service, not relieving for training, not forwarding the application for other or higher post, not considering for appointment under this or that pretext, not issuing caste certificates to SC applicants by the Pradhans of Gram Panchayats and as such.

Economic Disabilities

The phenomenon of poverty in India is comprehended on economic criteria. The Plan document mentioned the number of poor but the percentage of poor among the SCs is not separately shown. However, the Govt. documents admitted that the bulk of SCs was among the poorest of the population. But the figure 76.39% of the SC population indicated as cultivators and agricultural labourers reveals that their larger population belongs to the group of poor. The prevalence of bonded labour among the SC population can be considered for identification of poverty among them. In spite of the enactment in the year 1976 of the Central Law abolishing bonded labour and the new 20-Point Programme as well, the Reports of the Commissioner for SCs/STs inform us that the bonded labourers were identified mostly from the SCs. And the prevalence of bonded labour was attributed to indebtedness as a major cause. However, the Fifth Report of the Commissioner for SCs/STs informed that 80% of the bonded labourers who were identified in the country belonged to SCs and STs.

So far as the adoption of modern jobs is concerned a little progress has been revealed among some caste groups of untouchable category. Some recent studies, however, observed that the Bhangis were still in their caste-jobs of scavenging. Further it is interesting to know the share of SC households in the ownership of land among the total households in rural areas of the country. In this regard the Thirty-seventh NSS round has revealed that the SC households constituting 19.71% of total households had a share of only 7.89% which was the lowest in the total ownership of land holdings. Thus in spite of the various welfare programmes of the Government the economic condition of a majority of SCs/STs is still pathetic.

Educational Development

Despite the special educational facilities and anti-disabilities measures for SCs, the literacy rate in the year 1981 for SCs was only 21.38% against 36.17% at All-India level. The percentage of enrolment of SCs to total enrolment at High/ Higher Secondary stage during the year 1978-79 at All-India level was 9.9. These figures reveal a wide gap when compared with the enrolment of caste-Hindus to the enrolment of SCs. Despite reservation and other educational facilities many seats were not filled up by SC candidates in professional colleges, in Central institutions and at under-graduate and post-graduate levels. Thus the poor progress of SCs in education is alone of the indicators for their overall backwardness.

The policy of reservation is enshrined in Articles 16 (4) and *335* of the Constitution but during the recent years the caste-Hindus have expressed their resentment over it and so an organised anti-reservation widespread agitation led by the caste-

Hindus in Gujarat in the year 1981 is an example before all of us. Apart from the people's opposition in general, there are examples of non-SC/ST employees who had opposed reservation of vacancies on promotion. Despite the reservation measures for employment opportunities in India 16,61,081 educated Scheduled Caste job-seekers were on the liveregister as on 31.12.1979. The figure is indicative of the society of the problem of unemployment among the educated Scheduled Castes. However, the percentages of SC employees in various services show the slight progress. But it indicates for their marginal representation in the service sector of the country.

In this way the educational progress and a representation in services of the SCs/STs appear to be poor.

CASTE AND GENDER EQUATIONS IN INDIAN HISTORY

No aspect of Indian history has excited more controversy than India's history of social relations. Western indologists and Western-influenced Indian intellectuals have seized upon caste divisions, untouchability, religious obscurantism, and practices of dowry and sati as distinctive evidence of India's perennial backwardness. For many Indologists, these social ills have literally come to define India-and have become almost the exclusive focus of their writings on India. During the colonial period, it served the interests of the British (and their European cohorts) to exaggerate the democratic character of their own societies while diminishing any socially redeeming features of society in India (and other colonized nations). Social divisions and inequities were a convenient tool in the arsenal of the colonizers. On the one hand, tremendous tactical gains could be achieved by playing off one community against the other. On the other hand, there were also enormous psychological benefits in creating the impression that India was a land rife with uniquely abhorrent social practices that only an enlightened foreigner could attempt to reform. India's social ills were discussed with a contemptuous cynicism and often with a willful intent to instill a sense of deep shame and inferiority.

Strong elements of such colonial imagery continue to dominate the landscape of Western Indology. A liberal, dynamic West embracing universal human values is posed against an obdurate and unchanging East clinging to odious social values and customs. It is little wonder, therefore, that India's intellectuals have been unable to either fully understand the historic dynamics and context which gave life to these social practices or find effective solutions for their cure. Many historians and social activists appear to have tacitly accepted the notion that caste divisions in society are a uniquely Indian feature and that Indian society has been largely unchanged since the writing of the *Manusmriti* which provides formal sanction to such social inequities.

But caste-like divisions are neither uniquely Indian nor has Indian society been as socially stagnant as commonly believed. In all non-egalitarian societies where wealth and political power were unequally distributed, some form of social inequity appeared and often meant hereditary privileges for the elite and legally (or socially) sanctioned discrimination against those considered lower down in the social hierarchy. In fact, caste-like divisions are to be found in the history of most nations-whether in the American continent, or in Africa, Europe or elsewhere in Asia. In some societies, caste-like divisions were relatively simple, in others more complex. For instance, in Eastern Africa some agricultural societies were divided between land-owning and landless tribes (or clans) that eventually took on caste-like characteristics. Priests and warriors enjoyed special privileges in the 15th C. Aztec society of Mexico as did the Samurais (warrior nobles) and priests of medieval Japan. Notions of purity and defilement were also quite similar in Japanese society and members of society who carried out "unclean" tasks were treated as social outcasts-just as in India.

Amongst the most stratified of the ancient civilizations was the Roman Civilization where in addition to state-sanctioned slavery, there were all manner of caste-like inequities coded into law. Even in the Christian era, European feudalism provided all manner of hereditary privileges for the knights and landed barons (somewhat akin to India's Rajputs and Thakurs) and amongst the royalty, arranged marriages and dowry were just as common as in India. Discrimination against the artisans was also commonplace throughout Europe, and as late as the 19th century-artisans in Germany had to go through a separate court system to seek legal redress. They were not permitted to appeal to courts that dealt with the affairs of the nobility and the landed gentry. (For instance, Beethoven wrote numerous letters to German judicial authorities pleading that he not be treated as a second-class citizen-that as Germany's pre-eminent composer he deserved better treatment.) A common pattern that seems to emerge from a study of several such ancient and medieval societies is that priests and warriors typically formed an elite class in most medieval societies and social privileges varied according to social rank; in settled agriculture based societies, this was usually closely related to ownership of land.

For instance, we find no evidence of caste-like discrimination in societies where land was collectively owned and jointly cultivated, or where goods and services were exchanged within the village on the basis of barter, and there was no premium assigned to any particular type of work. All services and all forms of human labor were valued equally. Such village communes may have once existed throughout India and some appear to have survived until quite recently-especially in the hills, (such as in parts of Himachal and the North East, including Assam and Tripura), but also in Orissa and parts of Central India. In such societies, we also see little evidence of gender discrimination. In India, caste and gender discrimination appear to become more pronounced with the advent of hereditary and authoritarian ruling dynasties, a powerful state bureaucracy, the growth of selective property rights, and the domination of Brahmins over the rural poor in *agrahara* villages. But this process was neither linear nor always irreversible. As old ruling dynasties were overthrown, previously existing caste equations and caste hierarchies were also challenged and modified.

In many parts of India this process may have taken several centuries to crystallize and caste rigidity may be a much more recent phenomenon than has been commonly portrayed. The impression that caste divisions were always strictly enforced, or that there were no challenges to caste rigidity does not seem to square with a dispassionate examination of the Indian historical record. It should also be emphasized that caste-distinctions were not the only way, or even the most egregious way in which social inequities manifested themselves in older societies. In ancient Greece and Rome, the institution of slavery was at least as cruel a practice, if not worse. (It is therefore quite ironic how the slave-owning Greek states are revered by Western intellectuals as the world's first "democratic" societies but ancient India is denigrated for it's incomprehensible social ills.)

Levels and degree of caste discrimination in India have varied with time and there has been both upward and downward mobility of castes and social groups. Going by the strictures outlined in the *Manusmriti,* one might conclude that caste distinctions were set in stone, rigidly enforced and the possibilities of caste mobility completely circumscribed. But a closer examination of the historical record suggests otherwise.

Already in the Upanishadic period there were tensions between Brahmins and Kshatriyas, and there are explicit parables in the Upanishadic texts illustrating how an enlightened Kshatriya was able to exceed a Brahmin in spiritual wisdom and philosophical knowledge. In the Mahabharatha, there are references to a Brahmin warrior suggesting that caste categories were not entirely inflexible. There is also criticism of parasitism amongst Brahmins in some of the texts from the Upanishadic period, and social commentators emphasized how those who reneged on their social obligations were undeserving of their caste privileges.

This is an important point because it suggests that there was an implied social contract that involved both privileges and social obligations. The monarch might have enjoyed immense power and prestige, and exacted numerous rights over the common people, but also had the obligation to defend the people-to protect them from invaders, to dispense justice in an unprejudiced manner and assist in the development and preservation of irrigation facilities and roads. Failure to meet such expectations could and did lead to revolts, and dynasties rose and fell within a matter of few generations.

CHALLENGES TO BRAHMINICAL HEGEMONY AND CASTE-RIGIDITY

In the Upanishads, there is also recognition that conceptions of god could be quite varied, that Brahminical rituals were not essential to spiritual release, and that individuals might choose different deities or methods of worship. This ecumenical outlook facilitated the growth of alternative viewpoints not only in the realm of religious practice but also on norms of how society ought to be structured. Social challenges to absolute monarchical rule and the immense power of the priestly class probably led to a crescendo during the Buddhist period when Brahmin hegemony received challenges from several quarters-from radical atheists such as the *Lokayatas,* from Jain agnostics, and heterodox Hindus and Buddhists who wanted to reconstruct society on a less discriminatory and more humane basis.

Although it would be wrong to romanticize the Buddhists as being completely against caste distinctions {since there is evidence that they accepted caste distinctions in society outside their *sanghas* (communes)}, Buddhists along with other social critics undoubtedly played a powerful role in ensuring that caste was not the sole or even the dominant factor in shaping Indian society of that period. This is borne out by how so many ruling clans arose from a non-Kshatriya (and also non-Brahmin) background. The Nandas, the Mauryas, the Kalingas and the Guptas are just some of the more illustrious of India's ruling dynasties that did not arise from a Kshatriya background. (Of course, once some of these clans established themselves as ruling dynasties, they took on the Kshatriya mantle, and over time, the radical changes that accompanied their ascent to power gave way to social conservatism and a decaying of the radical currents that had contributed to their rise to power).

It is also worth noting that the classical four varna division of Hindu society (as described in the *Manusmriti)* does not appear to have had much practical significance if one were to go by the accounts of the Greek chronicler, Megasthenes. In his accounts of Mauryan India. Megasthenes appears to list a seven fold social order in which he differentiates between the priest and the philosopher (who he ranked much above the priest, and who could have been a Brahmin, Jain or Buddhist) and also gives special attention to court bureaucrats such as record keepers, tax collectors and judicial officials. He also ascribed to the peasantry a higher status than might be inferred from the *Manusmriti* and noted with amazement how the peasantry was left unharmed during battles.

According to Megasthenes, philosophers-whether Brahmins or Jain/Buddhist monks also had obligations in terms of offering advice to the ruler in matters of public policy, agriculture, health and culture. Repeated failure to provide sound counsel could lead to a loss of privileges-even exile or death. Thus, although many Brahmins may have held on to their privileges by being shameless sycophants-others made significant contributions in the realm of science, philosophy and culture. Social mobility was possible since learning was not an exclusive preserve of the Brahmins and both the Buddhist and Jain sanghas admitted people from different social backgrounds and also admitted women. (Jyotsna Kamat points to a Karnataka inscription from 1187 A.D. that suggests that Jain nuns enjoyed the same amount of freedom as their male counterparts.) The more advanced *sanghas* enforced a separate quorum for women to ensure that a largely male gathering may not take decisions that did not meet with the approval of the women members of the *sangha*.

Over time, it appears that the *sanghas* degenerated, losing their intellectual vitality and egalitarian spirit allowing the Brahmins to gradually consolidate their power and influence in the Gangetic plain. But even as late as the 6th-7th C, Gupta-period inscriptions describing land grants in Bengal appear to corroborate Megasthenes' view of how Indian society was structured. Social rank of senior court administrators (who may have risen from different caste backgrounds) invariably exceeded the rank of ordinary village priests. (In Orissa, Rajasthan and parts of Central and Southern India, this pattern prevailed till even later. Moreover, as society headed towards caste-ossification, it was the court administrators who after acquiring hereditary caste status, became the most privileged agents in society. In some instances, these administrative castes simply merged with other privileged castes such as Brahmin or Kshatriya, or else they were treated as equivalent, and the historic distinctions between then became blurred or obscured.)

In a sampling of Gupta period land grant decrees, it is intriguing that caste identities are omitted more often than explicitly included. Had caste been as important or dominant a social category, one might expect otherwise. Some of the most important figures appear to be officials involved in tax collection and land measurement. Various ranks of officials are mentioned without any explicit mention of their caste. Villagers are also frequently named without reference to their cast. Only occasionally, there are references to villagers who are also mentioned as being Brahmins. Some of the land grant records indicate that before land grants were made, certain categories of villagers-perhaps those considered more important-were consulted by the higher officials. Although Brahmins are mentioned in the list of those consulted, there are equal references to other categories of villagers such as *kutumbins* and *mahattaras* who may have been village officials or important landholders in the village.

Other references point to consultative committees that included the chief artisan, the chief scribe, the merchant and the guild-president of the town. It also appears that administrative changes led to the creation of new posts, the merger or elimination of older posts, and changes in ranks of various officials over time. An examination of the land grant decrees over a space of three centuries (5th-7th C Bengal) points to such changes and others-such as changes in procedures, or changes in the constitution of consultative committees, perhaps to reflect changing political alliances or changes in the economic status of different groups of townspeople and villagers. In a land allotment plate from Paschimbagh (Bengal) Brahmins are mentioned as tax payers, and the status of ordinary Brahmins does not seem at all exceptional. For instance, it points to a teacher or a Vedic scholar as being entitled to 10 *patakas* of land, but other Brahmins were entitled to only 2 *patakas*-a share less than that of a *Kayastha* (record-keeper) or *Vaidya* (medical practitioner). Carpenters, smiths and artisans were also put far above other service communities in terms of their share of land.

The Paschimbagh inscription also describes the grant of plots of land to florists, potters, carpenters, masons, blacksmiths and sweepers for serving a *matha* (monastery) indicating that when land was granted for a temple or monastery, priests were not the exclusive beneficiaries of land grants. (Two Bhaumakara charters from Talcher/Dhenkanal in Orissa similiarly refer to donations of land for a Buddhist temple, and allocations for its maintenance.) A study of land grants from 12th C Rajasthan (Pali) and Karnataka (Kalikatti) suggests that land grants had a limited life tenure even when initially decreed to be for life or for perpetuity. Beneficiaries of land grants were subject to transfers, and grants to a particular beneficiary were transferred to another beneficiary five or ten years later. It also appears that the beneficiaries were selected based on administrative rank rather than any particular caste-affiliation.

It is also not at all apparent that administrative rank was limited by birth. In Orissa, there is explicit evidence to the contrary. Ordinary peasants were able to rise up in the ranks of the military, and it is likely that a similar situation prevailed in the administrative ranks. Mayadhar Mansinha suggests that a combination of factors such as training, merit and personal determination played a role, (in addition to social standing and political connections) in determining rank and promotions. In Karnataka, there is evidence that some of the chief administrators were women.

Brahminical Ascendance

Nevertheless, the seeds for a more privileged role for the Brahmins were also being sown through the process of land grants to Brahmins. In some instances, thousands of Brahmins were granted rights to hitherto uncultivated land. In other cases, Brahmins were appointed as the local representatives of the state authorities in what are described as *agrahara* villages where Brahmins presided over small peasants, who in Bihar were mostly landless sharecoppers or bonded labourers. These *agrahara* villages were typically small villages and sattelites of bigger villages that included members of several castes and bigger land-holders. In Bihar, such *agrahara* villages proliferated and it is quite likely that in such *agraharas* oppressive social relations and some of the most egregious patterns of caste-centred discrimination and exploitation may have developed. (While early Gupta period records indicate the existence of rural consultative councils that mediated between the rulers and the artisans and peasants, it seems that such consultative councils became less important or were phased out with the growth of the *agraharas.* Thereafter, the Brahmins became the sole intermediaries between the village and the state, and over time, this may have enabled the Brahmins to exercise social and political hegemony over other inhabitants of the village. It also appears that the greatest incidence of the practice of untouchability occurs in conjunction with the growth in the power and authority of the Brahmins in such villages.)

But these developments took time to spread elsewhere in India, first spreading to Bengal and eastern UP, and very gradually elsewhere in India. However, this pattern was not necessarily replicated in identical form throughout India and some parts of India virtually escaped this trend. In *agrahara* villages in other parts of India, Brahmins did take on the role of local administrators and tax collectors, but the status of the small peasantry was not always as miserable as in Bihar. The degree of exploitation and oppression appears to be related to the extent of alienation from land-ownership. For example, evidence for Brahmin domination in Kalikatti, Southern Karnataka emerges after the 13th C. when villagers were instructed to pay taxes to the Brahmin assignees, leading to constant tensions and disputes, but without dramatic changes in the overall status of the tax-paying villagers.

Although Brahminization was an important factor in leading to caste ossification, it was not necessarily the sole or even the most important factor in the mix. The impact of the Islamic invasions, colonization by the British and ecological changes played an equally crucial if not decisive role in many instances. For instance, in Orissa, the ossification of the bureaucracy and its conversion into a group of privileged and exclusive castes appears to take place after the 14th-15th C. when we begin to see a general decline in its overseas trade due to the silting up of its rivers. At the same time, we see the growth of Brahminical hegemony in the realm of religion and military defeats at the hands of the Mughal armies led by Raja Man Singh of Jaipur. All these factors may have played a role in destroying the vibrancy of Oriya society and encouraging caste conservatism.

9

Religious Form of Caste System

In Hinduism there exists four castes arranged in a hierarchy. Anyone who does not belong to one of these castes is an outcast. The religious word for caste is 'Varna'. Each Varna has certain duties and rights. Each Varna members have to work in certain occupation which only that Varna members are allowed. Each Varna has certain type of diet. The highest Varna is of the Brahman. Members of this class are priests and the educated people of the society. The Varna after them in hierarchy is Kshatriya. The members of this class are the rulers and aristocrats of the society. After them are the Vaishya. Members of this class are the landlords and businessmen of the society. After them in hierarchy are the Sudra. Members of this class are the peasants and working class of the society who work in non-polluting jobs. The caste hierarchy ends here. Below these castes are the outcasts who are untouchable to the four castes. These Untouchables worked in degrading jobs like cleaning, sewage etc.

The first three castes had social and economical rights which the Sudra and the untouchables did not have. The first three castes are also seen as 'twice born'. The intention in these two births is to the natural birth and to the ceremonial entrance to the society at a much later age. Each Varna and also the untouchables are divided into many communities. These communities are called Jat or Jati (The caste is also used instead of Jat). For example the Brahmans have Jats called Gaur, Kokanastha, Sarasvat, Iyer and others. The outcasts have Jats like Mahar, Dhed, Mala, Madiga and others. The

Sudra is the largest Varna and it has the largest number of communities. Each Jat is limited to professions worthy of their Varna. Each Jat is limited to the Varna diet. Each Jat members are allowed to marry only with their Jat members. People are born into their Jat and it cannot be changed. This is the how the caste system is supposed to be in its religious form. But in reality it is much more complicated and different from its religious form.

BEGINNING OF THE CASTE SYSTEM

There are different theories about the establishment of the caste system. There are religious-mystical theories. There are biological theories. And there are socio-historical theories. The religious theories explain how the four Varnas were founded, but they do not explain how the Jats in each Varna or the untouchables were founded. According the Rig Veda, the ancient Hindu book, the primal man-Purush-destroyed himself to create a human society. The different Varnas were created from different parts of his body. The Brahmans were created from his head; the Kshatriyas from his hands; the Vaishyas from his thighs and the Sudras from his feet. The Varna hierarchy is determined by the descending order of the different organs from which the Varnas were created. Other religious theory claims that the Varnas were created from the body organs of Brahma, who is the creator of the world.

The biological theory claims that all existing things, animated and inanimated, inherent three qualities in different apportionment. Sattva qualities include wisdom, intelligence, honesty, goodness and other positive qualities. Rajas include qualities like passion, pride, valour and other passionate qualities. Tamas qualities include dullness, stupidity, lack of creativity and other negative qualities. People with different doses of these inherent qualities adopted different types of occupation. According to this theory the Brahmans inherent Sattva qualities. Kshatriyas and Vaishyas inherent Rajas qualities. And the Sudras inherent Tamas qualities. Like human beings, food also inherents different dosage of these qualities and it affects its eater's intelligence. The Brahmans and the Vaishyas have Sattvic diet which includes fruits, milk, honey, roots and vegetables. Most of the meats are considered to have

Tamasic qualities. Many Sudra communities eat different kinds of meat (but not beef) and other Tamasic food. But the Kshatriyas who had Rajasic diet eat some kinds of meat like deer meat which is considered to have Rajasic qualities. Many Marathas who claim to be Kshatriyas eat mutton. The drawback of this theory is that in different parts of India the same food was sometimes qualified to have different dosage of inherent qualities. For example there were Brahmans who eat meat which is considered Tamasic food.

The social historical theory explains the creation of the Varnas, Jats and of the untouchables. According to this theory, the caste system began with the arrival of the Aryans in India. The Aryans arrived in India around 1500 BC. The fair skinned Aryans arrived in India from south Europe and north Asia. Before the Aryans there were other communities in India of other origins. Among them Negrito, Mongoloid, Austroloid and Dravidian. The Negrito have physical features similar to people of Africa. The Mongoloid have Chinese features. The Austroloids have features similar the aboriginals of Australia. The Dravidians originate from the Mediterranean and they were the largest community in India. When the Aryans arrived in India their main contact was with the Dravidians and the Austroloids.

The Aryans disregarded the local cultures. They began conquering and taking control over regions in north India and at the same time pushed the local people southwards or towards the jungles and mountains in north India. The Aryans organized among themselves in three groups. The first group was of the warriors and they were called Rajayana, later they changed their name Rajayana to Kshatriya. The second group was of the priests and they were called Brahmans. These two groups struggled politically for leadership among the Aryans. In this struggle the Brahmans got to be the leaders of the Aryan society. The third group was of the farmers and craftsmen and they were called Vaishya. The Aryans who conquered and took control over parts of north India subdued the locals and made them their servants. In this process the Vaishyas who were the farmers and the craftsmen became the landlords and the businessmen of the society and the locals became the peasants and the craftsmen of the society.

In order to secure their status the Aryans resolved some social and religious rules which, allowed only them to be the priests, warriors and the businessmen of the society. For example take Maharashtra. Maharashtra is in west India. This region is known by this name for hundreds of years. Many think that the meaning of the name Maharashtra is in its name, Great Land. But there are some who claim that the name, Maharashtra, is derived from the Jat called Mahar who are considered to be the original people of this region. In the caste hierarchy the dark skinned Mahars were outcasts. The skin colour was an important factor in the caste system. The meaning of the word "Varna" is not class or status but skin colour. Between the outcasts and the three Aryan Varnas there is the Sudra Varna who are the simple workers of the society. The Sudras consisted of two communities. One community was of the locals who were subdued by the Aryans and the other were the descendants of Aryans with locals. In Hindu religious stories there are many wars between the good Aryans and the dark skinned demons and devils. The different Gods also have dark skinned slaves. There are stories of demon women trying to seduce good Aryan men in deceptive ways. There were also marriages between Aryan heroes and demon women. Many believe that these incidences really occurred in which, the gods and the positive heroes were people of Aryan origin. And the demons, the devils and the dark skinned slaves were in fact the original residence of India whom the Aryans coined as monsters, devil, demons and slaves.

As in most of the societies of the world, so in India, the son inherited his father's profession. And so in India there developed families, who professed the same family profession for generation in which, the son continued his father's profession. Later on as these families became larger, they were seen as communities or as they are called in Indian languages, Jat. Different families who professed the same profession developed social relations between them and organized as a common community, meaning Jat. Later on the Aryans who created the caste system, added to their system non-Aryans. Different Jats who professed different professions were integrated in different Varnas according to their profession. Other foreign invaders of ancient India-Greeks, Huns, Scythains and others-who conquered parts of India and created kingdoms were integrated in the Kshatriya Varna (warrior castes). But probably the Aryan policy was not to integrate original Indian communities within them and therefore many aristocratic and warrior communities that were in India before the Aryans did not get the Kshatriya status.

Most of the communities that were in India before the arrival of the Aryans were integrated in the Sudra Varna or were made outcast depending on the professions of these communities. Communities who professed non-polluting jobs were integrated in Sudra Varna. And communities who professed polluting professions were made outcasts. The Brahmans are very strict about cleanliness. In the past people believed that diseases can also spread also through air and not only through physical touch. Perhaps because of this reason the untouchables were not only disallowed to touch the high caste communities but they also had to stand at a certain distance from the high castes.

CASTE AND STAGES OF LIFE IN HINDUISM

The pattern of social classes in Hinduism is called the "caste system." The chart shows the major divisions and contents of the system. Basic caste is called *varna*, or "colour." Sub-caste, or *jati*, "birth, life, rank," is a traditional subdivision of *varna*.

The *Bhagavad Gita* says this about the varnas: The works of Brahmins, Kshatriyas, Vaishyas, and Shudras are different, in harmony with the three powers of their born nature. The works of a Brahmin are peace; self-harmony, austerity, and purity; loving-forgiveness and righteousness; vision and wisdom and faith.

These are the works of a Kshatriya: a heroic mind, inner fire, constancy, resourcefulness, courage in battle, generosity and noble leadership. Trade, agriculture and the rearing of cattle is the work of a Vaishya. And the work of the Shudra is service. There are literally thousands of sub-castes in India, often with particular geographical ranges, occupational specializations, and an administrative or corporate structure. When Mahatma Gandhi wanted to go to England to study law, he had to ask his sub-caste, the Modh Bania, for permission to leave India. ("Bania", means "merchant," and "Gandhi" means "greengrocer"—from *gandha*, "smell, fragrance," in Sanskrit—and that should be enough for a good guess that Gandhi was a Vaishya.) Sometimes it is denied that the varnas are "castes" because, while "true" castes, the jatis, are based on birth, the varnas are based on the theory of the gunas (the "three powers" mentioned in the Gita).

This is no more than a rationalization: the varnas came first, and they *are* based on birth. The gunas came later, and provide a poor explanation anyway, since the guna *tamas* is associated with both twice born and once born, caste and outcaste, overlapping the most important religious and social divisions in the system. Nevertheless, the varnas are now divisions at a theoretical level, while the jatis are the way in which caste is embodied for most practical purposes. Jatis themselves can be ranked in relation to each other, and occasionally a question may even be raised about the proper varna to which a particular jati belongs. As jati members change occupations and they rise in prestige, a jati may rarely even be elevated in the varna to which it is regarded as belonging.

Associated with each varna there is a traditional colour. These sound suspiciously like skin colours; and, indeed, there is an expectation in India that higher caste people will have lighter skin—although there are plenty of exceptions (especially in the South of India). This all probably goes back to the original invasion of the Arya, who came from Central Asia and so were undoubtedly light skinned. The people already in India were quite dark, even as today many people in India seem positively black. Apart from skin colour, Indians otherwise have "Caucasian" features—narrow noses, thin lips, etc.—and recent genetic mapping studies seem to show that Indians are more closely related to the people of the Middle East and Europe than to anyone else. Because Untouchables are not a varna, they do not have a traditional colour. I have supplied blue, since this is otherwise not found, and it is traditionally used for the skin colour of Vishnu and his incarnations. Chief among those is *Krishna* whose *name* actually means "black" or "dark," but he is always shown blue rather than with some natural skin colour. The first three varnas are called the *twice born*. This has *nothing* to do with reincarnation. Being "twice born" means that you *come of age* religiously, making you a member of the Vedic religion, eligible to learn Sanskrit, study the Vedas, and perform Vedic rituals. The "second birth" is thus like Confirmation or a Bar Mitzvah. According to the *Laws of Manu* (whose requirements may not always be observed in modern life), boys are "born again" at specific ages: 8 for Brahmins; 11 for Kshatriyas; and 12 for Vaishyas. A thread is bestowed at the coming of age to be worn around the waist as the symbol of being twice born. The equivalent of coming of age for girls is marriage.

The bestowal of the thread is part of the wedding ceremony. That part of the wedding ritual is even preserved in Jainism. Ancient Iran also had a coming of age ceremony that involved a thread. That and other evidence leads to the speculation that the *three* classes of the twice born are from the original Indo-European social system—the theory of George Dumezil. Even the distant Celts believed in three social classes. The three classes of Plato's *Republic* thus may not have been entirely his idea. Although there must have been a great deal of early intermarriage in India, nowhere did such an Indo-European social system become as rigid a system of *birth* as there. The rigidity may well be due to the influence of the idea of *karma*, that poor birth is morally deserved. According to the *Laws of Manu*, when the twice born come of age, they enter into the four *ashramas* or "stages of life."

1. The first is the *brahmacharya*, or the stage of the student (*brahmacharin*). For boys, the student is supposed to go live with a teacher (*guru*), who is a Brahmin, to learn about Sanskrit, the Vedas, rituals, etc. The *dharma* of a student includes being obedient, respectful, celibate, and nonviolent. "The teacher is God." For girls, the stage of studenthood coincides with that of the householder, and the husband stands in the place of the teacher. Since the boys are supposed to be celibate while students, Gandhi used the term *brahmachari* to mean the celibate practitioner that he thought made the best *Satyagrahi*, the best nonviolent activist.
2. The second stage is the *garhastya*, or the stage of the householder, which is taken far more seriously in

Hinduism than in Jainism or Buddhism and is usually regarded as mandatory, like studenthood, although debate continued over the centuries whether or not this stage could be skipped in favour of a later one. This is the stage where the principal *dharma* of the person is performed, whether as priest, warrior, etc., or for women mainly as wife and mother. Arjuna's duty to fight the battle in the *Bhagavad Gita* comes from his status as a householder. Besides specific duties, there are general duties that pay off the "three debts": (1) a debt to the ancestors that is discharged by marrying and having children; (2) a debt to the gods that is discharged by the household rituals and sacrifices; and (3) a debt to the teacher that is discharged by appropriately teaching one's wife, children, and, for Brahmins, other students. The three debts are sometimes associated with the three Gods of the Trimurti—the ancestor debt with Brahma, the gods debt with Vishnu, and the teacher debt with Shiva.

3. The third stage is the *vanaprastya*, or the stage of the forest dweller. This may be entered into optionally if (ideally) one's hair has become gray, one's skin wrinkled, and grandchildren exist to carry on the family. Husbands and wives may leave their affairs and possessions with their children and retire together to the forest as hermits. This does not involve the complete renunciation of the world, for husbands and wives can still have sex (once a month), and a sacred fire still should be kept and minimal rituals performed. This stage is thus not entirely free of *dharma*. The Forest Treatises were supposed to have been written by or for forest dwellers, who have mostly renounced the world and have begun to consider liberation. I am not aware that forest dwelling is still practiced in the traditional way. The modern alternatives seem to consist of the more stark opposition between householding and becoming a wandering ascetic. Nevertheless, forest dwelling is an institution that doesn't really develop as such in Jainism and Buddhism. The idea that husbands and wives would engage in ascetic practices together, without celibacy, would appear

extraordinary. In those terms, it is an unfortunate loss if the institution does not continue in modern Hinduism.

4. The fourth stage is the *sannyasa*, or the stage of the wandering ascetic, the *sannyasin* (or *sadhu*). If a man desires, he may continue on to this stage, but his wife will need to return home; traditionally she cannot stay alone as a forest dweller or wander the highways as an ascetic. The *sannyasin* has renounced the world completely, is regarded as dead by his family (the funeral is held), and is finally beyond all *dharma* and caste. When a *sannyasin* enters a Hindu temple, he is not a worshipper but one of the objects of worship. Not even the gods are *sanyasins* (they are householders), and so this is where in Hinduism, as in Jainism and Buddhism, it is possible for human beings to be spiritually superior to the gods. It has long been a matter of dispute in Hinduism whether one need really fulfil the requirements of the *Laws of Manu* (gray hair, etc.) to renounce the world. The Mahabharata says that Brahmins may go directly to Renunciation, but it also says that the three debts must be paid—and the debt to the ancestors could only be paid with husbands and wives living together either as householders or, if renunciates, as forest dwellers (indeed, the Pandavas are all born in that way). There are definitely no such requirements in Jainism or Buddhism. The Buddha left his family right after his wife had a baby, which would put him in the middle of his *dharma* as a householder. Buddhism and Jainism thus developed *monastic* institutions, with monks and nuns, but these did not really develop as such in Hinduism: While wandering ascetics are rather like mendicant monks, we lack monasteries and nuns, and the ascetics are, traditionally, supposed to have already lived something like a normal, lay life.

The four stages of life may, somewhat improbably, be associated with the four parts of the Vedas: the samhitas with the stage of the student, who is particularly obligated to learn them; the Brahmans with the stage of the householder, who is able to regulate his ritual behaviour according to them; the aranyakas with the stage of the forest dweller, who regulates his ritual behaviour according to them and who begins to contemplate liberation; and finally the upanishads with the stage of the wandering ascetic, who is entirely concerned with meditation on the absolute, *Brahman*.

The twice born may account for as much as 48% of Hindus, though I have now seen the number put at more like 18%—quite a difference but more believable. The Shudras (58% of Hindus) may represent the institutional provision that the Arya made for the people they already found in India. The Shudras thus remain once born, and traditionally were not allowed to learn Sanskrit or study the Vedas—on pain of death. Their *dharma* is to work for the twice born. But even below the Shudras are the Untouchables (24% of Hindus), who are literally "outcastes," without a varna, and were regarded as "untouchable" because they are ritually polluting for caste Hindus. Some Untouchable sub-castes are regarded as so polluted that members are supposed to keep out of sight and do their work at night: They are called "Unseeables."

In India, the term "Untouchable" is now regarded as insulting or politically incorrect (like *Eta* in Japan for the traditional tanners and pariahs). Gandhi's *Harijans* ("children of God") or *Dalits* ("downtrodden") are preferred, though to Americans "Untouchables" would sound more like the gangster-busting federal agent Elliot Ness from the 1920's. Why there are so many Untouchables is unclear, although caste Hindus can be ejected from their jatis and become outcastes and various tribal or formerly tribal people in India may never have been properly integrated into the social system. When Mahatma Gandhi's sub-caste refused him permission to go to England, as noted above, he went anyway and was ejected from the caste. After he returned, his family got him back in, but while in England he was technically an outcaste. Existing tribal people as well as Untouchables are also called the "scheduled castes," since the British drew up a "schedule" listing the castes that they regarded as backwards, underprivileged, or oppressed.

The Untouchables, nevertheless, have their own traditional professions and their own sub-castes. Those professions (unless they can be evaded in the greater social mobility of modern, urban, anonymous life) involve too much pollution to be performed by caste Hindus: (1) dealing with the bodies of dead animals (like the sacred cattle that wander Indian villages) or unclaimed dead humans, (2) tanning leather, from such dead animals, and manufacturing leather goods, and (3) cleaning up the human and animal waste for which in traditional villages there is no sewer system. Mahatma Gandhi referred to the latter euphemistically as "scavenging" but saw in it the most horrible thing imposed on the Untouchables by the caste system. His requirement on his farms in South Africa that everyone share in such tasks comes up in an early scene in the movie *Gandhi*. Since Gandhi equated suffering with holiness, he saw the Untouchables as hallowed by their miserable treatment and so called them "Harijans" (*Hari=Vishnu*). Later Gandhi went on fasts in the hope of improving the condition of the Untouchables, or at least to avoid their being politically classified as non-Hindus.

Today the status of the Shudras, Untouchables, and other "scheduled castes," and the preferential policies that the Indian government has designed for their advancement ever since Independence, are sources of serious conflict, including suicides, murders, and riots, in Indian society. Meanwhile, however, especially since economic liberalization began in 1991, the social mobility of a modern economy and urban life has begun to disrupt traditional professions, and oppressions, even of Untouchables. Village life and economic stasis were the greatest allies of the caste system, but both are slowly retreating before modernity in an India that finally gave up the Soviet paradigm of economic planning.

VARNA, CASTE, AND OTHER DIVISIONS

Although many other nations are characterized by social inequality, perhaps nowhere else in the world has inequality been so elaborately constructed as in the Indian institution of caste. Caste has long existed in India, but in the modern period it has been severely criticized by both Indian and foreign observers. Although some educated Indians tell non-Indians that caste has been abolished or that "no one pays attention to caste anymore," such statements do not reflect reality. Caste has undergone significant change since independence, but it still involves hundreds of millions of people. In its preamble,

India's constitution forbids negative public discrimination on the basis of caste. However, caste ranking and caste-based interaction have occurred for centuries and will continue to do so well into the foreseeable future, more in the countryside than in urban settings and more in the realms of kinship and marriage than in less personal interactions.

Castes are ranked, named, endogamous (in-marrying) groups, membership in which is achieved by birth. There are thousands of castes and sub-castes in India, and these large kinship-based groups are fundamental to South Asian social structure. Each caste is part of a locally based system of interdependence with other groups, involving occupational specialization, and is linked in complex ways with networks that stretch across regions and throughout the nation. The word *caste* derives from the Portuguese *casta*, meaning breed, race, or kind. Among the Indian terms that are sometimes translated as caste are *varna*, *jati*, *jat*, *biradri*, and *samaj*. All of these terms refer to ranked groups of various sizes and breadth. *Varna*, or colour, actually refers to large divisions that include various castes; the other terms include castes and subdivisions of castes sometimes called sub-castes.

Many castes are traditionally associated with an occupation, such as high-ranking Brahmans; middle-ranking farmer and artisan groups, such as potters, barbers, and carpenters; and very low-ranking "Untouchable" leatherworkers, butchers, launderers, and latrine cleaners. There is some correlation between ritual rank on the caste hierarchy and economic prosperity. Members of higher-ranking castes tend, on the whole, to be more prosperous than members of lower-ranking castes. Many lower-caste people live in conditions of great poverty and social disadvantage.

According to the Rig Veda, sacred texts that date back to oral traditions of more than 3,000 years ago, progenitors of the four ranked *varna* groups sprang from various parts of the body of the primordial man, which Brahma created from clay. Each group had a function in sustaining the life of society—the social body. Brahmans, or priests, were created from the mouth. They were to provide for the intellectual and spiritual needs of the community. Kshatriyas, warriors and rulers, were derived from the arms. Their role was to rule and to protect others. Vaishyas—landowners and merchants—sprang from the thighs, and were entrusted with the care of commerce and agriculture. Shudras—artisans and servants—came from the feet. Their task was to perform all manual labour.

Later conceptualized was a fifth category, "Untouchable" menials, relegated to carrying out very menial and polluting work related to bodily decay and dirt. Since 1935 "Untouchables" have been known as Scheduled Castes, referring to their listing on government rosters, or schedules. They are also often called by Mohandas Karamchand (Mahatma) Gandhi's term Harijans, or "Children of God." Although the term *Untouchable* appears in literature produced by these low-ranking castes, in the 1990s, many politically conscious members of these groups prefer to refer to themselves as Dalit, a Hindi word meaning oppressed or downtrodden. According to the 1991 census, there were 138 million Scheduled Caste members in India, approximately 16 percent of the total population.

The first four *varnas* apparently existed in the ancient Aryan society of northern India. Some historians say that these categories were originally somewhat fluid functional groups, not castes. A greater degree of fixity gradually developed, resulting in the complex ranking systems of medieval India that essentially continue in the late twentieth century.

Although a *varna* is not a caste, when directly asked for their caste affiliation, particularly when the questioner is a Westerner, many Indians will reply with a *varna* name. Pressed further, they may respond with a much more specific name of a caste, or *jati*, which falls within that *varna*. For example, a Brahman may specify that he is a member of a named caste group, such as a Jijotiya Brahman, or a Smartha Brahman, and so on. Within such castes, people may further belong to smaller sub-caste categories and to specific clans and lineages. These finer designations are particularly relevant when marriages are being arranged and often appear in newspaper matrimonial advertisements.

Members of a caste are typically spread out over a region, with representatives living in hundreds of settlements. In any small village, there may be representatives of a few or even a score or more castes.

Numerous groups usually called tribes (often referred to as Scheduled Tribes) are also integrated into the caste system to varying degrees. Some tribes live separately from others—particularly in the far northeast and in the forested centre of the country, where tribes are more like ethnic groups than castes. Some tribes are themselves divided into groups similar to sub-castes. In regions where members of tribes live in peasant villages with nontribal peoples, they are usually considered members of separate castes ranking low on the hierarchical scale.

Inequalities among castes are considered by the Hindu faithful to be part of the divinely ordained natural order and are expressed in terms of purity and pollution. Within a village, relative rank is most graphically expressed at a wedding or death feast, when all residents of the village are invited. At the home of a high-ranking caste member, food is prepared by a member of a caste from whom all can accept cooked food (usually by a Brahman). Diners are seated in lines; members of a single caste sit next to each other in a row, and members of other castes sit in perpendicular or parallel rows at some distance. Members of Dalit castes, such as Leatherworkers and Sweepers, may be seated far from the other diners—even out in an alley. Farther away, at the edge of the feeding area, a Sweeper may wait with a large basket to receive discarded leavings tossed in by other diners. Eating food contaminated by contact with the saliva of others not of the same family is considered far too polluting to be practiced by members of any other castes. Generally, feasts and ceremonies given by Dalits are not attended by higher-ranking castes.

Among Muslims, although status differences prevail, brotherhood may be stressed. A Muslim feast usually includes a cloth laid either on clean ground or on a table, with all Muslims, rich and poor, dining from plates placed on the same cloth. Muslims who wish to provide hospitality to observant Hindus, however, must make separate arrangements for a high-caste Hindu cook and ritually pure foods and dining area.

Castes that fall within the top four ranked *varnas* are sometimes referred to as the "clean castes," with Dalits considered "unclean." Castes of the top three ranked *varnas* are often designated "twice-born," in reference to the ritual initiation undergone by male members, in which investiture with the Hindu sacred thread constitutes a kind of ritual rebirth. Non-Hindu castelike groups generally fall outside these designations.

Each caste is believed by devout Hindus to have its own dharma, or divinely ordained code of proper conduct. Accordingly, there is often a high degree of tolerance for divergent lifestyles among different castes. Brahmans are usually expected to be nonviolent and spiritual, according with their traditional roles as vegetarian teetotaller priests. Kshatriyas are supposed to be strong, as fighters and rulers should be, with a taste for aggression, eating meat, and drinking alcohol. Vaishyas are stereotyped as adept businessmen, in accord with their traditional activities in commerce. Shudras are often described by others as tolerably pleasant but expectably somewhat base in behaviour, whereas Dalits—especially Sweepers—are often regarded by others as followers of vulgar life-styles. Conversely, lower-caste people often view people of high rank as haughty and unfeeling.

The chastity of women is strongly related to caste status. Generally, the higher ranking the caste, the more sexual control its women are expected to exhibit. Brahman brides should be virginal, faithful to one husband, and celibate in widowhood. By contrast, a Sweeper bride may or may not be a virgin, extramarital affairs may be tolerated, and, if widowed or divorced, the woman is encouraged to remarry. For the higher castes, such control of female sexuality helps ensure purity of lineage—of crucial importance to maintenance of high status. Among Muslims, too, high status is strongly correlated with female chastity.

Within castes explicit standards are maintained. Transgressions may be dealt with by a caste council, meeting periodically to adjudicate issues relevant to the caste. Such councils are usually formed of groups of elders, almost always males. Punishments such as fines and outcasting, either temporary or permanent, can be enforced. In rare cases, a person is excommunicated from the caste for gross infractions of caste rules. An example of such an infraction might be marrying or openly cohabiting with a mate of a caste lower than one's own; such behaviour would usually result in the higher-caste person dropping to the status of the lower-caste person.

Activities such as farming or trading can be carried out by anyone, but usually only members of the appropriate castes act as priests, barbers, potters, weavers, and other skilled artisans, whose occupational skills are handed down in families from one generation to another. As with other key features of Indian social structure, occupational specialization is believed to be in accord with the divinely ordained order of the universe.

The existence of rigid ranking is supernaturally validated through the idea of rebirth according to a person's karma, the sum of an individual's deeds in this life and in past lives. After death, a person's life is judged by divine forces, and rebirth is assigned in a high or a low place, depending upon what is deserved. This supernatural sanction can never be neglected, because it brings a person to his or her position in the caste hierarchy, relevant to every transaction involving food or drink, speaking, or touching.

In past decades, Dalits in certain areas (especially in parts of the south) had to display extreme deference to high-status people, physically keeping their distance—lest their touch or even their shadow pollute others—wearing neither shoes nor any upper body covering (even for women) in the presence of the upper castes. The lowest-ranking had to jingle a little bell in warning of their polluting approach. In much of India, Dalits were prohibited from entering temples, using wells from which the "clean" castes drew their water, or even attending schools. In past centuries, dire punishments were prescribed for Dalits who read or even heard sacred texts.

Such degrading discrimination was made illegal under legislation pased during British rule and was protested against by pre-independence reform movements led by Mahatma Gandhi and Bhimrao Ramji (B.R.) Ambedkar, a Dalit leader. Dalits agitated for the right to enter Hindu temples and to use village wells and effectively pressed for the enactment of stronger laws opposing disabilities imposed on them. After independence, Ambedkar almost single-handedly wrote India's constitution, including key provisions barring caste-based discrimination. Nonetheless, discriminatory treatment of Dalits remains a factor in daily life, especially in villages, as the end of the twentieth century approaches. In modern times, as in the past, it is virtually impossible for an individual to raise his own status by falsely claiming to be a member of a higher-ranked caste. Such a ruse might work for a time in a place where the person is unknown, but no one would dine with or intermarry with such a person or his offspring until the claim was validated through kinship networks. Rising on the ritual hierarchy can only be achieved by a caste as a group, over a long period of time, principally by adopting behaviour patterns of higher-ranked groups. This process, known as Sanskritization, has been described by M.N. Srinivas and others. An example of such behaviour is that of some Leatherworker castes adopting a policy of not eating beef, in the hope that abstaining from the defiling practice of consuming the flesh of sacred bovines would enhance their castes' status. Increased economic prosperity for much of a caste greatly aids in the process of improving rank.

THE INDENTURE SYSTEM

In the colonies of the British, French and the Dutch, exploitation in one form or the other stalked the Indian indentured labourers. The Coolies who arrived to work in the sugar estates in the West Indies were marched to their barracks known as 'Nigger Yard.' It was the same in Mauritius--only the language was different, 'camps des Noirs' or the backbreaking work in the canefields.

In 1843 the first shipload of 217 Indian labourers arrived in Port of Spain in Trinidad in the Caribbean. And in the same decade, others were taken to British Guiana in South America, and Mauritius off the coast of Africa; in the 1860's to the British colony of Natal in South Africa; in the 1870's to the Dutch colony of Surinam; in the 1880's to Fiji. By 1917-20 the indenture system was abolished but not before 1.5 million Indian bonded labourers had been induced move to remote parts of the globe in the service of British capitalism. In South Africa they worked from daybreak to nightfall, from four in the morning to seven in the night, and far beyond their capacity. They were strictly confined to the limits of their master's estate. Beating and flogging was part of the regular routine in the plantations. In the West Indies the cattle whip was employed; in Malaya it was the cane, and in South Africa it was the rawhide cattle lash. One callous estate manager reportedly said "As long as the coolie is working for you, you have the right to do what you like with him-that is, short of killing".

Some Caribbean planters solved the problem of the sick by abandoning them to fate. In Grenada the majority of the 2000 Indians were kicked off the estates when they became ill and allowed to die on the road. The editor of a Jamaica newspaper wrote in 1863: 'One must see these wretched hungry, houseless and outcast specters picking up in the streets a chance bone or any putrid offal.... and so crippled, nude, skeletoned before their death, they live on, no parish authority taking them in'. Unlike the Chinese and the Blacks, the Indians were also wary of the penchant for proselytizing among white missionaries who were on the lookout for 'heathen converts'. Indians were always branded as the dregs of their country, low-born, even criminal. Inspite of this, the Europeans managed to take Indian women for sexual purposes-usually the daughter of a coolie.

Dave Freedholm teaches world religion and philosophy at a nationally recognized independent college preparatory school in the US. and a practitioner of Hindu spirituality for some years, says: 'Caste' was used to justify Christian proselytizing and for continued domination over the Indian population, and this continues to be the case today. Also, the ills of contemporary Indian society (poverty, caste, etc.), which were exacerbated in part due to centuries long foreign occupation, exploitation and domination, are blamed primarily on Hindu thought. Thus, some Western scholars, ignoring the historic subversion of Indian society and Hinduism by the West, align themselves with the 'oppressed' against the 'evils' of Hinduism. The victim is made to feel guilty and hence the 'Hindu shame' I find amongst some Hindus.

Most Christians today (and most scholars of religion) would be scandalized if the feudal system, slavery, capitalist exploitation or anti-Judaism were used to define the essence of Christianity. They would understand these things to be historically and socially bound and not part of Christian universal ideals. In short, descriptions of Christianity in textbooks would distinguish the core or essence of Christian theology from specific social, historical and political contexts.

However, Hinduism is not treated in the same way. It does seem that the caste system, as understood today, was foisted on Indian society by its Western (Christian) oppressors, the British. Efforts within Hindu society to reform itself, and to provide a new vision of Hinduism, are too often ignored or downplayed.

INDIAN CASTE

A Graver intellectual confusion than that caused by the non-translation of the word Caste there has seldom been. The assumed impossibility of finding an equivalent for the idea in English has led to the belief that there is something mysterious and unprecedented in the institution. People become bewildered as to whether it is a religious or a social obligation. Every one demands of the reformer a conflict with it. The whole question grows obscure and irritating. Yet all this time we have had an exact synonym for the word, and the parallel is the closer since our word connotes the same debatable borderland between morals and good taste. Caste ought to stand translated as honour. With Oriental quaintness, it is true, India has given a certain rigidity to this idea, but her analysis of the thing itself is as profound as it is acute.

Our conduct is commonly governed far more by social habit than by considerations of right and wrong. When the tide of the ethical struggle has once set in over some matter, we may regard ourselves as already half-lost. Why are my friend's open letters absolutely safe in my presence, though I am longing for the information they convey? Why can money given for one purpose not be used for another, when all the canons of common sense and expediency urge that it should? Who will confess to an effort in speaking the truth at any cost whatever? Why, when I am annoyed, do I not express myself in the language of Billingsgate? To each of which questions one would reply, somewhat haughtily, that the point was one of honour, or, that such happened to be the custom of one's class. Yet if we examine into the sanction which honour can invoke there is nothing beyond a rare exercise of the power of ostracism. The Church excommunicates, the law imprisons, but society merely "cuts" the offender in the street. Yet which of these three inflicts the deepest wound? It is as true of London as of Benaras that caste-law is the last and finest that controls a man. For it comes into operation at that precise point where tribunals fail. It takes cognisance of offences for which no judge could inflict penalties. It raises standards and demands virtues that every man will interpret according to the stringency of his pride, and yet that no one can feel himself to have wholly fulfilled. And it does all this without once permitting the sensation of merit. Having done all, one remains an unprofitable servant. For no one would count the punctual discharge of debts (all debts are debts of honour), the hauteur that brooks no stain upon the name, and the self-respect that builds the whole ethical code upon itself, as religious observances. These things were due, we say, to our birth or blood, or position before men. It is true that their non-fulfillment would leave a stain upon the conscience, and it is also true that the attempt to work out the obligations of honour must be the immediate test of the sincerity of one who proposes to lead a life of greater devotion and earnestness than common. Still, caste is not the same thing as personal piety and perhaps for this reason complete renunciation of its claims and benefits is essential in India to the monastic life.

There is another point about our Western conception of noblesse oblige. Few as the persons may be who could formulate their sentiment; the fact pervades the whole of the social area. Each class has its own honour. If honourable employers feel compelled to think of the comfort of their workers, honourable servants feel equally compelled to keep their lips shut on their masters' affairs, and either responds to an appeal in the name of his ideal. The priest may find the honour of his profession in conflict with that of the detective, but all the world will uphold the faithfulness of both. The efficient realisation of his ideals by the schoolmaster will involve an occasional pardon, even of a grave offence, if he conceives forgiveness to be the best formative influence which at the moment he can command. The very same effort in the merchant will require a distribution of punishment that is rigorous and just, since order, integrity, and unfailing promptitude—not the development of human character—are his ends. Thus every man, in every critical act of his life, calls silently for the judgment of his peers and refuses all other. The weaknesses of caste everywhere are manifold. For society, like the individual, is always apt to insist upon the tithing of mint and rue, and to neglect the weightier matters of the law. But it is not usually the martyr who marks its worst failure. He is the white dove cast forth by crows, that is, a member of a higher tried by consensus of the lower castes. We have here a case of government usurping the functions of society, much as if the headmaster should exercise authority in a dispute among boys.

For it is essential to the very idea of honour that every caste should be autonomous. The true failure of caste occurs whenever it establishes such an ascendancy of social opinion over the individual's conscience that his power of advance is impeded and he becomes less of a man, or less really beneficent socially, by remaining more of a gentleman—a state of things which is not uncommon among ourselves. For we may postulate that all ideals are helpful only in so far as they subserve a man's manhood and freedom, and destructive the instant they render him less able to express his own inmost will. It is he; therefore, who ought to have been a martyr and chose ease who is the true caste victim, not the hero of an auto-da-fe.

That this is a real danger we all know. What Protestant has never exalted the creed of his sect over freedom of thought? What Catholic has never put comfort above spirituality? What politician has not preferred party above principle? What student of science has never been prejudiced against new truth? And if we look without, where do we not see the mere breaker of conventionality treated as outside brotherhood? Where do we not find persons conforming to usages that displease them, merely because they would be inconvenient to dispute?

A certain sweeping justification of such facts may be urged, inasmuch as there are circumstances under which the cohesion of the group is well worth the sacrifice of the liberty of a few individuals. And the habitual outrage of custom without reason is perhaps rightly held to be as anti-social as any felony. In the last resort, however, social pressure must be held in bounds, for nothing should interfere with a man's right to try himself, or sap the roots of his independence. And society is a vague and irresponsible magistrate, with so little illumination as to his own purposes and tendencies that he frequently mistakes the pioneers of his march for deserters and orders the stoning of prophets, whose sepulchers and monuments will be erected by his children. The question of the inner trend or intention of the social movement must form the law in whose name all doubtful cases are tried. And, while it is never easy to determine the point accurately for one's own people, in the case of the Hindu race the supreme purpose of their past evolution is quite apparent.

Even a cursory reading of the Laws of Manu displays Indian society as united in a great cooperation for the preservation of the ancient race-treasure of Sanskrit literature. The feeling must have grown up when the Vedas alone required conserving, and the families entrusted with various portions were encouraged to become in all ways dependent on the community, that every energy might be devoted to the task in hand. This is the real meaning of prostration at the feet of Brahmans, of the great merit acquired by feeding them, and of the terror of the crime of killing one. It is not the man; it is race-culture that is destroyed by such an act.

As ages went on and the Upanishads and other things were added to the store, that which was hitherto memorised became entrusted to writing. The Vedas became Scriptures—and now the method, of psychology, of astronomy, of mathematics, made themselves felt as integral parts of the Aryan treasure, in common with Sanskrit literature. This widened the conception of culture without liberalising the social bearings of the question, and the Brahman caste continued to be recognised as the natural guardians of all learning, the old religious compositions being still regarded as the type.

If we ask how it happened that the Aryan folk became so early conscious of their responsibility in the matter of Sanskrit letters, there can be only one answer. They found themselves in the presence of other and unlearned races. This point brings us to the question of the origin of strongly differentiated castes in general. In its nature caste is, as we have seen, honour; that is to say, an ideal sentiment by whose means society spontaneously protects itself from some danger against which it is otherwise defenceless. For instance, life in Texas having been for many years dependent on the possession of horses, and safeguards against the horse-thief being few and difficult, he came to be the object of unprecedented social abhorrence. Horse-stealing was the last crime a lost soul would stoop to.

In a similar way, as some think, may have grown up the Indian feeling about cow-killing. If the cattle, in time of stress, were killed for food, agriculture would be unable to take a new start, and so a people accustomed to eat beef grasped the situation perhaps, and renounced the practice. But since these two sentiments pervade whole nations, they are not exactly what we are accustomed to think of as caste, inasmuch as in the latter there is a distinct gradation of rank connected with the sentiment.

In the term "blackleg" applied by trade unionists to competing forms of labour, we have an instance of the kind we want. Here we have an occupational group giving birth immediately to the ideal which is necessary to its safety.

Throughout the worlds of love, of war, and of work, indeed, honour is an instinct of the very greatest potency. How few men, after all, desert to an enemy as spies! How strong is the feeling of class-obligation amongst servants and working men! This element is very evident in the Indian industrial castes, which are often simply hereditary trade-unions. No Englishman is so powerful, nor is any Hindu so hungry, that one man could be bribed to take up the trade of another. Nothing would induce the dairyman, for instance, to take charge of a horse, or a laundryman to assist the household. But the very strongest, and perhaps also ugliest, of all possible roots of caste is the sense of race, the caste of blood. We have an instance of this in the animosity that divides white men from negroes in the United States, and we have other instances, less talked of, all up and down our vast British possessions. There is probably no other emotion so inhuman which receives such universal sympathy as this.

For it is fundamentally the physical instinct of a vigorous type to protect itself from fusion. And both sides participate in the revulsion. Here we have the secret of rigid caste, for the only rigid caste is hereditary, and of hereditary caste the essential characteristic is the refusal of intermarriage. Granting, then, what could not well be denied, that the Aryan forefathers found themselves in India face to face with inferior and aboriginal races, what may we gather, from the nature of the caste system today, to have been the elements of the problem, as they more or less clearly perceived it?

Those elements we may infer to have been four in number:

1. They desired above all things to preserve the honour of their daughters from marriage with lower and savage peoples. Exclusion from marriage with any but one's own caste became the rigorous rule, the penalty fell on the father and the family that permitted a woman to go unguarded on this head. To this day, if a son marry beneath caste he degrades himself; but if a daughter be wrongly given, the whole family becomes out-casted.
2. They seem to have desired to preserve the aboriginal races, on the one hand from extermination, and on the other from slavery of the person two solutions which seemed later the only alternatives to Aryan persons in a similar position! Those aborigines, therefore, who became dependent on the Aryan population, had their definite place assigned them in the scale of labour, and their occupations were secured to them by the contempt of the superior race.

   We must not forget, in the apparent harshness of this convention, its large factor of hygienic caution. The aborigines were often carrion-eaters, and always uncleanly in comparison with their neighbours. It was natural enough, therefore, that there should be a refusal to drink the same water, and so on.

   On the other hand, it is one of the mistakes of caste everywhere, that it institutionalises and perpetuates an inequality which might have been minimised. But we must not forget, in the case of the Indian system, the two greater evils which were avoided altogether.
3. The Aryans realised very clearly that it was not only their race but also their civilization that must be maintained in its purity. The word Aryan implies one acquainted with the processes of agriculture, an earer of the ground, to use an Elizabethan word—accustomed therefore to a fixed and industrialised mode of living, evidently in contrast to others who were not.

   Fire and the processes of cooking and eating food are easily distinguished as the core of the Personal life and establishment in a climate where habits can at any time be made so simple as in India. It is these that can never be dispensed with, though they may be arranged for to-night in a palace, and tomorrow in the jungle under a tree.

In view, then, of the necessity of safeguarding the system of manners grew up the restrictions against eating with those of lower caste, or allowing them to touch the food and wants of their betters. The fact that the Aryan could eat food cooked by Aryan hands alone implied that the strictest preliminaries of bathing had been complied with.

By a continuous crystallisation, all caste laws—from being the enunciation of broad canons of refinement as between Aryan and non-Aryan—came to be the regular caste-barriers between one class and another of the same race. In this way they lost their invidious character.

It is undeniable that this caste of the kitchen, so wittily named "don't touchism" by a modern Hindu leader, lends itself to abuse and becomes an instrument of petty persecution more readily than the intermarriage laws. Some of the saddest instances of caste-failure have occurred here. Nevertheless, the original intention remains clear and true, and is by no means completely obscured, even with the lapse of ages.

4. It was, however, in their perception of the fourth element of the problem that the early Aryans triumphantly solved the riddle of Humanity. They seem to have seen clearly that amongst the aborigines of India themselves were many degrees of social development already existent, and that these must be preserved and encouraged to progress.

From such a comprehension of the situation sprang the long and still growing graduation of non-Aryan castes, some of which have established themselves in the course of ages within the Aryan pale. Marriage, for instance, is an elabourate and expensive social function in the highest classes. But as we descend it becomes easier, till amongst the Baghdis, Bauris, and other aboriginal castes, almost any connection is ratified by the recognition of women and children. This is a point in which Eastern scores over Western development; for in Europe the Church has caused to be reckoned as immoral what might, with more philosophy, have been treated as the lingering customs of sub-organised race-strata.

As is the nature of caste, mere social prestige constitutes a perpetual stimulus and invitation to rise, which means in this case to increase the number of daily baths and the cleanliness of cooking, and to restrict to purer and finer kinds the materials used for food, approximating continually toward the Brahman standard. For is it not true that noblesse oblige? This fact it is that makes Hinduism always the vigorous living banyan, driving civilization deeper and wider as it grows, and not the fossilised antiquity superficial observers have supposed.

Such, then, is the historic picture of the rise of caste. The society thus originated fell into four main groups:

(1) Priests and learned men—the Brahmans;

(2) The royal and military caste;

(3) Professional men and merchants—the middle-class or bourgeoisie, as we say in Europe; and

(4) The working people, or sudras, in all their divisions.

(Of the second group only the Rajput branch remains now stable. For the military caste, finding itself leaderless under the Maurya dynasty, is said to have become literary, and is certainly now absorbed in the bourgeoisie.)

This functional grouping, however, is traversed in all directions nowadays by the lines of caste. In the mountains it is no uncommon thing to find the Brahman acting as a labourer, impressed as a coolie, or working as a farmer, and in the cities he belongs largely to the professional ranks. Many of India's most learned and active sons, on the other hand, belong to the third and even fourth divisions. And the new castes, which are of constant growth, are less easy than the old to classify. Every new community means a new caste in India. Thus we have the Mohammedan, the Christian, and the modern reform castes—of all of which one peculiarity is non-belief in the caste principle!—as well as others. And who shall determine, for instance, to which of the four main grades Islamism, with its inclusion of peasant, citizen, and prince, belongs?

The fact is, if a man's mode of life be acceptable to his own caste-fellows, the rest of Indian society has no quarrel with it. And this autonomy of castes it is which is the real essential for social flexibility and fundamental equality. As bearing on this point, few utterances have ever been so misquoted as the great dictum of Buddha, that "he who attains to God is the true Brahman." For this is misquoted whenever it is made to imply that the Brahman holds in any sense a monopoly in religion. No possible statement could be more foreign to the genius of Hinduism. When we read that shortest and greatest of India's gospels, the "Bhagavad Gita" (a poem composed by Brahmans, preserved by Brahmans, and distributed through the length and breadth of the country, always by Brahmans), we find ourselves in the presence of the most comprehensive mind that ever contemplated Hindu life.

The compassion of Buddha, perhaps, looms greater across the centuries, but in dealing with social problems his very tenderness and spiritual fire make him second to Krishna, who was always calm, broad, and consistently national in his outlook. We must accept the Gita as an authoritative pronouncement on Hindu society. And the Gita rings with the constantly reiterated implication that "he who attains to God is the true man," while it interprets all life and responsibility as a means to this end. Thus, "Better one's own duty, though imperfect, than the duty of another well discharged. Better death in one's own duty; the duty of another brings on danger." We have to remember, too, that the Gita is made up of the very best of the Vedas and Upanishads, and was specially written for the benefit of women and the working classes, who, as destitute of classical learning, had little chance of studying these great scriptures.

But its contents were to depend upon Brahman effort for promulgation. Another witness to the fact that spirituality has always been regarded in India as the common human possession lies in the Hindu word for religion itself—dharma, or the manness of man. This is very striking. The whole weight, of the conception is shifted away from creed, much more from caste or race, to that which is universal and permanent in each and every human being. And, last of all, we may remember that the greatest historical teachers of Hinduism—Rama, Krishna, and Buddha, besides many of the Upanishadic period—were men of the second, or military, caste. No, the Brahman was never in any sense the privileged monopolist of religion: he was a common channel of religious lore, because his actual function was Sanskrit culture, and Sanskrit happens to be the vehicle of the most perfect religious thought that the world ever produced, but "realisation" itself has always been recognised as a very different matter from this, and, Brahman or non-Brahman, has been accepted wherever it appeared. The advantage that the priestly caste did undoubtedly enjoy, however, lay in the fact that in their case the etiquette of rank led directly to the highest inspiration, as the scholar's life, even in its routine, will be nearest to that of the saint.

One peculiarity of the place of the religious life in the Indian system is that it is an inclusive term for all forms of higher individuation. Theoretically, to the Hindu mind, all genius is inspiration, the perception of unity; and the mathematics of Euclid or the sculpture of Michael Angelo would be as authentic an expression of the religious consciousness as the sainthood of Francis. Only the result of this method of interpretation is that sainthood takes precedence of all others as the commonest form of greatness. Scientific research, as in the astronomy of Bhashkar Acharya and the psychology of Patanjali, has not had sufficient opportunity of securing defined and independent scope. And literature has been yoked to the car of mythology as much as the art of medieval Italy.

Nevertheless, India is too well acquainted with genius to forget that the caste of the spirit is beyond human limitation, often beyond recognition. It is held that the best lower men can do for that brotherhood which asserts itself in the consciousness of greatness is to give it freedom. Hence a man can always be released from social obligations if he desire to live the life of ideas, of the soul. Only, it is held that if he will not fulfil the law, neither shall he add to the burdens of the community. So he who claims to be one of the great spiritual beyond-castes must renounce family and property, relying upon the charity of men for his daily bread, and knowing well that for any work of scholarship—such as the observatories at Benaras and Jeypore—a Hindu government at least would provide him ample means. It is only as long as one avails oneself of the benefits of the social structure that it is held not unreasonable to require conformity to its usages. This renunciation is Sannyas, the Indian form of monasticism, and Sannyas, theories to the contrary notwithstanding, has always been open to all castes. Indeed, it is held that when the responsibilities of life are over, a man's duty is to leave the world and spend the remainder of his days in that state; and in some parts of Northern India one meets with "Tyagi Mehtars," or monastics who were by birth the lowest of the low.

Theoretically, the monk is caste-fellow of the whole world, prepared to eat with any one; and where, by sheer dint of spirituality and self-discipline, such a feeling is realised; every Hindu in India considers the broken bread of this lover of mankind as sacramental food. It is usual, too, to eat from the hands of holy men without inquiry as to their standing when in the world. One of the most interesting points in all this to a Western mind is the difference implied and established between the caste of priests or chaplains on the one hand, and the fact of spiritual realisation, outside all caste, on the other. Nothing in the Indian thought about life can be more striking than this. The family chaplain in Bengal may be the official teacher, but every man and woman discards his authority silently the instant they find some soul (in the world or out of it; it may be husband or child, or the holy man living in his garden; usually it is an ascetic), with a quickening spiritual touch upon their own. He or she then becomes the guru, or teacher, and this relationship is made the central fact of life. The appearance of this new teacher, when he is powerful enough to be an important social phenomenon, is the historic origin of almost all new castes. The Sikh nation was formed in this way by a succession of gurus. Chaitanya welcomed all castes to Vaishnavism and made it possible for them to rise thereby. The scavengers, too low to venture to claim either Hinduism or Islamism as their own, were raised in consideration and self-respect by Guru Nanak and Lal Begi Mehtar—the last a saint of their own degree.

The preacher arises and proclaims the new idea. He gathers about him men of all classes: the educated won to the service of his thought, the ignorant swept in by the radiance of his personality. Amongst his disciples distinctions of caste break down. The whole group is stamped with his character and prestige. Eventually, if it contain a preponderance of Brahman elements, it may take rank with the best, carrying certain individuals up with it. But if it be composed chiefly of the scum of society, it will remain little considered; and yet, in the strength of its religious and intellectual significance may certainly claim to have progressed beyond its original point. Such is likely to be the fate of the present Christian converts. Those who are recruited from the lowest pariahs may acquire a certain prestige from their new faith and take a better place in the social scale, consequently, in centuries to come. At the same time we must not forget that forty or fifty years ago, conversions were made that undoubtedly involved great sacrifices, and the descendants of these Christians may lose rather than gain in the long run.

Taking the history of Hinduism as a whole, we observe a great systole and diastole of caste, the Buddhist and the present Christian periods ranking as well-marked eras of fusion, while the intervening centuries are characterised by progressive definition, broken every now and then by a wave of reform which thought itself a movement towards caste abolition, but ended simply in the formation of a new group. For this is the fact in which all would-be reformations in India find at once their opportunity and their limit. It may now be taken as proved that in order to affect caste widely the agitator would need to aim deeper than the external phenomena, at underlying spiritual impulses.

If this theory of caste be valid, then, we find that the word signifies not so much mere rank in society as the standard of honour which is associated with rank. And as the private's conduct may be governed as much as his officer's by enlightened self-respect, we have seen that honour is something which applies to the whole of society equally. Even Tennyson, it will be remembered, pictures the country youth as outvaunting Lady Clara Vere de Vere in her pride of birth. The word caste, therefore, is by no means that antithesis of democracy which has been so commonly assumed. Neither, amongst a people familiar with the process of self-organisation, would it prove any barrier to efficient cooperation. For the one essential to this power is an established habit of ignoring all points of mutual difference not germane to the matter in hand. What we call good-breeding, or what India calls caste, ought to make this easier. For any group of men met together for a common purpose find their individual rights secured to them in this way, and are free, by age-long acceptance, from any suspicion of another's desire to interfere with them. This is a basis of strength and not of weakness; so that it seems, if Indian men and women are not at present capable of combined action to any great degree, it is a matter of their own neglect of the habit, and not a necessary consequence of their institutions. We need not too readily accept the statement of such weakness, either, as infallible. My own observation has been that the Hindu people are capable enough of vigorous cooperation along the lines natural to them, those of the undivided family, the village community, and others. That inability which Europeans would show to face these tests, they may be expected to display before ours

To be absolutely just, however, we must admit that the observance of caste law has entailed many foolish and irritating losses upon society during the last fifty years. We have seen that there are definite reasons, not wanting in cogency, why a man of good birth should not eat in all companies, or of food cooked by hands supposed less cleanly. Such rules, however, cannot be kept by those who, for any reason, cross the seas to Europe. This fact, more than any other detail, makes it a matter of out-casting to take the journey and persecutions have sometimes ensued which are shocking to contemplate. A man may care little about the loss of station for his own sake, but the shoe pinches when he finds himself unable to make worthy marriages for his daughters; hence he will often submit to a heavy fine in order to buy back his position.

Bibliography

Ainapur, L. S.: *Dynamics of Caste Relations in Rural India*, Jaipur, Rawat Publications, 1986.

Andre, Beteille: *The Backward Classes and the New Social Order*, Oxford University Press, Delhi, 1981.

Atal, Yogesh: *The Changing Frontiers of Caste*, Delhi, National Publishing House, 1968.

Benjamin, Joseph: *Scheduled Castes in Indian Politics and Society*, New Delhi, Ess Ess Publications, 1989.

Blunt, E. A. H. *Caste System of Northern India*, London, Oxford University Press, 1931.

Burman, B.K.: *Beyond Mandal and After Backward Classes in Perspective*, New Delhi, Mittal, 1992.

Chatterjee, Partha: *Caste and Subaltern Consciousness*, Delhi, Oxford Unviersity Press, 1994.

Deshpande, Vasant: *The Mhaisal Untouchables*, Pune, Dastane Ramchandra & Co., 1983.

Devendra, M. : *Scheduled Castes and Tribes: Socio-Economic Upliftment Programmes*, Ashish Publishing House, New Delhi, 1994.

Dumont, Louis: *The Caste System and Its Implications*, London, Granada Pub. Ltd., 1970.

Gorhe, Neelam: *Social Development and Dalit Women*, Gyan Pub. House, New Delhi, 1995.

Gurukal, Rajan: *The Formation of Caste Society in Kerala*, Rawat Publications, New Delhi, 1994.

Hutton, J. H.: *Caste in India: Its Nature, Function and Origins*, London, Cambridge University Press, 1946.

Jaiswal, S.: *Caste: Origin, Function and Dimensions of Change*, New Delhi, Manohar, 1998.

James M.: *Untouchable : An Indian Life History*, CA, Stanford University Press, 1979.

Joshi, R. : *Daughters of Independence: Gender, Caste, and Class in India.* NJ, Rutgers University Press, 1986.

Juergensmeyer, Mark: *Religion as Social Vision: The Movement Against Untouchability in 20th Century Punjab*, University of California Press, Berkeley, 1979.

Kakade, S. R.: *Scheduled Castes and National Integration: A Study of Marathwada*, New Delhi, Radiant Pub., 1990.

Kamble, N. D.: *Deprived Castes and their Struggle for Equality*, Ashish Publishing House, New Delhi, 1983.

Kaul, Rekha: *Caste, Class and Education: Politics of the Capitation Fee Phenomenon in Karnataka,* New Delhi, Sage Publications, 1993.

Kinsley, D.: *Hindu Goddesses. Vision of the Divine Feminine in the Hindu Religious Tradition*, Delhi, Motilal Banarsidass, 1987.

Kumar, Pradip : *Social Mobility and Caste Violence: A Study of the Gujarat Riots*, Delhi, Adjanta Publications, 1985.

Lakshmanna, C.: *Caste Dynamics in Village India*, Nachiketa Publications, Bombay, 1973.

Lal, Shyam: *Caste and Political Mobilisation: The Bhangis*, Jaipur, Panchsheel Prakashan, 1981.

Mayer, A.: *Caste in an Indian Village: Change and Continuity 1954-1992*, Delhi, OUP, 1996.

Mishra, J.: *Equality vs Justice. The Problem of Reservations for Backward Classes,* New Delhi, Deep & Deep, 1996.

Mohan, P.E.: *Scheduled Castes: History of Elevation, Tamil Nadu, 1900-1955*, Madras, New Era Pub., 1993.

Nagaraja, A. : *Caste and Land in Colonial South India*, Rawat Publications, New Delhi, 1994.

Narayan, K.: *Storytellers, Saints, and Scoundrels*, Philadelphia, University of Pennsylvania Press, 1989.

O'Hanlon, R.: *Caste, Conflict and Ideology*, New York, Cambridge University Press, 1985.

Oddie, G.A.: *Hindu and Christian in South-East India*, London, Curzon Press, 1991.

Omvedt, Gail: *Land, Caste and Politics in Indian States,* Authors Guild Publications, Delhi, 1982.

Parmaji, S.: *Caste Reservations and Performance*, Mamata Publications, Warangal, 1985.

Patwardhan, Sunanda: *Change Among India's Harijans: Maharashtra a Case Study*, New Delhi, Orient Longmans, 1973.

Quigley, D.: *The Interpretation of Caste*, Cambridge, CUP, 1993.

Rajshekar, V. T. : *Dalit Movement in Karnataka*, Madras, Christian Literatuure Society, 1978.

Ram, Jagivan: *Caste Challenge in India*, New Delhi, Vision Books, 1980.

Robert L. Jr.: *The Dravidian Movement*, Bombay, Popular Book Depot, 1965.

Sara S.: *Dharma's Daughters: Contemporary Indian Women and Hindu Culture,* NJ, Rutgers University Press, 1991.

Sarkar, J.: *Caste, Occupation and Change*, Delhi, B. R. Publishing Co., 1984.

Sharma, B. D.: *Dalits Betrayed*, New Delhi, Har-Anand Publications, 1994.

Silverberg, James: *Social Mobility in the Caste System in India*, Mouton Publishers, The Hague, 1968.

Singh, S. N.: *Reservation: Problems and Prospects*, New Delhi, Uppal Publishing House, 1987.

Subhamani N.: *Mahatma Gandhi and Babasaheb Ambedkar: Crusaders Against Caste and Untouchability*, Andhra Pradesh: Saroja Publications, Hyderabad, 1997.

Tiwari, P. O.: *Dimensions of Scheduled Caste Development in India*, Uppal Publishing House, New Delhi, 1991.

Tripathy, R. B.: *Dalits: A Sub-Human Society*, New Delhi, Ashish Publishing House, 1994.

Verma, B. M.: *Development of Scheduled Castes and Administration*, New Delhi, Uppal Publishing House, 1993.

Webster, John: *The Christian Dalits: A History,* Delhi, Indian Society for Promoting Christian Knowledge (ISPCK), 1994.

Index